T0330324

PIRATES AND PRIVATEERS

EXETER MARITIME STUDIES
Series Editors: Michael Duffy and David J. Starkey

PIRATES AND PRIVATEERS

New Perspectives on the War on Trade in the
Eighteenth and Nineteenth Centuries

Edited by

DAVID J. STARKEY
E.S. VAN EYCK VAN HESLINGA
J.A. DE MOOR

UNIVERSITY
of
EXETER
PRESS

First published in 1997 by
University of Exeter Press
Reed Hall, Streatham Drive
Exeter, Devon EX4 4QR
UK
www.exeterpress.co.uk

Printed digitally since 2010

British Library Cataloguing in Publication Data
A catalogue record for this book is
available from the British Library

ISBN 978 0 85989 481 4

Typeset in 11.5/13pt Garamond 3
by Exe Valley Dataset Ltd, Exeter

Printed and bound by CPI Group (UK) Ltd, Croydon, CR0 4YY

CONTENTS

MAPS

TABLES

FIGURES

Notes on Contributors

J. L. Anderson was formerly Senior Lecturer in Economics at La Trobe University, Australia, his research interests being chiefly in economic history and maritime history. His publications include a number of works on piracy in world history.

Patrick Crowhurst is the author of *The Defence of British Trade, 1689–1815* and *The French War on Trade 1793–1815* as well as numerous articles on the war on trade in the eighteenth century. He formerly taught History at Leicester Polytechnic and now teaches English in Bratislava.

Ole Feldbaek is Professor of History at the University of Copenhagen. He has published extensively on Danish trade, shipping, naval development and diplomacy in the eighteenth century.

Corrie Reinders Folmer studied History at the Free University Amsterdam, before gaining a Master's degree from the University of Leiden. She is currently completing a doctoral thesis on the Middelburg Commerce Company.

Erik Goebel is Senior Research Archivist at the Danish National Archives. He specialises in seventeenth- and eighteenth-century Danish economic and social history, particularly colonial trade and shipping.

Els van Eyck van Heslinga formerly taught maritime history at the University of Leiden and is now Director of Collections at the Netherlands Maritime Museum, Amsterdam. She has published widely on Dutch seafaring in the early modern period and on the Dutch East India Company.

Faye Kert was awarded a Master's degree by Carleton University for her dissertation on Nova Scotian privateering. She is currently President of the Canadian Nautical Research Society.

Goncal López Nadal is Lecturer in Economic History at the Universitat de les Illes Balears, Palma. He specialises in the maritime economic history of the Mediterranean, especially in the organization of trade and privateering.

Ghislayne Loyré has published various works on the Muslim communities of the Philippines, including *A la recherche de l'Islam philippin: La communauté maranao* and *The Institutions of Maguindanao.*

Jaap de Moor is Assistant Professor of History at the University of Leiden. He specializes in overseas and military history, and his recent publications include *European Expansion and Law: The Encounter between European and Indigenous Law in Nineteenth- and Twentieth-Century Africa and Asia.*

Dian Murray is the author of several works on Chinese maritime history including *The Origin of the Tiandihui: The Chinese Triads in Legend and History* and *The Pirates of the South China Coast 1790–1810.* She is Professor of History and Associate Dean at the University of Notre Dame, Indiana.

Jan Parmentier is Assistant-Professor in the Department of Maritime and Overseas History at the University of Ghent. He has published widely on European trade with Asia in the seventeenth and eighteenth centuries.

Marcus Rediker teaches History at the University of Pittsburgh. He is the author of the award-winning book, *Between the Devil and the Deep Blue Sea: Merchant Seamen, Pirates and the Anglo-American Maritime World.*

Robert C. Ritchie is Director of the Huntingdon Library and the author of *Captain Kidd and the War against the Pirates.*

David J. Starkey is Wilson Family Lecturer in Maritime History at the University of Hull. He has published extensively on British shipping and trade in the eighteenth and nineteenth centuries and is the author of *British Privateering Enterprise in the Eighteenth Century.*

Jan van Zijverden holds a Master's degree in Maritime History from the University of Leiden and currently works as Information Officer at the Netherlands Maritime Museum, Amsterdam.

Preface

The literature on piracy and privateering, already extensive, has expanded considerably in the last twenty or so years. Though much of this recent work is of high quality, it tends to focus on particular strains of commerce-raiding activity in certain regions of the globe: buccaneering in the Caribbean, the corsairs of the Mediterranean, privateering authorized by one or other of the European states, piracy in the South China Sea, and so forth. This fragmented approach is perfectly understandable given the scope and complexity of the subject matter, but it raises many questions of a comparative nature: did piratical operations in the East Indies resemble those in the West Indies? How similar were the aims and structures of privateering ventures set forth from the different countries of the North Atlantic region? Why did the responses of European states to the problems and opportunities thrown up by attacks on sea-borne commerce differ so widely? To address such issues, and thereby to provide a broad perspective on the war on trade, we invited a select number of regionally and thematically specialized historians to attend a conference on piracy and privateering. The papers delivered at the meeting, which was held in the Netherlands in May 1991, are presented in this volume.

Middelburg, in the province of Zeeland, was chosen as the venue for the conference, not least because this region, more than any other in the Netherlands, is historically associated with privateering and piratical activities. The meeting was a successful and memorable event, owing not only to the lively contributions of the participants, to whom we offer our thanks, but also to the invaluable support offered by many individuals and institutions. We were greatly assisted by the enthusiastic co-operation of the provincial authorities of Zeeland, the municipal authorities in Middelburg, and the personnel of the Zeeuwse Bibliotheek where the conference sessions were held. The Province of

Zeeland (College van Gedeputeerde Staten) provided generous financial support, and further subsidies were received from the Koninklijke Nederlandse Academies van Wetenschappen (Amsterdam), the Faculty of Letters, University of Leiden, the Stichting Leids Universiteits Fonds, the Stichting Ondersteuningsfonds Nationaal Instituut voor Scheepvaart en Scheepsbouw (Rotterdam), and the Oostersche Handel en Reederijen (Amsterdam). A special publication grant was made by Donald A. Petrie in New York to assist in the preparation of this volume. To all of these sponsors, we are most grateful. Finally we would like to thank Simon Baker and his staff at the University of Exeter Press for their help in bringing this project to fruition.

David J. Starkey
E.S. van Eyck van Heslinga
J.A. de Moor

Introduction

David J. Starkey

Attacks upon sea-borne trade have been a feature of human maritime activity since the seas were first used for the transport of goods and people. Such violent assaults have been perpetrated by various types of aggressor, the status of whom has largely depended on his or her standing in that changing and subjective notion, the law of nations. In general, three forms of commerce-raider can be identified. Firstly, there is the pirate, the maritime assailant who acts beyond the law, robbing and plundering sea travellers without the authority of any recognized state. While the pirate has always preyed on trade, the second form of commerce-raider, the privateer, was active in various guises between early medieval times and the mid-nineteenth century. Sanctioned by a state, the privateer's predatory operations were restricted to specified targets and subject to the due process of law. One of the potential attributes of these privately owned ships-of-war was the support they provided to the third kind of commerce-raider, the state navy, which emerged as a permanent facet of European maritime activity in the early seventeenth century. Though public navies were relatively slow to develop, and were not solely concerned with the war on trade, their increasingly significant presence, and the growth of state power that they embodied, had a vital bearing on the evolution and extent of the private strains of commerce-raiding activity—piracy and priva-teering—which form the principal concern of this volume.

Our knowledge of private commerce-raiding has expanded consider-ably since the International Commission of Maritime History organized a major conference on piracy and privateering in 1975. A common cry arising from the 50 or so papers and reports presented at that meeting was the need for further research on these important, but neglected, dimensions of trade, shipping and naval history.[1] In many respects, this plea has been heeded and by dint of the exertions of numerous historians we now know a good deal about the character and significance of private forms of maritime predation as practised over the ages. For instance, the works of Andrews, Senior, Hebb, Stradling, van Vliet and Appleby have greatly enhanced our understanding of commerce-raiding and naval activity in European waters in the late sixteenth and early seventeenth centuries.[2] Great strides have been made in the study of Caribbean buccaneering, with Hill, Bromley and Burg offering stimulating, at times controversial, insights into the social, political and economic mores of buccaneer communities,[3] themes pursued from differing perspectives by Rediker, Ritchie and Zahadieh.[4] Among the proliferation of general pirate histories, Cordingley's discussion of the images of piracy, Stanley's treatment of women pirates, and Marley's illustrated history of the adventurers of the high seas are perhaps the most valuable.[5] A body of work has also been published on eighteenth-century privateering, with Bromley and Crowhurst focusing on French corsairs,[6] Starkey, Bromley, Raban and others on British privateering enterprise,[7] and Swanson and Garitee adding an American dimension to the literature.[8]

In spite of this flurry of research and publication, many aspects of the history of piracy and privateering remain uncharted. Our knowledge of the war on trade in the late eighteenth and nineteenth centuries, for instance, is comparatively thin, with important topics such as *la course independante*, that upsurge of predatory activity which formed a significant part of the Spanish American Wars of Liberation, still requiring rigorous analysis.[9] Coverage from a spatial point of view is also unbalanced in that predatory activity undertaken in the Indian Ocean, the East Indies and the Pacific has received far less attention than that conducted in the Atlantic. Even here, in the well-regulated privateering businesses of the European powers, lacunae in our knowledge exist: how were privateering ventures organized in the various belligerent nations? Was the commerce-raiding business profitable? What factors determined the scale of activity? What part did the neutral states play in the maritime conflicts of the long eighteenth century?

This volume, in providing comparative perspectives on piracy and privateering in the Atlantic and the eastern seas during the 1700–1850 period, addresses some, but by no means all, of these issues. It commences with Robert C. Ritchie's examination of the measures taken by European and American governments to regulate private commerce-raiding, chiefly by repressing piracy and applying tighter controls on privateering—leading ultimately to the abolition of this ancient activity in 1856. In essence, this process should be viewed in the context of the growth of state power, a theme that has stimulated much discussion in recent years. Especially relevant to private commerce-raiding are the analyses of Brewer and Baugh which point to the importance of an aggressive, 'blue water' colonial and commercial policy, and with it an extensive navy, in the early emergence and effectiveness of the 'military-fiscal state' in Britain.[10] While this gave a decisive advantage in the Second Hundred Years War, it also meant that Britain took the lead in constraining piratical and privateering activity. This was more than a policing role, however, for, as Ritchie points out, it was British policy as well as British naval forces that exerted a growing influence over the business of maritime predation. In this respect, Ritchie lends clarity and accurate detail to Thomson's assertions that between 1700 and 1850 states increasingly monopolized violence, eradicating firstly non-state unauthorized violence (including piracy), and then non-state authorized violence (including privateering).[11]

In treating piracy and privateering separately, Ritchie's chapter largely reflects the reality that pirates and privateers were essentially distinct species of predator in the post-1700 maritime world. Demarcation questions still arose, most notably during the wave of commerce-raiding that washed over the Caribbean and North Atlantic in the wake of the Spanish American revolutions, when the dubious legitimacy of the letters of marque granted by the 'Carthaginian Republic' and the 'Republic of Buenos Ayres' echoed doubts concerning the authorizations issued to Caribbean buccaneers over a century earlier. But, in general, pirates and privateersmen were distinguished by more than the technical definitions laid down in the law; they lived and worked in very different environments. Pirates, by going 'on the account', put themselves beyond the law and the confines of established society to live in outlaw communities and deploy their labour in risk- and profit-sharing ventures. Privateersmen, on the other hand, deployed their labour in the vessels and with the equipment— that is, the capital—owned by merchants and shipowners, and it was back to work as wage-earning seafarers that most returned once their commerce-raiding diversion had ended. Thus, piracy, as it developed after 1700, was increasingly a way of life, while privateering was but one of a number of wartime opportunities for shipowners and seafarers. This demarcation provides the agenda for the rest of the volume.

Four chapters consider different strains of piracy. Marcus Rediker discusses the utopian dimensions of Atlantic piracy in the early eighteenth century, while Dian Murray, Ghislaine Loyré and J.L. Anderson examine, from different vantage points, various forms of piracy in the eastern seas during the 1750–1850 period. All demonstrate that piracy was a significant factor in each respective setting: thus, Rediker argues that piracy challenged the social and political structures of the Anglo-American maritime world; Murray estimates that the Chinese pirate confederation, mustering an astonishing 50,000–70,000 members, performed many of the maritime functions of the imperial state in the early nineteenth century; in the southern Philippines, as Loyré establishes, piracy was no less than a way of life in coastal communities, permitting inhabitants to achieve a strong degree of independence from local and colonial authorities; and by Anderson's reckoning, piracy increased the net costs borne by traders and societies, both indigenous and European, in the eastern seas. A number of more contentious issues also arise. Rediker emphasizes the ideological underpinnings of Atlantic piracy in the 1714–26 period, and the links that it provides between the radical outlaws at sea of the seventeenth century and the revolutions of the late eighteenth century. This accords little with Murray's assertion that the Chinese pirate confederation emerged in response to short-term economic problems and mirrored rather than rejected social structures ashore. Anderson likewise identifies economic factors, not the socio-political protest at the heart of Rediker's analysis, as causing the parasitic, episodic and intrinsic strains of piracy evident in the eastern seas.[12] Loyré, in discussing intrinsic forms of piracy in the Philippines, finds that the penetration of these regions by European traders did not precipitate piracy, but affected pre-existing patterns of predatory activity, a conclusion that adds evidence to the recent debate concerning pirates and empires.[13] Clearly, given its vast scope and contrasting forms, there is much room for further research and debate on the social, political and economic causes and consequences of piracy.

This is perhaps less true of privateering, partly because this business was sanctioned by states, and therefore generated much more documentary source material than the other, illegal form of private commerce-raiding. Nevertheless, some new perspectives emerge from the nine chapters that deal with the private war at sea in this volume. For instance, the privateering enterprise of a range of belligerents is examined, indicating that the character and significance of the activity varied considerably over time and between the different powers. One such variant was evident in the Mediterranean, where the *corso*, an endemic form of commerce-raiding rooted in the 'eternal war' between Islam and Christendom, left a distinctive stamp on the war on trade in the region after 1714. As Gonçal López Nadal demonstrates, privateering activity was increasingly confined to periods of general war, with profit the principal motive of the Spanish, French and North African corsairs who operated in the Mediterranean. State naval power, particularly that wielded by the British, is identified as an important influence in the process by which this ancient struggle evolved from a crusade into a business opportunity, from the *corso* to the *corsarismo*, during the eighteenth century.

As such, it increasingly resembled the private commerce-raiding operations of the North Atlantic. In Britain, as David J. Starkey indicates, the level of such privateering enterprise between 1739 and 1815 was subject to short-term fluctuations, the most pronounced occurring in the early stages of the Fourth Anglo-Dutch War in 1780–1 when some 450 private ships-of-war and over 19,000 privateersmen were engaged in a brief surge of commerce-raiding activity. The long-term, underlying trend, however, was one of contraction from the heady days of 1744–57 when large-scale, 'deep-water' pirate ships-of-war formed the most dynamic sector of the privateering fleet. Demand, in the guise of the perceived extent and vulnerability of enemy trade, was the factor chiefly conditioning this pattern. This was also the case in North America, with British colonial privateering stimulated by the volume and proximity of Bourbon trade in the Caribbean in the 1740s and 1750s,[14] a pattern evident, though with the Americans now independent and British trade now the target, in the American Revolutionary War and again, as Faye Kert shows, in the 1812–14 war. However, in British North America, most notably in Nova Scotia, privateering against the United States was a further feature of the Anglo-American War. On both sides of the border, as Kert concludes, supply-side factors were significant as trade was disrupted by the war, and local merchants and seafarers turned to privateering as one of the alternative avenues for investment and employment.

In his analysis of French privateering expeditions in the

Revolutionary and Napoleonic Wars, Patrick Crowhurst likewise identifies the supply of factors as being critical to the scale and success of private commerce-raiding. This was a high risk business, largely because potential British prizes, though numerous and valuable, were well protected by the Royal Navy. Accordingly, privateering was not an easy option; rather, as Crowhurst's case studies indicate, it was the resort of merchants and shipowners shorn of viable commercial alternatives. Such *armateurs*, moreover, needed to trim their costs to the bone, recruit a skilled and experienced captain and crew, and enjoy a large degree of good fortune in order to profit from their privateering investments. Such ingredients were not always forthcoming as the studies of Dutch privateering by Corrie Reinders Folmer and Jan van Zijverden demonstrate. In the first of these accounts, a large-scale privateering venture promoted by the Middelburg Company in 1747 is analysed. Alas, despite the company's meticulous planning and the viability of the scheme—British ventures of a similar strength returned vast profits at this time[15]—the project foundered due to a shortage of labour. In the Fourth Anglo-Dutch War, the Republic's privateering business was again muted at a time when British private ships-of-war proliferated, only 29 vessels sailing with Dutch letters of commission in the war as a whole. On this occasion, as van Zijverden notes, it was not a lack of labour, but the availability of a profitable alternative occupation—trading under neutral colours—that explained the apparent reluctance of the Dutch to set forth privateers.

Indeed, neutral trading is a much neglected factor in the literature on the maritime wars of the 1689–1815 period, notwithstanding the works of Pares, Carter and Feldbaeck.[16] Numerous insights into this complex issue are presented in this volume. While Starkey and van Zijverden cite the ability of belligerents to trade under neutral flags as one of the factors depressing levels of British and Dutch privateering activity, three further chapters focus specifically on the neutral traders. Jan Parmentier analyses Ostend's apparent emergence as a major shipping centre during the Anglo-Dutch conflict of 1780–3, a seemingly meteoric rise explained by the re-registration of Dutch, French and British vessels in the small imperial port. This early case of flagging out brought income and business to Ostend, and permitted merchants and shipowners based in the belligerent states to continue commercial operations armed with neutral papers—sometimes forged—instead of carriage guns and cutlasses. Attention is then afforded to Denmark's exploitation of the neutrality option, a strategy that was also pursued by Sweden, Russia and, most notably, the Dutch Republic. Ole Feldbaeck examines the maritime policy of successive Danish governments between 1750 and 1807, revealing that shipping belligerents' goods was a relatively safe and profitable business, though it inevitably led to increasingly fraught diplomatic relations with the dominant sea power, Britain. The practicalities of this policy are considered in Eric Goebel's discussion of the fateful voyage of the *Bornholm,* a Danish man-of-war charged with escorting neutral vessels in the Caribbean between 1780 and 1782. This was not a simple task; as well as the physical problems associated with assembling and protecting merchantmen, Peter Schionning, the *Bornholm*'s commander, had to contend with the aggressive enthusiasm of British privateers-men and naval seafarers in prosecuting their right to stop and search neutral vessels, a zeal that in his case extended to the capture of the Danish naval escort.

Such incidents indicate that commerce-raiding in the 1700–1850 period entailed much more than well-regulated attacks on the enemy's commerce. To comprehend fully the complexities of the war on trade during this era, further research of a comparative nature is required on European privateering and neutral trade, as well as on piracy in all its manifestations across the globe. Despite the many advances in our knowledge that have been made in the interim, this message carries echoes of that issued by the 1975 San Francisco conference. One further conclusion of that meeting bears repetition here: piracy and privateering, as this volume of essays clearly shows, were highly significant factors in the war on trade which raged through the eighteenth and nineteenth centuries.

Notes

1. Michel Mollat (ed.), *Course et piraterie* (Paris, 1975) 2 vols.
2. Kenneth R. Andrews, *Ships, Money and Politics: Seafaring and Naval Enterprise in the Reign of Charles I* (Cambridge, 1991); C.M. Senior, *A Nation of Pirates: English Piracy in its Heyday* (Newton Abbot, 1976); David D. Hebb, *Piracy and the English Government 1616–1642* (Aldershot, 1994); R.A. Stradling, *The Armada of Flanders: Spanish Maritime Policy and European War 1568–1668* (Cambridge, 1992); A.P. van Vliet, *Vissers en Kapers: De zeevisserij vanuit het Maasmondgebeid en de Duinkerker kapers 1580–1648* (Gravenhage, 1994); John C. Appleby, 'English Privateering during the Spanish and French Wars, 1625–1630' (unpublished Ph.D. thesis, University of Hull, 1983).
3. Christopher Hill, 'Radical Pirates' in *The Collected Essays of Christopher Hill: Vol. 3, People and Ideas in 17th Century England* (Brighton, 1986); J.S. Bromley, 'Outlaws

at Sea: Liberty, Equality and Fraternity among Caribbean Freebooters' in J.S. Bromley, *Corsairs and Navies 1660–1760* (London, 1987); B.R. Burg, *Sodomy and the Perception of Evil: English Sea Rovers in the Seventeenth-Century Caribbean* (New York, 1983).

4. Marcus Rediker, *Between the Devil and the Deep Blue Sea: Merchant Seamen, Pirates and the Anglo-American Maritime World 1700–1750* (Cambridge, 1987); Robert C. Ritchie, *Captain Kidd and the War against the Pirates* (Cambridge, Mass., 1986); Nuala Zahadieh, '"A Frugal, Prudential and Hopeful Trade": Privateering in Jamaica 1655–89' *Journal of Imperial and Commonwealth History*, 18 (1990); Nuala Zahadieh, 'Trade, Plunder and Economic Development in early English Jamaica, 1655–89' *Economic History Review*, 39 (1986).

5. David Cordingly, *Life Among the Pirates: The Romance and the Reality* (London, 1995); Jo Stanley, *Bold in her Breeches: Women Pirates across the Ages* (London, 1995); David F. Marley, *Pirates: Adventurers of the High Seas* (London, 1995).

6. J.S. Bromley, 'The French Privateering War' in Bromley, *Corsairs and Navies*; Patrick Crowhurst, *The French War on Trade: Privateering 1793–1815* (Aldershot, 1989).

7. David J. Starkey, *British Privateering Enterprise in the Eighteenth Century* (Exeter, 1990); chapters by John Bromley, Alan G. Jamieson and William R. Meyer in Alan G. Jamieson (ed.), *A People of the Sea: The Maritime History of the Channel Islands* (London, 1986); Peter Raban, 'The Profits of Privateering: A Guernsey Fleet, 1756–62' *Mariner's Mirror*, 81 (1994).

8. Carl E. Swanson, *Predators and Prizes: American Privateering and Imperial Warfare 1739–1748* (Columbia, S.C., 1991); Jerome R. Garitee, *The Republic's Private Navy: The American Privateering Business as Practised by Baltimore during the War of 1812* (Middletown, Conn., 1977).

9. See Anne Pérotin-Dumon, 'La contribution de *corsarios insurgentes* a l'independance Americaine, 1810–1830' in Mollat (ed.), *Course et piraterie*; Basil Lubbock, *Cruisers, Corsairs and Slavers: An Account of the Suppression of the Picaroon, Pirate & Slaver by the Royal Navy during the 19th Century* (Glasgow, 1993).

10. John Brewer, *The Sinews of Power: War, Money and the English State, 1688–1783* (London, 1989); Daniel A. Baugh, 'Maritime Strength and Atlantic Commerce: The Uses of A Grand Marine Empire' in Lawrence Stone (ed.), *An Imperial State at War: Britain from 1689 to 1815* (London, 1994).

11. Janice E. Thomson, *Mercenaries, Pirates and Sovereigns: State-building and Extraterritorial Violence in Early Modern Europe* (Princeton, 1994).

12. See J.L. Anderson, 'Piracy and World History: An Economic Perspective on Maritime Predation' *Journal of World History*, 6 (1995); and David J. Starkey, 'Pirates and Markets' in Lewis R. Fischer, *The Market for Seamen in the Age of Sail* (St John's, Newfoundland, 1994).

13. Anne Pérotin-Dumon, 'The Pirate and the Emperor: Power and the Law on the Seas, 1450–1850' in James D. Tracy (ed.), *The Political Economy of Merchant Empires* (Cambridge, 1991).

14. See Swanson, *Predators and Prizes*; and James G. Lydon, *Pirates, Privateers, Profits* (Upper Saddle River, N.J., 1970).

15. Starkey, *British Privateering Enterprise*, 117–60.

16. Richard Pares, *Colonial Blockade and Neutral Rights 1739–1748* (Oxford, 1938);

Alice Carter, *Neutrality or Commitment: The Evolution of Dutch Foreign Policy 1667–1795* (London, 1975); Ole Feldbaeck, 'Eighteenth Century Danish Neutrality: Its Diplomacy, Economics and Law' *Scandinavian Journal of History,* 13 (1983).

CHAPTER 1

Government Measures against Piracy and Privateering in the Atlantic Area, 1750–1850

Robert C. Ritchie

Introduction

Piracy and privateering accompanied the rise of the European empires. Both activities thrived with state sponsorship as the competition for trade and empire caused a scramble for the spoils of the emerging world economy. The undernourished state of international law and policing gave states considerable leeway. The imperial states reached far and wide in their grasp for power and profit and then set about providing the administrative apparatus to control what they had seized. The interval between ambitious grab and adequate means of control was quite long in places. These intervals allowed the development of piracy on a unique scale.

Privateering was a slightly different matter. The competition for empire brought a wider geographic dimension to the nearly endemic wars that accompanied the rise of European nation-states. Attacks on enemy commerce by privateers were a vital part of these wars, and while subject to considerable abuse, were brought to a high degree of organization as a matter of state policy and were recognized internationally as an appropriate state activity.

Thus, piracy and privateering shared a continuum from completely illegal to entirely authorized attacks on private property. How states came to regard and deal with this continuum is the topic of this chapter. While it concentrates on the period from 1750 to 1850, it also considers the earlier period because the policies that were developed during the late seventeenth and early eighteenth centuries set many of the parameters that applied in the period under discussion.

Pirates

The excesses of pirates were the first to require control. Europe had suffered from indigenous pirates such as those of Dunkirk or the south-western ports of England for a very long time, but the race for empire and the struggle for religious and political freedom by various peoples brought new elements into piracy. In addition, the struggles for empire brought England, France, the Netherlands and other smaller states into conflict with Spain and Portugal over the spoils derived from the expanding world economy. Governments and merchant groups found commerce-raiding in war and peace a convenient way of weakening rivals and acquiring a share of the new wealth. Given the state of international law and of the mechanisms for enforcing it, there were few impediments to commerce-raiding. And for emerging states such as the Dutch, who were struggling for survival, or for the English, locked in combat with the Spanish, there were few rules worth bothering about. Merchants, companies, governments and government officials all exploited the situation to enrich themselves.[1]

By the middle of the seventeenth century order, at least in home waters, became a priority for the new states and the growing navies policed the waters around Europe with increasing effectiveness, bringing about a general decline of piracy. The Mediterranean remained more dangerous to commerce because of the Barbary corsairs, but treaties, pay-offs and the occasional armed raid brought peace for the major trading states.[2] The real problem now lay out in the empires where piracy still flourished.

The Caribbean, the scene of treasure ships and increasingly wealthy sugar islands, was the major arena for state rivalry. Out of this competition there arose the buccaneers, an indigenous body of free-booters. Confusion reigned as international competition made it easy for the buccaneers to acquire privateering commissions from one or other of the imperial powers who were so frequently locked in war. Also, many men were willing to sail without papers because there were always merchants in the West Indies or the North American colonies who were willing to do business with them, regardless of the legal niceties. During the 1680s the buccaneers expanded their activities to the Pacific, West Africa and the Indian Ocean and their attacks on shipping became ever more sophisticated. By 1700, however, the metropolitan governments and merchants were no longer willing to permit such widespread lawlessness and so they created policies and institutions that would bring an end to large-scale European piracy.[3]

The English were well known as the 'nation of pirates', and as the emerging naval power their actions regarding piracy were particularly important. The first significant change was in the attitude of merchants and government officials who had often sponsored piracy in the past. Now they were more intent on enjoying the profits of empire and regular trade and were less willing to suffer losses from uncontrolled brigandage. The English government was now willing to impose tighter rules on privateering, making sharper the distinctions between it and piracy. The law relating to piracy was revised so that it could be brought to bear anywhere in the empire and Vice-Admiralty courts were established in the colonies with powers to act against pirates. Moreover, the Royal Navy underwent a series of changes that would make it a formidable tool in the new campaign. Because of the nearly continuous wars from 1688 to 1713, the navy gained an enormous number of ships and most of the new ships were in the lesser rates that could be used in commerce protection. In addition, seven naval warrant officers, sitting as a court, could hold a trial for piracy, and ships and goods captured from pirates were treated as prize, giving the navy a financial incentive to hunt for pirates.[4]

In the peace that followed the Treaty of Utrecht the war against the pirates gained momentum. By 1730 the heyday of buccaneering was over as the navy hunted pirates in the Caribbean, North America and even in the Indian Ocean. The navy also solidified its role in commerce protection by extending the number of cruisers that remained active in dangerous areas and off port cities in the colonies, and by creating permanent stations. This was a new policy, but after the creation of a permanent base at Antigua, the Royal Navy gradually added bases that would ultimately extend into places as far afield as the north-west Pacific and Australia.[5] Naval stations and cruising areas gradually covered the shipping zones of the world and made possible the *Pax Britannica*. The Royal Navy, however, was not the only force active in commerce protection. Even the infant navy of the United States managed to enter the campaign against robbery at sea.[6]

Figure 1.1 Bombardment of Algiers by combined Dutch/British naval force, 26 August 1816. (Netherlands Maritime Museum, Amsterdam)

All of these activities brought to a close the first phase of empire-building that had so often been characterized by official and unofficial brigandage. While the days were over when Morgan could raise 2,000 men and assault Panama, or when it was possible to operate a pirate base on the island of Saint Marie near Madagascar, it obviously did not mean an end to piracy. As long as valuables were moved by sea, theft would always follow. There were still enough episodes to provide for the literary appetite for books and pamphlets started by Exquemelin and nourished by Daniel Defoe. Works such as *Pirate Barbarity: Or the Female Captive . . . the Unparalleled Sufferings of Miss Lucretia Parker*, or *The Surprising Adventures of Henry Twisdon . . . Horrid Proceedings on board the Corsair: His Arrival at an Astonishing Cave in Africa* kept piracy from fading from public consciousness.[7] Such episodes concerned governments if a pirate crew became too successful, but generally they aroused little concern.

However, there were other forms of piracy. Many sea-going peoples continued to practice piracy as a traditional activity and, with the expansion of the empires and their navies, conflict was inevitable. The oldest of these communities and ones familiar to all the European powers were the city states of North Africa with their long tradition of corsairing. For centuries bought off with subsidies and treaties, the Barbary corsairs were in terminal decrepitude by the early nineteenth century. States still sent the occasional expedition to punish them until a joint Dutch and English squadron overwhelmed them in 1816 and then the French occupied the whole area in 1830, bringing an end to a long episode in Mediterranean maritime history.[8] There were many other traditional seafaring communities with a penchant for piracy and, while this topic lies outside the scope of this chapter, the Arab, Malay, Filipino and Chinese maritime communities all came into contention with European commercial interests. One example was the conflict with the Joasmi Arabs in the Persian Gulf. After a series of incidents the Royal Navy attacked them twice, until in 1819 the final expedition demanded and received local concessions that left Britain the major maritime power in the region. The same scenario of a naval expedition destroying local shipping and leading to a demand for concessions so that there would be no more depredations against 'legitimate' commerce would be played out a number of times. Such ploys, no matter what the provocation, provided a convenient means of expanding imperial control into new areas, bringing ever-larger regions into the orbit of the European world order.[9]

Fig. 1.2   Dutch privateers bringing the French man-of-war *Bourbon* into Flushing roadstead, 1702
(Hisrerisch Sheepvaart Museum, Amsterdam)

While the navies, especially the British, managed to suppress piracy except for these occasional outbursts, the age of revolution would present new challenges. In revolutionary times it was difficult to tell the patriots from the traitors and the revolutionaries from the royalists. In American waters, and especially in the Caribbean, recognizing appropriate authority was extremely difficult. Even the shrewdest captain could make mistakes, whether it was a navy captain trying to do his duty, or a merchant captain attempting to sail safely.[10] Royalist regimes were replaced with revolutionary ones and they in turn were often replaced by a new colonial government put in charge by the British. Each might issue 'commissions' regarded as legitimate by them if by no one else. The accompanying slave rebellions and the revolution in Haiti brought 'picaroons' out as a new element in commerce-raiding.[11] A similar situation developed with the break-up of the Spanish empire. During the wars for independence, various governments authorized privateering, stimulating the *course independante*. Privateers set forth from Columbia, Cuba, Argentina and Mexico, but some were of dubious virtue. French and Americans from New Orleans sailed under the Mexican flag, using it as a cover for old piratical habits. Columbian privateers moved to Haiti after the Spanish regained control of Cartagena. In Argentina the Caudillo Arigas sent out ships from Buenos Aires that raided as far afield as the Pacific and the West Indies. Cuba became a centre for piracy and the attacks of many small ships on American commerce outraged the new government of the United States.[12] The swirl of events and the confused status of so many governments made it possible for pirates to take advantage of the situation. The Caribbean again resembled the glory days of buccaneering.

This was not exclusively an American phenomenon. The Greek independence movement, in attempting to free Greece from Turkey, led to an outbreak of piracy in the eastern Mediterranean.[13] The revolutionary movement sent ships to raid Turkish commerce, but again many slipped from the leash and there was always the question of the validity of the government's commissions. In the end the Royal Navy established order.

During this era navies were absorbed in fighting in home waters and the number of ships available, particularly in the early months of the conflict, was limited and trade protection suffered. Even once sufficient force could be brought to bear, the situation could be so confusing that commanders had great difficulty in separating the legitimate commerce-raiders from the bogus or merely piratical. Once the revolutions were crushed, contained or accepted and international order restored, peace and the navies reasserted their dominance and the pirates soon found that they were just as vulnerable as the buccaneers had been in similar circumstances. As in the past, piracy might occur randomly or in special circumstances, but a sustained attack on major commercial interests would soon be defeated.[14]

One other change affected piracy in the Atlantic area and that was a steady erosion of support for the pirates among maritime communities. In North America, for instance, the pirates found a warm welcome when the infant port towns of the American colonies sought any sort of trade goods. Once the merchants had created regular trade and a steady prosperity, however, the need to do business with pirates waned and so did their support. The merchants quickly joined the anti-piracy crusade and instead of finding a warm welcome, the pirates were confronted by the hangman and a long rope.[15]

Privateers

No such fate awaited privateers. During most of the period under consideration privateering commissions were sought in many merchant communities as soon as war was declared. In fact, as soon as war was imminent petitioning started to force the government to produce commissions early and allow the privateers to catch enemy commerce unprepared. In Britain and France the merchants interested in privateering formed a potent lobby to ensure their profits. In France, for instance, the policy of ransoming, or allowing a ship and cargo to go free on the payment of a ransom, was pursued even though it was not in the best interests of the state. The rationale of the war against commerce was to deprive the enemy of ships and cargoes and ransoming undermined this policy. However, it was very popular with the privateers who could stay at sea longer and capture more ships for greater profits. The success of the privateering campaign and the resistance of the privateers to giving up ransom finally forced the government to change policy in 1706 and provide a legal basis for ransom.[16] British privateering interests were also adept at getting their way, but they did have to face the opposition of the Royal Navy, which was always short of men and hated to see the privateersmen take away prime sailors and exacerbate the manning problem. Navy captains, themselves hungry for prize money, also disliked the competition.[17]

What lured the merchants into seeking commissions was the profitability of the business. While there could be and often were losers, privateering remained highly profitable for the lucky and the skilled. In the colonies the returns from privateering provided much-needed capital to develop young economies. In the navy an appointment to a frigate was like money in the bank, especially if assigned to the Mediterranean. Thus, privateering had considerable support and would continue to be an important wartime activity.[18]

Privateering, like piracy, reached its apogee in the late seventeenth and early eighteenth centuries. The two great wars at the turn of the century gave ample scope to privateering on a hitherto unknown scale. Record numbers of ships obtained licences and they in turn captured ships on a grand scale. This activity forced the warring states, especially England and France, to define privateering and to bring it under control. One of the oldest and most abused forms of commerce-raiding, the letter of reprisal in peacetime, was more or less abandoned. Since it was permitted as a way of allowing recovery of goods seized by piratical act, the decline of piracy in European waters meant that it was less needed and, because it was quite often used as a means of stealing goods far in excess of the original loss, it was frequently an embarrassment to nation-states involved in strengthening diplomatic ties and creating a web of treaties to regularize their affairs. It was best not to allow individuals to take matters into their own hands, but to provide institutional means for recovery.[19]

Wartime witnessed no such reticence. Commerce-raiding or preying on private property at sea was still regarded as a legitimate war aim. In the case of France an early commitment to the *guerre d'escadre* changed to the *guerre de course* and an enhanced institutional framework to commission the privateers and adjudicate their prizes was created.[20] This change in policy proved decisive and the French privateering war that followed damaged British trade. England, on the other hand, remained committed to both a great fleet and to privateering, and while the scale of the privateering effort never equalled that of the French it was still considerable. In the process the government refined the rules relating to prize and passed a number of statutes that set out the conditions for commissions and for treating prizes. In general the regulations were tightened to allow only wealthy investors to enter the business and to allow the broadest scope to their activities.[21] To get into the business investors had to post bonds and agree to a long set of rules governing their activities. Privateering had become a regulated business from the initial licence to the final decree in prize court. Yet there was still scope to abuse ships and men, particularly those of neutrals whose status was always problematic. These episodes led to charges that the privateers were frequently lawless and nothing more than licensed pirates.

The two great wars (the Nine Years War, 1688–97, and the War of the Spanish Succession, 1702–13) fought under these rules saw unprecedented privateering activities.[22] While the devastation reached new levels the two main participants never considered abandoning their commitment to commerce-raiding. If anything, they urged their privateers to greater efforts. Both Britain and France passed legislation to remove the state's share from prize adjudication, allowing the privateers to keep all of the prizes for themselves.[23] They did, however, try to mitigate its worst effects on their own commerce. The key policy was convoying. All the maritime powers had experience with convoys, but the unprecedented attacks on commerce meant that they needed to protect larger fleets of merchant ships and convoy them to many more places. This meant far greater co-ordination with various merchant groups, either the great companies that monopolized trade in commodities or to whole areas, such as the Levant, or the 'free' trades such as sugar or tobacco, where no company dominated. The need for constant contact between the government and the merchants helped create effective lobbies that would continue after the war. As allies, and with the most to lose because of their large carrying fleets, the Dutch and the English had to develop the most sophisticated systems. From the Baltic to the East Indies, ships needed protection either from vessels that sailed with them or from cruisers at the nodal points of navigation. The Royal Navy gained bitter experience in attempting to control the wayward ways of merchant ships whose captains were intent on sailing in safety while enhancing their own commercial advantages. To force the merchants to obey the rules a Convoy Act was passed in 1708 that gave the navy more authority to discipline the unruly. France also developed a convoy system, but it was never as successful as the allies, who would always have the edge due to greater naval power.[24]

One other development aided shipowners in surviving the war years, and that was insurance. Already well developed on the continent, the London market received a great impetus during the wars and emerged much stronger. By the middle of the eighteenth century London had emerged as the premier insurance centre. This also helped ameliorate the effects of war, even on the French who used the London insurance market in wartime until the British government made this illegal. French ships sailed without insurance or with extremely expensive insurance thereafter, adding another burden to French trade in wartime.[25] Thus by the Peace of Utrecht in 1713 the maritime states had controlled privateering to some extent and created the means to mitigate its effects. Given the devastation wrought by the privateers, it is a wonder that the peacemakers did not address the issue in the treaty process, but there were still too many interests favouring its retention and opponents were few and weak.

Opposition came from the neutral states. Little new policy with regard to the rights of neutrals developed during the wars. However, the whole issue of neutrality came to be critical as Dutch economic vitality waned around mid-century and the Netherlands' naval power declined compared to that of France and Britain. As a result of these and other factors, the Netherlands turned towards a neutral stance in great power affairs. What would propel the Dutch into controversy was the continuing vitality of their carrying fleet which might not be conveying as many Dutch goods as before, but now carried greater amounts of the trade of other nations.[26]

The problems of neutrals would come to the fore in the wars that started in 1739. The War of Jenkin's Ear and King George's War were primarily wars of empire that pitted first Spain and then France against the British. They highlighted the importance of colonial trade and ushered in a new era of commerce-raiding in the colonies. This was especially true in the North American ports where appetites that had been whetted in the earlier wars could be more fully satisfied now that prosperity had generated more shipping resources. The result was that New York, Boston, Newport and Philadelphia would send more ships and men to sea than ever before and reap very considerable profits from privateering.[27] Most of their raiding was confined to the West Indies where the French sugar colonies had to sustain a major attack on their trade. This raised serious issues for neutrals such as the Dutch and the Danes, who carried French colonial goods in their ships. The Dutch based their policy on the treaty of 1674 with England that permitted free ships to carry free goods. As long as England and the Netherlands were allies this rule was easy for each side to honour. But British attitudes hardened towards neutrals during this period, particularly with regard to the carrying of Baltic naval supplies to the French, and when war was declared again in 1756 the British were ready to change the rules.[28]

The 'rule' of 1756, as declared unilaterally by Britain, defined neutral commerce in a way that suited Britain. Any trade that was denied to other states in peacetime by the mercantile system of the imperial powers was denied to them in wartime. Thus French colonial trade, a monopoly of French ships and merchants in peacetime, could not be carried by neutrals in wartime. Added to this rule was another innovation relating to continuous voyages. This meant that if the ultimate destination of a cargo was an enemy port it could be taken at any point along the voyage and claimed as prize. By these two measures Britain had seriously hampered the rights of neutrals, most particularly the Dutch and the Danes, and exposed their trade to serious threat.[29] In fact, the attacks on Dutch shipping became so indiscriminate in the Channel that new rules on privateering were issued to confine it to major ships, thus denying legitimacy to the very small craft that were taking prizes in home waters.

The second half of the eighteenth century had started with the greatest naval power substantially limiting the rights of neutrals and opening up considerable trade to threat by privateering. The Seven Years War (1756–63) would witness another war on trade that weakened the rights of neutrals and made the war on commerce a major aspect of English policy. Although the British occasionally mitigated the effects of their privateers on neutral commerce, as the dominant naval power the actions of the English had broader implications.[30] As long as the British openly favoured the extension of privateering in this way, it would continue to play a role in wartime.

As has already been shown in the discussion of piracy, the age of revolution put great pressure on the web of agreements relating to trade and privateering. During the wars that accompanied the American Revolution, the French Revolution and the Napoleonic era there were few attempts by the new states to take the initiative to end privateering. More often than not all sides would continue to prey on commerce and use the old rules. The new American government, for instance, immediately allowed privateering and each of the new states created prize courts and started to issue commissions. The French government took a different tack. In 1792 it requested negotiations towards ending privateering. This would, of course, please the neutrals, but found no favour with the British government so the initiative came to nothing. By 1793 the government allowed privateering and in 1796 the Directory allowed attacks on neutral commerce.[31] The neutrals, in their turn, tried to stay out of the wars and to this end revived the League of Armed Neutrality in 1800, but met with scant success again.

In general the era was one of turmoil and confusion as to rights of war and navigation. The problems are obvious. Old imperial states treated newly proclaimed independent nations as traitors and their privateering commissions were seen as worthless and the men who sailed with them were considered pirates. This led to great confusion. When Benjamin Franklin provided commissions and aid to American privateers in France, the French government stopped him in order to live up to old treaty agreements with England.[32]

In the West Indies there was even more confusion. On occasion royalist sympathizers controlled French colonial governments and permitted ships to sail with royal commissions.[33] When the Haitian revolutionary government permitted privateers to operate from its ports nearly all established governments refused to recognize them as legitimate.[34] These were the two extremes in the Caribbean, but nearly every other possibility existed as war and revolution swirled among the islands producing headaches for any naval commander. As we have already seen, pirates lurked everywhere. These problems remained intractable and were a constant throughout the whole period.[35]

In European waters the war between Napoleon and Britain was more straightforward. One side introduced the Continental Blockade and the other a blockade on European trade and with this the possibilities for privateering were great. However, as the dominant naval power, Britain made the rules, and in this nearly total war the neutrals suffered once again. When Denmark attempted to carry on what it regarded as normal and legal trade the Royal Navy swept in and defeated the Danish fleet. After that Danish trade continued but with convoys from the Royal Navy. This long era of war and revolution did little to curb privateering. New rules were set, such as the reorganization of the *Conseil de prize* in 1800, but on the whole the system was much as before.[36] The British faced a lesser challenge from the French due to the navy's ability to maintain a blockade on French ports and to run a better convoy system, but even with such dominance the British could not completely do away with privateers. As long as a major state with a significant number of ports wanted to permit privateering it was nearly impossible to stop it from doing so.

The End of Privateering

After the Napoleonic War there was a long era of peace between the major European powers. Privateering faded into memory as amity grew between the major powers. On the few occasions it occurred it had minor effects.[37] Meanwhile the age of industrialism and liberal capitalism got under way and the growth of trade was important to many governments. The British especially pursued their advantages and pushed greater trade freedom. In this atmosphere it seemed more and more anomalous to allow private warships to attack commerce. The long process whereby the state came to monopolize force, first by banning private armies, came to its logical end in questioning the continuation of private warships. As an American statesmen put it, 'War is now an affair of Governments'.[38] Should an era that espoused the growth of trade and industry allow attacks on private property at sea by 'licensed pirates'? Obviously not, for as Queen Victoria put it, 'privateering is a kind of piracy which disagrees with our Civilization, its abolition throughout the World would be a great step in its advance'.[39] Lord Clarendon, the English foreign minister, considered it 'inconsistent with modern civilization', and James Buchanan, the United States minister in Britain, stated that 'the genuine dictate of Christianity and civilization would be to abolish war against private property upon the ocean altogether'.[40] Such sentiments foretold the end of privateering.

The occasion came with the Crimean War. Prior to the war various states made declarations regarding neutral rights. The Swedes and the Danes refused to admit privateers to their ports altogether. Prussia, a long-time advocate of neutral rights, declared against privateering during the war. The French and British governments, with differing policies regarding neutrals, and now joined together as allies, decided to reduce the confusion and please the neutrals by following them.[41] Cynics might say that this was not much of a sacrifice as Russia was hardly a great maritime power and it was easy to bottle up its trade. None the less, for the first time in a major European war there was to be no privateering.

The British government had a major concern about this general declaration because the United States refused to go along with any general agreement on privateering. Because it had a small navy and growing carrying fleet, the United States refused to join in the ban. Britain feared that the United States would harbour Russian privateers or even allow its citizens to accept Russian commissions. After receiving private assurances that this would not be permitted, the government relaxed, but it was still concerned about an American campaign to ban all attacks on private property at sea in wartime.[42]

Thus, when Count Waleski, the French plenipotentiary to the peace conference after the war, suggested that the conference should undertake a broad general statement regarding maritime law, the British government agreed.[43] The delegates at the conference quickly produced a statement banning privateering and defining neutral rights. The Declaration of Paris in 1856 was signed by the seven nations who attended the conference and they invited other nations to join them. During the next two years most major nations followed them. A few nations such as Spain, Mexico and, most importantly, the United States refused to do so, as all of them had long coast lines and weak navies and believed they had to allow privateering to protect themselves. Thus in one grand diplomatic gesture the major maritime powers abandoned privateering.[44]

The United States was soon forced to attempt a last minute agreement to the Declaration prior to the secession of the southern states. This attempt came to nothing as the United States wanted to attach a rider to its signature that was unacceptable to the other powers. To the deep misgiving of the Union, the Confederacy allowed privateers to operate. This would be the last privateering campaign of note, although it was not very large or successful. The Confederacy would rely more on naval raiders to damage Union commerce.[45] Other than this episode the ban would continue in place.

While successful, the ban remained controversial. Many in England questioned its necessity and accused the government of 'treasonous' behaviour. They had 'cut off [Britain's] right arm' and given away a fundamental right.[46] In France, the *Jeune Ecole* urged a revival of the policy of the *guerre de course* when the confluence of affordable new torpedo boats and the seemingly unaffordable new battleships and weapon systems made privateering a suitable policy, but these arguments never found favour with the government and they remained nothing more than a discussion point with naval theorists.[47] The great powers preferred the state's continued monopoly of violence and an armaments race. Over the horizon the ultimate weapon for commerce destruction, the submarine, allowed the war on commerce to proceed firmly under the control of governments and the destruction of trade to reach unprecedented heights. It would have been better if they had followed the advice of secretary of state William L. Marcy in 1856:

> The United States consider powerful navies and large standing armies, as permanent establishments, to be detrimental to national prosperity and to civil liberty. The expense of keeping them up is burdensome to the people; they are, in the opinion of this Government, in the same degree a menace to peace among nations. A large force, ever ready to be devoted to the purposes of war, is a temptation to rush into it. The policy of the United States has ever been, and never more than now, adverse to such establishments; and they can never be brought to acquiesce in any change in international law which may render it necessary for them to maintain a powerful navy or large regular army in time of peace.[48]

Notes

1. There are numerous sources, among them Clive Senior, *A Nation of Pirates: English Piracy in its Heyday* (London, 1976); Wesley F. Graven, 'The Earl of Warwick, A Speculator in Piracy' *Hispanic American Historical Review,* 10 (1930), 457–79; Kenneth R. Andrews, *The Spanish Caribbean, Trade and Plunder, 1530–1630* (New Haven, 1978).
2. Peter Earle, *Corsairs of Malta and Barbary* (London, 1970); William Spencer, *Algiers in the Age of the Corsairs* (Norman, Okla., 1976); C. Lloyd, *English Corsairs on the Barbary Coast* (London, 1981); Seton Dearden, *A Nest of Corsairs: The Fighting Karamanlis of the Barbary Coast* (London, 1976).
3. C.H. Haring, *The Buccaneers in the West Indies in the Seventeenth Century* (London, 1910); M. Besson, *The Scourge of the Indies: Buccaneers, Corsairs and Filibusters . . .* (London, 1929); A.G. Course, *Piracy in Eastern Seas* (London, 1966); P.K. Kemp and C. Lloyd, *The Brethren of the Coast. The British and French Buccaneers in the South Seas* (London, 1960); L.C. Vrijman, *Kaapvaart en Zeerooverij. Uit de Geschiedenis der Vrije Nering in de Lage Landen* (Amsterdam, 1938).
4. See Robert C. Ritchie, *Captain Kidd and the War Against the Pirates* (Cambridge, Mass., 1986), 127–59.
5. Daniel A. Baugh, *British Naval Administration in the Age of Walpole* (Princeton, 1965), 341–72; Barry M. Gough, *The Royal Navy and the Northwest Coast of North America, 1810–1914: A Study of British Maritime Ascendancy* (Vancouver, 1971); John Bach, *The Australia Station: A History of the Royal Navy in the Southwest Pacific, 1821–1913* (Kensington, New South Wales, 1986); Barry M. Gough, 'Sea Power and South America: The Brazils or South American Station of the Royal Navy, 1808–1837' *American Neptune,* 50 (1990), 26–34; and for the origins of cruising, Ruth Bourne, *Queen Anne's Navy in the West Indies* (New Haven, 1939), 58–107.
6. Gardner W. Allen, *Our Navy and the West Indian Pirates* (Cambridge, Mass., 1919) and his *Our Navy and the Barbary Corsairs* (Connecticut, 1905); Francis B.C. Bradlee, *Piracy in the West Indies and its Suppression* (Salem, Mass., 1923).
7. *Pirate Barbarity* (New York, 1806) and Twisdon, *Surprising Adventures* (London, n.d.). Some of these episodes were the result of crews mutinying against

repressive regimes. Alexander Wallace, *Piratical Seizure of the Brig Admiral Trowbridge, by part of her crew while lying at anchor of the Island of Sooloo, August 21, 1807* (London, 1807).

8. R. Perkins, *Gunfire in Barbary: Admiral Lord Exmouth's Battle with the Corsairs of Algiers in 1816* (Havant, 1982); G.S. van Krieken, 'Het Engels-Nederlandse bombardement van Algiers in 1816' *Tijdschrift voor Zeegeschiedenis*, 2 (1987), 138–50.

9. For the Persian Gulf, see Sultan Muhammad Al-Qasimi, *The Myth of Arab Piracy in the Gulf* (London, 1986); and for the other point of view, Charles R. Low, *History of the Indian Navy, 1613–1863* (London, 1877) vol. I, 310–66; H. Moyse Bartlett, *The Pirates of Trucial Oman* (London, 1966); Grace Fox, *British Admirals and Chinese Pirates, 1832–1869* (London, 1940); Nicolas Tarling, *Piracy and Politics in the Malay World: A Study of British Imperialism in the Nineteenth Century South East Asia* (Nendelin, 1978); Alfred P. Rubin, *Piracy, Paramountcy and Protectorates* (Kuala Lumpur, 1974).

10. For the confusion of earlier times, Richard Pares, *War and Trade in the West Indies, 1739–1763* (Oxford, 1936); Alan G. Jamieson, 'American Privateers in the Leeward Islands, 1776–78' *American Neptune*, 43 (1983), 20–30; U. Bonnel, *La France, les Etats-Unis et la Guerre de Course (1797–1815)* (Paris, 1961), 187–226; N. Gallois, *Les Corsairs français sous la République et l'Empire* (Paris, 1847); Michael Duffy, *Soldiers, Sugar and Seapower: The British Expeditions to the West Indies and the War Against Revolutionary France* (Oxford, 1987).

11. H.J.K. Jenkins, 'Privateers, Picaroons, Pirates: West Indies Commerce Raiders, 1793–1801' *Mariner's Mirror*, 73 (1987), 181–6; Michael Palmer, *Stoddert's War: Naval Operations During the Quasi-War with France, 1798–1801* (Columbia, S.C., 1987), 146–81; H.J.K. Jenkins, 'The Leeward Island Command, French Royalism and the *Bienvenue*, 1792–1793' *Mariner's Mirror*, 71 (1985), 477–8, and by the same author, 'Admiral Laforey and the Saint Pierre Raiders, 1790–1791, *Ibid.*, 218–20; John Pelzer, 'Armed Merchantmen and Privateers: Another Perspective on the American Quasi-War with France' *American Neptune*, 50 (1990), 270–81.

12. Francis B.C. Bradlee, *Piracy in the West Indies and its Suppression* (Salem, Mass., 1923); Anne Pérotin-Dumon, 'La contribution des Corsarios insurgentes à l'Independence Americaine; course et piraterie dans le golf du Mexique et la mer des Antilles (1810–1830)' in M. Mollat (ed.), *Course et Piraterie: Etudes presentées à la Commission Internationale d'Histoire Maritime à l'occasion de son XV Collogue* (Paris, 1975), 666–75; Augustin Beraza, *Los Corsairos de Artigas* (Montevideo, 1978) and by the same author, *Los Corsairos de Montevideo* (Montevideo, 1978); *State Papers and Publick Documents of the United States* (Boston, 1817) vol. V, 243–7.

13. Sir Edward Codrington, *Piracy in the Levant, 1827–1828* (London, 1934).

14. For piracy in recent times see Roger Villar, *Piracy Today: Robbery and Violence at Sea since 1980* (London, 1985); Eric Allen, *Piracy at Sea* (Paris, 1989).

15. Ritchie, *Captain Kidd*, ch. 10.

16. Stark, *Abolition*, 98–9.

17. Baugh, *British Naval Administration*, 113–17. For the finances of a successful captain, see Julian Gwyn, *The Enterprising Admiral: The Personal Fortune of Sir Peter Warren* (New York, 1974).

18. Among the many studies, Carl F. Swanson, 'The Profitability of Privateering:

Reflections on British Colonial Privateering during the War of 1776–1783' *American Neptune*, 42 (1982), 36–59; Patrick Crowhurst, 'Profitability in French Privateering, 1793–1815' *Business History*, 24 (1982), 48–60; P.L. Wickens, 'The Economics of Privateering: Capital Dispersal in the American War for Independence' *Journal of European Economic History*, 13 (1984), 375–95; David J. Starkey, *British Privateering Enterprise in the Eighteenth Century* (Exeter, 1990), 59–81; James G. Lydon, *Pirates, Privateers and Profits* (Upper Saddle, N.J., 1970), 225–59.

19. The Peace of Utrecht recognized reprisal but only in cases where justice had been denied to those losing a cargo. However, the representative of the offending nation was to be given four months notice prior to the issue of the commission in order to do justice to the claimant. *A Collection of all the Treaties of Peace, Alliance and Commerce, Between Great Britain and the Other Powers . . .* (London, 1785) vol. V, 37. The drastic decline of piracy in European waters reduced the need for reprisal.

20. Geoffrey Symcox, *The Crisis of French Sea Power, 1688–97: From Guerre d'Escadre to Guerre de Course* (The Hague, 1974).

21. For an excellent discussion of British privateering activity, Starkey, *British Privateering Enterprise*.

22. Some of the best work on privateering in this era was done by J.S. Bromley and many of his essays have been brought together in *Corsairs and Navies, 1660–1760* (London, 1987). See also the essays by J. Delameau, W. Minchinton, D. Aldridge in Mollat (ed.), *Course et Piraterie*; J. Th. Verhees-van Meer, *De Zeeuwse Kaapvaart tijdens de Spaanse Successieoorlog, 1702–1713* (Middelburg, 1986); Starkey, *British Privateering*, ch. 4.

23. In England the change was legislated in 6 Anne c. 13, 1708; in France it was covered by the Ordinance of 1709. Stark, *Abolition*, 98–9.

24. Patrick Crowhurst, *The Defence of British Trade, 1689–1815* (Folkestone, 1977), especially ch. 2 and the area by area discussion in chapters 4–7; Owen Rutter, *Red Ensign: A History of Convoy* (London, 1942); Patrick Villiers, 'La Lutte Contre la Course Anglaise en Atlantique Pendant La Guerre d'Independance des Etats-Unis d'Amerique, 1778–1783' in Mollat (ed.), *Course et Piraterie*, 572–83; Bourne, *Queen Anne's Navy*, 108–40.

25. Crowhurst, *Defence of British Trade*, 81–103; Barry Supple, *Royal Exchange Assurance* (London, 1970).

26. Alice Carter, *Neutrality and Commitment: The Evolution of Dutch Foreign Policy, 1667–1795* (London, 1975); by the same author, *The Dutch Republic in Europe in the Seven Years War* (London, 1971); Jonathan Israel, *Dutch Primacy in World Trade, 1585–1740* (Oxford, 1989).

27. Lydon, *Piracy, Privateering*, passim; H.M. Chapin, *Privateering During King George's War, 1739–1748* (Providence, 1928); Carl E. Swanson, 'American Privateering and Imperial Warfare, 1739–1748' *William and Mary Quarterly*, 42 (1985), 357–82. There was also increased privateering from the British outports, see J.W.D. Powell, *Bristol Privateers and Ships of War* (Bristol, 1930); and J.E. Mullins, *Liverpool Privateering, 1756–1815* (Nova Scotia, 1936).

28. The most complete discussion is in Richard Pares, *Colonial Blockade and Neutral Rights, 1739–1763* (Oxford, 1938). Also see his *War and Trade in the West Indies, 1739–1763* (Oxford, 1936).

29. Pares, *Colonial Blockade*, 180–204, 204–24; Starkey, *British Privateering*, 161–92.

30. Starkey, *British Privateering*, 170.
31. Gardner W. Allen, *Massachusetts Privateers and the Revolution* (Cambridge, Mass., 1927); Stark, *Abolition*, 104–5. See also, David J. Starkey, 'British Privateering against the Dutch in the American Revolution' in Stephen Fisher (ed.), *Studies in British Privateering, Trading Enterprise and Seamen's Welfare, 1775–1900* (Exeter, 1987), 1–17, and also his *British Privateering*, 194–217; Ulane Bonnel, 'Apogée et Declin de la Course en Atlantique fin 18–19e siècle' in Mollat (ed.), *Course et Piraterie*, 512–54.
32. W.B. Clark, *Ben Franklin's Privateers: A Naval Epic of the American Revolution* (New York, 1956).
33. On the French royalists see the articles by Jenkins cited in note 11. See also U. Bonnel, *La France, Les Etats-Unis et la guerre de course, 1797–1815* (Paris, 1961), 187–226.
34. Jenkins, 'Privateers' *Mariner's Mirror*, 73 (1987), 181–6.
35. The Americans were particularly active at this time. Jerome R. Garitee, *The Republic's Private Navy: The American Privateering Business as Practised by Baltimore during the War of 1812* (Middleton, Conn., 1977); M.H. Jackson, *The Privateers of Charleston, 1793–1796* (Washington, 1969).
36. Bonnel, *La France*, 141; Patrick Crowhurst, *The French War on Trade. Privateering, 1793–1815* (Aldershot, 1989); Alice Carter, 'The Dutch Privateering Arm in the Mid and Late Eighteenth Century' in Mollat (ed.), *Course et Piraterie*, 441–52; A.N. Ryan, 'The Price of Protection: Foreign Flags under British Convoy in Baltic Trade, 1807–1812' *Ibid.*, 632–45.
37. Stark, *Abolition*, 29.
38. Secretary William L. Marcy as quoted in Sir Francis Piggott, *The Declaration of Paris, 1856: A Study, Documented* (London, 1919), 397.
39. As quoted in H.W. Malkin, 'The Inner History of the Declaration of Paris' *The British Yearbook of International Law*, 8 (1927), 30.
40. James Buchanan to Secretary of State, 25 March 1854, in *British and Foreign State Papers, 1855–1856* (London, 1865) vol. 46, 831–2.
41. Malkin, 'Inner History', 1–20.
42. Malkin, 'Inner History', 20–4.
43. Sir A.W. Ward and G.P. Gooch, *The Cambridge History of British Foreign Policy, 1783–1919* (London, 1923) vol. II, 279.
44. Stark, *Abolition*, 140–7.
45. Malkin, 'Inner History', 35. For the Confederacy, William M. Robinson, *The Confederate Privateers* (New Haven, 1928); A.F. Warburton, *The Trial of the Officers and Crew of the Privateer Savannah, on the Charge of Piracy* (New York, 1862).
46. See the debate in Hansard, *Parliamentary Debates*, 3rd Series, vol. 142, 488–501; for later attacks, Piggott, *Declaration*, passim; and Stark, *Abolition*, 145. But a virulent denunciation is to be found in Thomas G. Bowles, *The Declaration of Paris 1856: Being an Account of the Maritime Rights of Great Britain . . . A History of Their Surrender . . .* (London, 1900).
47. Arthur J. Marder, *British Naval Policy, 1880–1905: The Anatomy of British Sea Power* (London, 1940), 86–8; Geoffrey Symcox, 'Admiral Mahan, the Jeune Ecole and the Guerre de Course' in Mollat (ed.), *Course et Piratarie*, 676–701.
48. Piggott, *Declaration*, 397.

CHAPTER 2

Hydrarchy and Libertalia: The Utopian Dimensions of Atlantic Piracy in the Early Eighteenth Century

Marcus Rediker

A Pirate Utopia

Edward Braithwaite, a clever and knowledgeable seventeenth-century observer of things maritime, once remarked that sailors lived 'in a Hydrarchy'. By this he meant that sailors were a peculiar lot whose customs and social lives were formed by their long, isolated stints of work at sea. In this chapter I will use Braithwaite's term to designate the self-rule and social order devised and deployed by pirates during the early eighteenth century, though I also wish to suggest that Hydrarchy was not entirely peculiar, either to pirates or to sailors. Rather, I will argue that it was a volatile, serpentine tradition of opposition—now latent, now mobilized—within both maritime and working-class culture. Within the history of early modern Atlantic radicalism it reared its head again and again, emerging as a distinctly proletarian form of republicanism in the age of revolution.[1]

A version of Hydrarchy appeared in the first chapter of volume II of *A General History of the Pyrates* (1728), which tells the tale of Captain Misson and his fellow pirates who established a utopian republic in Madagascar called 'Libertalia'.[2] Their settlement looked backward to the ancient prophecy that paradise would be found on the east coast of Africa; it was itself a prophetic glance toward future societies to be based on the revolutionary ideals of liberty, equality and fraternity. Libertalians would be 'vigilant Guardians of the People's Rights and Liberties'; they would stand as 'Barriers against the Rich and Powerful'. By waging war on behalf of 'the Oppressed' against 'the Oppressors', they would see that 'Justice was equally distributed'.[3]

When it came to self-rule, Misson's pirates 'look'd upon a Democratical Form, where the People themselves were the Makers and Judges of their own Laws, [as] the most agreeable'. They sought to institutionalize their commitment to 'a Life of Liberty', which they took for a natural right. They stood against monarchy, preferring to elect and rotate their leaders: 'Power . . . should not be for Life, not hereditary, but determinate at the end of three Years'. They limited the power of their principal leader, who was never to 'think himself other than their Comrade' and was to use his power 'for the publick Good only'. They chose their council, their highest authority, 'of the ablest among them, without Distinction of Nation or Colour'.[4]

Misson's pirates were anti-capitalist, opposed to the dispossession that necessarily accompanied the historical ascent of wage labour and capitalism. They insisted that 'every Man was born free, and had as much Right to what would support him, as to the Air he respired'. They resented the 'encroachments' by which 'Villains' and 'unmerciful Creditors' grew 'immensely rich' as others became 'wretchedly miserable'. They spoke of the 'Natural right' to 'a Share of the Earth as is necessary for our Support'. They saw their piracy as a war of self-preservation.[5]

Men who had been 'ignorant of their Birth-Right, and the Sweets of Liberty' would recapture lost freedoms and guarantees of well-being in Libertalia, and they would do so by redefining fundamental relations of property and power. They had no need for money 'where every Thing was in common, and no Hedge bounded any particular Man's Property', and they decreed that 'the Treasure and Cattle they were Masters of should be equally divided'. Formerly seamen, wage labourers, and perhaps even victims of dispossession themselves, these pirates would finally have 'some Place to call their own', where 'the Air was wholesome, the Soil fruitful, the Sea abounding with Fish', where they would enjoy 'all the Necessaries of Life'. '[W]hen Age or Wounds had render'd them incapable of Hardship', Libertalia would be a place 'where they might enjoy the Fruits of their Labour, and go to their Graves in Peace'.[6]

Concerns over 'Birth-rights', 'the Sweets of Liberty' and the 'Fruits of Labour' were broad enough to include the abolition of slavery. Misson observed that 'Trading for those of our own Species, cou'd never be agreeable to the Eyes of divine Justice: That no Man had power of Liberty of another'. He 'had not exempted his Neck from the Galling Yoak of Slavery, and asserted his own Liberty, to enslave others'. Misson and his men thus took slaves from captured slave ships and incorporated them into their own social order as 'Freemen'. They were literally a motley crew, half black and half white on some of their vessels, made up of African, Dutch, Portuguese, English and French (Catholic and Huguenot) seamen. Misson 'gave the Name of *Liberi* to his People, desiring in that might be drown'd the distinguish'd Names of *French, English, Dutch, Africans, &c*'. Libertalia made room for many cultures, races and nations.[7]

Thus did Misson and his men create a radical-democratic utopia that condemned dispossession, capitalist property relations, slavery and nationalism, as it affirmed justice, democracy, liberty and popular rights. Of course it was all a fiction, or so we have been told by scholars who have for many years insisted that the author of *A General History of the Pyrates* was in fact Daniel Defoe, writing under the pen name Captain Charles Johnson.[8] But was it a fiction? Since a man named Misson and a place named Libertalia apparently never existed, the literal answer must be yes. But in a deeper historical and political sense Misson and Libertalia were not simply fictions. Christopher Hill has recently detected in Misson's utopia the lingering influence of the popular radicalism of the English Revolution. A group of pirates had, after all, settled in Madagascar in a place they had 'given the name of Ranter Bay', named, it would seem, after the most radical of the Protestant sects of the English Revolution.[9]

In this chapter I wish to carry Hill's argument further by suggesting that Libertalia was a fictive expression of the living traditions, practices and dreams of an Atlantic working class, many of which were observed, synthesized and translated into discourse by the author of *A General History of the Pyrates*. A mosaic assembled from the specific utopian practices of the early eighteenth-century pirate ship, Libertalia had objective bases in historical fact.[10] Hydrarchy came ashore as Libertalia.

The Maritime World Turned Upside Down

The pirate ship, like Libertalia, was a 'world turned upside down', made so by the articles of agreement that established the rules and customs of the pirates' social order. Pirates 'distributed justice', elected their officers, divided their loot equally, and established a different discipline. They limited the authority of the captain, resisted many of the practices of capitalist merchant shipping industry, and maintained a multicultural, multiracial, multinational social order. They demonstrated quite clearly—and subversively—that ships did not have to be run in the brutal and oppressive ways of the merchant service and the Royal Navy.[11]

On the high seas, as in Libertalia, pirates elected their leaders democratically. They gave their captain unquestioned authority in chase and battle, but otherwise insisted that he be 'governed by a Majority'. As one observer noted, 'they permit him to be Captain, on Condition, that they may be Captain over him'.[12] They gave him few privileges: no extra food, no private mess, no special accommodations. Moreover, the majority giveth and it taketh away, deposing captains for cowardice, cruelty, refusing 'to take and plunder English Vessels', or even for being 'too Gentleman-like'.[13] Captains who dared to exceed their authority were sometimes executed. Most pirates, 'having suffered formerly from the ill-treatment of their officers, provided carefully against any such evil' once free to organize the ship after their own hearts.[14] Further limitations on the captain's power appeared in the person of the quartermaster, who was elected to represent and protect 'the Interest of the Crew', and in the institution of the council, the democratic gathering that usually involved every man on the ship and always constituted its highest authority.[15]

The 'equal division' of property in Libertalia had its basis in the pirates' shipboard distribution of plunder, which levelled the elaborate hierarchy of pay ranks common to maritime employments and dramatically reduced the distance between officers and common men. Captain and quartermaster received one and a half to two shares; minor officers and craftsmen, one and a quarter or one and a half; all others got one share each. Such egalitarianism flowed from crucial, material facts. By expropriating a merchant ship (after a mutiny or a capture), pirates seized the means of maritime production and declared it to be the common property of those who did its work. They also abolished the wage relation central to the process of capitalist accumulation. So rather than work for wages using the tools and larger machine (the ship) owned by a merchant capitalist, pirates now commanded the ship as their own property, and shared equally in the risks of their common adventure.[16]

Pirates acted as 'vigilant Guardians of the Peoples Rights and Liberties' and as 'Barriers against the Rich and Powerful' when they took revenge against merchant captains who tyrannized the common seaman and against royal officials who upheld their bloody prerogative to do so. The Libertalian's comment about overseeing 'the Distribution of Justice' referred to a specific practice among pirates by the same name. After capturing a prize vessel, pirates 'distributed justice' by inquiring about 'the Commander's Behaviour to their Men'. They 'whipp'd and pickled' those 'against whom Complaint was made'.[17] Bartholomew Roberts's crew considered the matter so important that they formally designated one of their men—George Willson, no doubt a fierce and lusty man—as the 'Dispencer of Justice'. Pirates 'barbarously used' and occasionally executed some captured captains, and a few even bragged of their avenging justice upon the gallows.[18] Pirate captain Howell Davis claimed that 'their reasons for going a pirating were to revenge themselves on base Merchants and cruel commanders of Ships'.[19] Still, pirates did not punish captains indiscriminately. They often rewarded the 'honest Fellow that never abused any Sailors' and even offered to let one decent captain 'return with a large sum of Money to London, and bid the Merchants defiance'.[20] Pirates thus stood against the brutal injustices of the merchant shipping industry, one crew claiming to be 'Robbin Hoods Men'.[21]

Like their comrades in Libertalia, pirates revelled in their 'Share of the Earth' that came in the form of food and drink, for these very items had, for many, figured crucially in the decision to 'go upon the account'. A mutinous sailor aboard the *George Galley* in 1724 responded to his captain's orders to furl the mizen-top by saying 'in a surly Tone, and with a kind of Disdain, So as we Eat so shall we work'. Other mutineers simply insisted that 'it was not their business to starve', and that if a captain was making it their business, hanging could be little worse.[22]

Many observers of pirate life noted the carnivalesque quality of their occasions—the eating, drinking, fiddling, dancing, and merriment—and some considered such 'infinite Disorders' inimical to good discipline at sea.[23] Men who had suffered short or rotten provisions in other maritime employments now ate and drank 'in a wanton and riotous Way', which was indeed their 'Custom'. They conducted so much business 'over a Large Bowl of Punch' that sobriety might even bring 'a Man under a Suspicion of being in a Plot against the

Commonwealth'. The very first item in Bartholomew Roberts's articles guaranteed every man not money but rather 'a Vote in Affairs of Moment' and 'equal Title' to 'fresh provisions' and 'strong Liquors'. For some who joined, drink 'had been a greater motive . . . than Gold'. Most would have agreed with the motto: *'No Adventures to be made without Belly-Timber'*.[24]

The real pirates of the Atlantic made efforts to provide for their health and security, their own 'self-preservation', as did the settlers at Libertalia. The popular image of the freebooter as a man with a patched eye, a peg leg and a hook for a hand is not wholly accurate, but still it speaks an essential truth: sailoring was a dangerous line of work. Pirates therefore put a portion of all booty into a 'common fund' to provide for those who sustained injuries of lasting effect, whether the loss of eyesight or any appendage. They tried to provide for those rendered 'incapable of Hardship' by 'Age or Wounds'.[25]

One of the most distinctive features of Misson's utopia was its attack on slavery. Did it have basis in historical fact? The answer to this question—and indeed the entire record of relations between pirates and people of African descent—is ambiguous, even contradictory. A substantial minority of pirates had worked in the slave trade and had therefore been part of the machinery of enslavement and trans-portation. And when pirates took prize vessels, as they did near African and New World ports, slaves were sometimes part of the captured 'cargo', and were in turn treated as such, traded or sold as if commodities like any other. Pirates were occasionally said to have committed atrocities against the slaves they took.[26]

But it must also be noted that people of African descent made up crucial parts of pirate crews. A few of these men ended up 'dancing to the four winds', like the mulatto who sailed with Black Bart Roberts and was hanged for it in Virginia in 1720.[27] Another 'resolute Fellow, a Negroe' named Caesar stood ready to blow up Blackbeard's ship rather than submit to the Royal Navy in 1718; he too was hanged. Black pirates also made up part of the pirates' vanguard, the most trusted and fearsome members of the crew who boarded a prospective prize. The boarding party of the *Morning Star* had 'a Negro Cook doubly arm'd'; more than half of Edward Condent's boarding party on the *Dragon* was black.[28]

These were not exceptional cases, for 'Negroes and Molattoes' were present on almost every pirate ship, and only rarely did the many merchants and captains who commented on their presence call them 'slaves'.[29] Black pirates sailed with Captains Bellamy, Taylor, Williams, Harris, Winter, Shipton, Lyne, Skyrm, Roberts, Spriggs, Bonnet, Phillips, Baptist, Cooper, and others. In 1718, 60 of Blackbeard's crew of 100 were black, while Captain William Lewis boasted '40 able Negroe Sailors' among his crew of 80. In 1719 Oliver La Bouche had a ship that was, like Misson's, 'half French, half Negroes'.[30] Black pirates were common enough—and nightmare enough—to move one newspaper to report that an all-mulatto band of sea-robbers was marauding the Caribbean, eating the hearts of captured white men![31]

Some black pirates were free men, perhaps like the experienced 'free Negro' seaman from Deptford, England, who in 1721 led a 'a Mutiny that we had too many Officers, and that the work was too hard, and what not'. Others were runaway slaves. In 1716 the slaves of Antigua had grown 'very impudent and insulting', causing their masters to fear an insurrection. Hugh Rankin writes that a substantial number of the unruly 'went off to join those pirates who did not seem too concerned about color differences'.[32] The 'Negroes' captured with the rest of Black Bart's crew in 1722 grew mutinous over the poor conditions and 'thin Commons' they suffered at the hands of the Royal Navy, especially since 'many of them' had 'lived a long time' in the 'pyratical Way'. 'The pyratical way' must have meant, to them as to others, more food and greater freedom.[33]

We also know that a good many pirates settled in West Africa, joining and intermixing with the native Kru, who were themselves known for their skills in things maritime (and also, when enslaved, for their leadership of revolts in the New World).[34] And of course pirates had for many years mixed with the native population in Madagascar, helping to produce 'a dark Mulatto Race there'.[35] Cultural exchanges among pirates, seamen and Africans were extensive, resulting, for example, in the well-known similarities of form between African songs and sea shanties. In 1743 some seamen were court-martialled for singing a 'negro song' 'in defiance of discipline'.[36] There are also intriguing instances in which mutineers engaged in totemistic practices that resembled the rites performed by slaves before a revolt. In 1731 a band of mutineers drank 'rum and gunpowder', while on another occasion a sailor signalled his rebellious intentions by 'Drinking Water out of a Musket barrel'.[37] The direction of influence here is not clear, but influence itself seems likely.

Too little is known about black pirates, yet we must conclude that pirates as a whole in the early eighteenth century did not self-consciously attack slavery as was done in Misson's utopia, neither did pirates adhere to the strict racial logic that polarized a great many societies around the Atlantic. Some slaves and free blacks seem to have found relative freedom aboard the pirate ship, which was no easy thing for many to find, especially in the Carribean The very existence of black pirates, contradictory though their lives probably were, may well have moved the author of *A General History of the Pyrates* to imagine the deeper critique of slavery at work in Libertalia.

Africans and African-Americans were but one part of a motley crew, in Libertalia and aboard most pirate ships. Governor Nicholas Lawes of Jamaica echoed the thoughts of royal officials everywhere when he called pirates a 'banditti of all nations'. Black Sam Bellamy's crew was 'a mix't multitude of all Country's', as were the principal mutineers aboard the *George Galley* in 1724: an Englishman, a Welshman, an Irishman, two Scots, two Swedes and a Dane, all of whom became pirates. Benjamin Evans's crew consisted of men of English, French, Irish, Spanish and African descent. When hailed by other vessels, pirates emphasized their rejection of nationality by replying that they came 'From the Seas'. And as a mutineer had muttered in 1699, 'it signified nothing what part of the World a man liv'd in, so he Liv'd well'.[38] Such was the separatist logic that led to the founding of Libertalia.

The War against Libertalia

The utopian features of the pirate ship were crucial to both the recruitment and reproduction of the group, and eventually to its suppression, for both pirates and the English ruling class recognized the power of Hydrarchy and its alternative social order. Some worried that pirates might 'set up a sort of Commonwealth' in areas where 'no Power' would be 'able to dispute it with them'. Colonial and metropolitan merchants and officials feared the incipient separatism of Libertalia in Madagascar, Sierra Leone, Bermuda, the Bay of Campeche, and other regions.[39] If Libertalia was a working-class dream, it was equally (and necessarily) a ruling-class nightmare.

Colonel Benjamin Bennet wrote of pirates to the Council of Trade and Plantations in 1718: 'I fear they will soon multiply for so many are willing to joyn with them when taken.' Multiply they did: after the War of the Spanish Succession, as working conditions in the merchant shipping industry deteriorated, seamen turned to the black flag by the thousands. Edward England's crew took nine vessels off the coast of Africa in the spring of 1719 and found 55 of the 143 seamen ready to sign their articles. Such desertion to Hydrarchy was common between roughly 1716 and 1722, when, as one pirate told a merchant captain, 'people were generally glad of an opportunity of entring with them'.[40]

It is not hard to understand why these men joined. The prospect of plunder and 'ready money', the food and the drink, the camaraderie, the democracy, equality, and justice, the promise of care for the injured—all of these must have been appealing. The attractions were perhaps best summarized by Bartholomew Roberts, who remarked that in the merchant service 'there is thin Commons, low Wages, and hard Labour; in this, Plenty and Satiety, Pleasure and Ease, Liberty and Power; and who would not ballance Creditor on this Side, when all the Hazard that is run for it, at worst, is only a sower Look or two at choaking. No, *a merry Life and a short one*, shall be my motto.'[41]

The English ruling class was less than keen about the merriment, but more than happy to oblige Roberts and his men in making their lives short ones. The 5,000 or so pirates who haunted the sea lanes of the Atlantic had made a great deal of 'Noise in the World'—they had refused nationalism by attacking English vessels and they had done great damage to the world's capitalist shipping industry. English rulers, Whig and Tory alike, responded by drawing upon and continuing the reforms of the 1690s, hanging sea robbers by the hundreds. Merchants petitioned Parliament, which obliged with deadly new legislation; meanwhile, prime minister Robert Walpole took an active, personal interest in putting an end to piracy. Many historians have claimed that the hangman was not nearly as busy as he might have been in this age of rapidly expanding capital punishments, but the point cannot be proved by pirates. They—and their dreams of Libertalia—were clearly marked for extinction.[42]

The Origins and Subsequent History of Libertalia

We may conclude by considering two questions. From where did Hydrarchy and Libertalia come? And where, once piracy had been formally suppressed, did they go?

First it should be said that the maritime utopia of the early eighteenth century may well be unique in the annals of piracy (though not, as suggested below, in the annals of the working class). It took a long time for seamen to get, as one man put it, 'the choice in themselves'—that is, the autonomous power to organize the ship as they wanted.[43] Anglo-Atlantic piracy had long served the needs of the state and the merchant community. But there was a long-term tendency for the control of piracy to devolve from the top of society toward the bottom, from the highest functionaries of the state (late sixteenth century), to big merchants (early seventeenth century), to smaller, usually colonial merchants (late seventeenth century), and finally to the common men of the deep (early eighteenth century). When this devolution reached the bottom, when seamen (as pirates) organized a social world apart from the dictates of mercantile and imperial authority and used it to attack merchants' property (as they had begun to do in the 1690s), then those who controlled the state resorted to massive violence, both military (the navy) and penal (the gallows), to eradicate piracy. The social organization of Hydrarchy represented the victory by which the maritime working class had seized control of piracy; the separatism of Libertalia was a necessary response to the state's campaign of terror to reverse that victory.[44]

The sources of the pirates' social order in the early eighteenth century were many, but probably the greatest of them was, as I have argued elsewhere, the experience of work, wages, culture and authority accumulated in the normal, rugged course of maritime life and labour. The pirates' social order cannot be comprehended apart from their previous experiences on merchant, naval or privateering vessels. They transformed harsh discipline into a looser, more libertarian way of running a ship that depended on 'what Punishment the Captain and Majority of the Company shall think fit'. They transformed the realities of chronically meagre rations into near-chronic feasting, an exploitative wage relation into collective risk-bearing, and injury and premature death into concerns for health and security. Their democratic selection of officers stood in stark, telling contrast to the near-dictatorial arrangement of command in the merchant service and Royal Navy. The pirates' social order thus realized tendencies that were both dialectically generated and in turn suppressed in the course of work and life at sea. The culture and experiences of the common seaman constituted the pre-eminent source of Hydrarchy.[45]

A second, closely related source of the pirate social order was the 'Jamaica Discipline' or the 'Law of the Privateers', the body of custom bequeathed to them by the buccaneers who had haunted the Caribbean from roughly 1630 to 1680. This custom boasted a distinctive conception of justice and 'a kind of class consciousness' against 'the great'—shipmasters, shipowners, 'gentlemen adventurers'. It also featured democratic controls on authority and provision for the injured.[46]

The buccaneers were 'the outcasts of all nations' except Spain, their common enemy. They drew their numbers from the convicts, prostitutes, debtors, vagabonds, runaway slaves and indentured servants, religious radicals and political prisoners who had migrated or been exiled to the Caribbean. According to one official, the buccaneers were 'white servants and all men of unfortunate and desperate condition'. Many French buccaneers, like Alexander Exquemelin, had been indentured servants (*engagés*) and, before that, textile-workers and day labourers. Most of the buccaneers were English or French in background, but there were also Dutch, Irish, Scottish, Scandinavian, West Indian and African men involved.[47]

Christopher Hill has suggested the English Revolution as a source of the buccaneers' social order: 'A surprising number of English radicals emigrated to the West Indies either just before or just after 1660', including Ranters, Quakers, Familists, Anabaptists, radical soldiers, and others who 'no doubt carried with them the ideas which had originated in revolutionary England'. A number of buccaneers, we know, went about their work in the 'faded red coats of the New Model Army'. In the New World they insisted upon the democratic election of their officers just as they had done in a revolutionary army on the other side of the Atlantic.[48]

Another intriguing suggestion about the sources of buccaneering culture comes from the late J.S. Bromley. Many French freebooters came, as *engagés*, 'from areas affected by peasant risings against the royal *fisc* and the proliferation of crown agents' in the 1630s. In these regions protesters had shown a capacity for self-organization, the constitution of 'communes', election of deputies and promulgation of *Ordonnances*, all in the name of 'du Commun peuple'.[49] Such experiences may have informed the social code of the 'Brethren of the Coast' in America.

The buccaneers originated as a kind of multiracial maroon society based on hunting and gathering, formed by unfree labourers (indentured servants and a few slaves) and others who ran from the brutalities of a nascent plantation system. They hunted wild cattle and gathered the king of Spain's gold. They combined the diverse experiences of peasant rebels, demobilized soldiers, dispossessed smallholders, unemployed workers, and others from several nations and cultures, including the Carib and Cuna Indians. Buccaneers knew that their survival in a strange land depended upon their willingness to adapt by drawing on all resources. The 'Custom of the Coast' survived even when high mortality meant that many of the 'Brethren' themselves did not.[50]

How the social and cultural transition from seventeenth-century buccaneer to eighteenth-century pirate worked is, and will probably remain, largely a mystery. But some continuities are clear. Traditions sometimes lived on because a few hearty souls survived the odds against longevity in seafaring work. Some of the old buccaneers themselves served on Jamaican privateers during the War of the Spanish Succession, then took part in the new piracies in peacetime. The 'Jamaica Discipline' and the exploits it made possible also lived on in folktale, song, ballad and memory, not to mention the popular published (and much-translated) accounts of Alexander Exquemelin, Père Labat, and others.[51]

Another kind of continuity appeared in the mutiny aboard HMS *Chesterfield* in October 1748, off the west coast of Africa, not far from Cape Coast Castle. One of the ringleaders of mutiny, John Place, had been there before. He had sailed with the pirate Bartholomew Roberts and had been captured off Cape Coast Castle by Captain Challoner Ogle in HMS *Swallow* in 1722. When the time came, a quarter of a century later, for the know-how of mutiny and an alternative social order, Place was apparently the man of the moment, the one to help the mutineers do as Misson had done, 'to settle a colony'. Place embodied a tenacious tradition that had lived in tales, in action, in sullenly silent memory, on the lower deck of the *Chesterfield* and, no doubt, countless other vessels. He was obviously a patient man, but still victory would not be his. He was hanged, but Hydrarchy did not die with him.[52]

During the American Revolution, many thousands of captured American seamen were charged as 'pirates' and 'traitors' and herded into British prisons and prison ships, where they quickly organized themselves in the ways of Hydrarchy. According to Jesse Lemisch, these seamen, now autonomous because their officers had asked to be separated from them, 'governed themselves in accord with abstract notions of liberty, justice, and right' and created a social world characterized by 'egalitarianism', 'collectivism' and commitment to revolutionary ideals. What had functioned as 'articles' among seaman and pirates now became a constitution of sorts, 'a Code of By-Laws . . . for their own regulation and government'. As always they used democratic practices, worked 'to assure the equitable distribution of food and clothing', concerned themselves with questions of health, and established their own distinctive discipline. A captain who looked back at the prison Hydrarchy with considerable surprise remarked that seamen were 'of that class . . . who are not easily controlled, and usually not the most ardent supporters of good order'. What he and others like him failed to understand was that seamen had no trouble supporting an 'order' of their own making.[53]

There was also a maritime dimension to the utopia conceived by the English radical Thomas Spence. Spence's brave new world had its origins in a dying man's gift of a ship to his sons. It was, the man specified, to be 'COMMON PROPERTY. You all will be EQUAL OWNERS, and shall share the profits of every voyage equally among you.' Like pirates before him, the man insisted that the division of resources heed no office. His injunctions were drawn up as a Constitution (much like the pirates' articles), his plan soon implemented. But the marine republicans grew weary of the larger, oppressive government in their own land and decided to 'set sail for America, where they expected to see government administered more agreeably to their notions of equality and equity'. When their ship was wrecked on an uninhabited island, they used their principles to establish the Republic of Spensonia, which according to A.L. Morton, 'looks backward to the medieval commune and forward to the withering away of the state'.[54] Hydrarchy had come ashore as Libertalia once more.

Hydrarchy appeared in another, more material form only a few years later, in the world-shaking mutinies of English (and Irish and African and other) sailors at Spithead and the Nore in 1797. Sailors had been restless and more than normally mutinous since the American Revolution, and finally they exploded in revolt. In 1797 they removed disagreeable officers, elected their own delegates and set up their own 'council', imposed their own discipline, and established their own 'shipboard democracy'. They also made demands for food, health and liberty (the last of which, after all, had a special meaning for seamen). They drew on the radical practices of America's revolutionary seamen and some even spoke of settling a 'New Colony', perhaps in America, perhaps even in Madagascar.[55]

Our discussion of Hydrarchy and Libertalia raises questions about the process by which subversive popular ideas and practices are kept alive, underground and over water, for long periods of time. Indeed, the pirates' alternative social order might be seen as a maritime continuation of the traditional peasant utopia, in England and continental Europe, called 'The Land of Cockaygne'. The dislike of work, the abundance of food, the concern with good health, the levelling of social distinctions and the turning of the world upside down, the re-division of property, the ease and the freedoms—all of the elements of primitive communism that informed the medieval myth were expressed in Libertalia and at least partially realized on the pirate ship.[56]

And yet if Hydrarchy and Libertalia echoed the dreams of Cockaygne in centuries gone by, so did they speak to the future, to the development of mass radical-democratic movements. Hydrarchy and Libertalia may be intermediate popular links between the defeated republicans of the English Revolution and the victorious republicans of the age of revolution more than a century later. The relative absence of piracy in the Atlantic between 1750 and 1850 may in the end owe something to the utopian prospects of an earlier age and the ruthless repression they called forth. But so too might the age of revolution owe something to the utopian dimensions of earlier popular struggles. Many pirates themselves may have died upon the gallows, defeated, but Hydrarchy and Libertalia had many victories yet to claim.

Notes

This essay is dedicated to the memory of William Appleman Williams, who long ago emphasized to me the importance of the themes of this essay. Thanks to Wendy Goldman, Christopher Hill, Jesse Lemish and Peter Linebaugh for their help with this essay.

1. Braithwaite quoted in Christopher Lloyd, *The British Seaman, 1200–1860: A Social Survey* (Rutherford, N.J., 1970), 74. The themes of this essay will be treated at greater length and in a broader context in Peter Linebaugh and Marcus Rediker, *The Many-Headed Hydra: The Atlantic Working Class in the Seventeenth and Eighteenth Centuries*, forthcoming.

2. On Misson, see Herbert Deschamps, *Les Pirates à Madagascar aux XVIIe et XVIIIe siècles* (Paris, 1972), ch. 9, and Joel H. Baer, 'Piracy Examined: A Study of Daniel Defoe's *General History of the Pyrates* and its Milieu', (unpublished Ph.D. dissertation, Princeton University, 1970), ch. 5.

3. Captain Charles Johnson, *A General History of the Pyrates*, ed. Manuel Schonhorn (1724, 1728; reprint Columbia, S.C., 1972), 392, 425 (hereafter cited as *History*).

4. *History*, 432, 391, 393, 392, 403, 433, 434.

5. *History*, 389, 392, 390. The essential background here is Christopher Hill, 'Pottage for Freeborn Englishmen: Attitudes to Wage Labour', in his *Change and Continuity in Seventeenth-Century England* (Cambridge, Mass., 1975), 219–38.

6. *History*, 427, 432, 394, 415, 423, 435. Individual plots of land were to be permitted in Libertalia; see 432–4.

7. *History*, 392, 425, 417, 403, 427. Libertalia was eventually destroyed by natives of Madagascar who apparently feared that the new settlement would upset the balance of power on the island. The end came 'without the least Provocation given, in the Dead of Night, [when] the Natives came down upon them in two great Bodies, and made a great Slaughter, without Distinction of Age or Sex, before they could put themselves in a Posture of Defence'. See *History*, 437.
8. The case for Defoe's authorship was made by John Robert Moore in *Defoe in the Pillory and Other Studies* (Bloomington, 1939), 129–88, but his argument has recently been challenged, convincingly in my estimation, by P.N. Furbank and W.R. Owens, *The Canonisation of Daniel Defoe* (New Haven, 1988), 100–21. It should be said that the overall reliability of the *History* has been established regardless of specific authorship.
9. Information of Clement Downing (1724), High Court of Admiralty Papers (hereafter HCA) 1/55, f. 79, Public Record Office, London. Ranter Bay is also mentioned in Information of Charles Collins (1724), HCA 1/55, f. 77. Christopher Hill, 'Radical Pirates?' in Margaret Jacob and James Jacob (eds), *The Origins of Anglo-American Radicalism* (London, 1984), 17–32.
10. Hill was the first to note the 'survival of Utopian and radical ideas' among pirates; 'Radical Pirates?', 18. Other important works on the social history of pirates in this era are J.S. Bromley, 'Outlaws at Sea, 1660–1720: Liberty, Equality, and Fraternity among the Caribbean Freebooters' in Frederick Krantz (ed.), *History From Below: Studies in Popular Protest and Popular Ideology in Honour of George Rudé* (Montreal, 1985), 301–20, Robert C. Ritchie, *Captain Kidd and the War against the Pirates* (Cambridge, Mass., 1987).
11. Many of the arguments below draw on evidence presented in my earlier work, ' "Under the Banner of King Death": The Social World of Anglo-American Pirates, 1716 to 1726', *William and Mary Quarterly* 3rd ser. 38 (1981), 203–27; and *Between the Devil and the Deep Blue Sea: Merchant Seamen, Pirates, and the Anglo-American Maritime World, 1700–1750* (Cambridge, 1987), ch. 6. My principal (though not exclusive) subject here will be the pirates of the Anglo-Atlantic world.
12. *History*, 213.
13. Examination of John Brown (1717) in John Franklin Jameson (ed.), *Privateering and Piracy in the Colonial Period: Illustrative Documents* (New York, 1923), 294; William Snelgrave, *A New Account of Some Parts of Guinea and the Slave Trade* (London, 1734; reprint London, 1971), 199.
14. Arthur L. Hayward (ed.), *Lives of the Most Remarkable Criminals . . .* (London, 1735), 37; *History*, 42, 296, 337.
15. *History*, 423.
16. The pirates' emphasis on equality did not sit well with the merchant captains whose place in the world depended upon maritime hierarchy and privilege. To such people it was galling that 'there is so little Government and Subordination among [pirates], that they are, on Occasion, all Captains, all Leaders'. See *An Account of the Conduct and Proceedings of the Late John Gow, alias Smith, Captain of the Late Pirates . . .* (London, 1725; reprint Edinburgh, 1978), introduction.
17. *History*, 338, 582.
18. Proceedings of the Court held on the Coast of Africa', HCA 1/99, f. 101; *Boston Gazette*, 24–31 Oct. 1720; *Boston Gazette*, 21–28 Mar. 1726.

19. Snelgrave, *New Account*, 225.
20. *Boston News-Letter*, 14–21 Nov. 1720; Snelgrave, *New Account*, 241.
21. Testimony of Thomas Checkley (1717) in Jameson (ed.), *Privateering and Piracy*, 304; *The Trials of Eight Persons Indited for Piracy* (Boston, 1718), 11.
22. *An Account of . . . the Late John Gow*, 3. Immediately after the mutiny, the pirates sought a prize vessel 'with Wine, if possible, for that they wanted Extreamly', 13. See also *History*, 307, 319.
23. *History*, 244, 224. Bartholomew Roberts's crew was taken in 1722 because many of the men were drunk when the time came for an engagement. See *History*, 243, and John Atkins, *A Voyage to Guinea, Brazil, & the West Indies . . .* (London, 1735; reprint London, 1970), 192. It would have been for such reasons that drunkenness was banned in Libertalia.
24. *History*, 129, 135, 167, 222, 211, 280, 205. See also 209, 312, 353, 620; *American Weekly Mercury*, 17 Mar, 1720; Snelgrave, *New Account*, 233–8.
25. *History*, 212, 308, 343.
26. Hugh F. Rankin, *Golden Age of Piracy* (New York 1969), 34, has claimed that some free blacks who signed pirates' articles were taken to the West Indies and sold as slaves, but I have found no evidence of such practices.
27. *American Weekly Mercury*, 17 Mar. 1720. Such hangings were rare, for the British state preferred to sell captured black pirates as slaves to stock its New World plantations.
28. *History*, 82; Information of Joseph Smith and Information of John Webley (1721), HCA 1/18, f. 35; Information of William Voisy (1721) HCA 1/55, f. 12. Native Americans also turned up on pirate ships, though in much smaller numbers. See *The Trials of Five Persons for Piracy, Felony, and Robbery* (Boston, 1726).
29. One of the references to slaves came in the legal efforts of a group of merchants to recover property taken by a pirate crew; see Masters vs. *Revenge*, Minutes of the Vice-Admiralty Courts of Charleston, South Carolina (1718), Manuscript Division, Library of Congress, f. 308. See also Jameson (ed.), *Privateering and Piracy*, 344.
30. *Boston News-Letter*, 17–24 June 1717; *The Tryals of Major Stede Bonnet and Other Pirates* (London, 1719), 46; *History*, 173, 427, 595. Rankin notes that a 'surprising number of Negroes and mulattoes were listed among the members of pirate crews' but that one captain, Edward Low, seems to have opposed letting African-Americans serve aboard his vessel (*The Golden Age of Piracy*, 24–5, 148). See also *Boston News-Letter*, 29 Apr.–6 May 1717.
31. *Boston News-Letter*, 4–11 Apr. 1723.
32. R. Reynall Bellamy (ed.), *Ramblin' Jack: The Journal of Captain John Cremer* (London, 1936), 144; Rankin, *The Golden Age of Piracy*, 82.
33. *History*, 273.
34. H. Ross, 'Some Notes on the Pirates and Slavers around Sierra Leone and the West Coast of Africa, 1680–1723' *Sierra Leone Studies*, 11 (1928), 16–53. Some of these were probably men from Roberts's crew who escaped into the woods before being taken by the Royal Navy in 1722. See *American Weekly Mercury*, 31 May –7 June 1722.
35. *History*, 131.
36. L.G. Carr Laughton, 'Shantying and Shanties' *Mariners' Mirror*, 9 (1923), 48–50.

37. Trial of John McPherson and others, Proceedings of the Court of Admiralty, Philadelphia, 1731, HCA 1/99, f. 3; Information of Henry Hull (1729) HCA 1/56, ff. 29–30.

38. Lawes to Council of Trade and Plantations, 31 Jan. 1719, in W. Noel Sainsbury et al. (eds), *Calendar of State Papers, Colonial Series, America and the West Indies 1719–20* (London, 1860), 19; Walter Hamilton to CTP, 6 Jan. 1717, Colonial Office (CO) 152/12, f. 211, PRO; Representation from Several Merchants trading to Virginia to Board of Trade, 15 April 1717, CO 5/1318, ff. 12–13; *History*, 468, 474, 359; *Boston Gazette*, 6–13 July 1725; 'A Discovery of an Horrid Plot aboard the *Antelope*', CO 323/3, ff. 92–3.

39. Cotton Mather, *Instructions to the Living, From the Condition of the Dead: A Brief Relation of Remarkables in the Shipwreck of above One Hundred Pirates* . . . (Boston, 1717), 4; meeting of 1 Apr. 1717, in H.C. Maxwell Lyte (ed.), *Journal of the Commissioners for Trade and Plantations* . . . (London, 1924), vol. III, 359; *History*, 7; *American Weekly Mercury*, 24 Nov. 1720; *New England Courant*, 19–26 March 1722.

40. *History*, 115–16; Snelgrave, *New Account*, 203.

41. *History*, 244; Bromley 'Outlaws at Sea', 11, 12; Atkins, *A Voyage*, 191.

42. *History*, 43 (quotation); Leo Francis Stock, *Proceedings and Debates of the British Parliaments respecting North America* (Washington, D.C., 1930), vol. III, 364, 433, 453, 454; Ritchie, *Captain Kidd*, 235–7. Walpole's direct involvement can be seen in Treasury Warrant to Capt. Knott, T52/32 (10 Aug. 1722), PRO, and in the *American Weekly Mercury*, 1–8 July 1725.

43. Hayward, *Lives of the Most Remarkable Criminals*, 37.

44. Ritchie, *Captain Kidd*, 147–51. Piracy was coloured less by religious and national antagonism in the eighteenth than in the seventeenth century, when hatred for Catholic Spain had energized a great many buccaneers.

45. This paragraph summarizes some of the arguments of my *Between the Devil and the Deep Blue Sea*. It should also be noted that pirates drew upon national and international maritime custom, occasionally reaching back to ancient and medieval seafaring life: they divided their money and goods into shares; they consulted collectively and democratically on matters of moment; they elected a quartermaster, who, like the medieval 'consul' (and the seventeenth-century equivalent in the army) adjudicated the differences between captain and crew. See William McFee, *The Law of the Sea* (Philadelphia, 1951), 50, 54, 59, 72; Bromley, 'Outlaws at Sea', 5.

46. P.K. Kemp and Christopher Lloyd, *Brethren of the Coast: Buccaneers of the South Seas* (New York, 1960); Carl and Roberta Bridenbaugh, *No Peace Beyond the Line: The English in the Caribbean, 1624–1690* (New York, 1972); C.H. Haring, *The Buccaneers in the West Indies in the XVII Century* (London, 1910; reprint Hamden, Conn., 1966) 71, 73; Bromley, 'Outlaws at Sea', 6.

47. Kemp and Lloyd, *Brethren of the Coast*, 3; Bridenbaugh, *No Peace Beyond the Line*, 62, 176; Bromley, 'Outlaws at Sea', 7 (quotation), 8.

48. Hill, 'Radical Pirates?', 20, 25; Kemp and Lloyd, *Brethren of the Coast*, 17 (quotation); Bromley, 'Outlaws at Sea', 6.

49. Bromley, 'Outlaws at Sea', 8, 9.

50. Bromley, 'Outlaws at Sea', 15; Richard Price (ed.), *Maroon Societies: Rebel Slave Communities in the Americas* (2nd edn, Baltimore, 1979).

51. Bromley, 'Outlaws at Sea', 17; Marcus Rediker, 'The Common Seaman in the Histories of Capitalism and the Working Class' *International Journal of Maritime History*, 1 (1989), 352–3.

52. W.E. May, 'The Mutiny of the *Chesterfield*' *Mariners' Mirror*, 47 (1961), 178–87. For a similar example see Information of William Omara (1737), HCA 1/57, ff. 8–9: in planning a mutiny in 1736, Nicholas Williams announced to his fellow conspirators, 'I have brought in Johnson, who is a special good fellow for this purpose and has several times been upon the Account'.

53. Jesse Lemisch, 'Listening to the "Inarticulate": William Widger's Dream and the Loyalties of American Revolutionary Seamen in British Prisons' *Journal of Social History*, III (1969–70), 1–29, quotations at 27, 21, 23, 24; Larry G. Bowman, *Captive Americans: Prisoners during the American Revolution* (Athens, Ohio, 1976), 40–67; John K. Alexander, 'Forton Prison During the American Revolution: A Case Study of the British Prisoner of War Policy and the American Prisoner Response to that Policy' *Essex Institute Historical Collections*, CII (1967), 369.

54. See Thomas Spence, 'The Marine Republic (1794)', *Pigs' Meat* (2nd edn), vol. II, 68–72 (emphasis in original); A.L. Morton, *The English Utopia* (London, 1952) 164, 165 (quotation).

55. Henry Baynham, *From the Lower Deck: The Royal Navy, 1780–1840* (Barre, Mass., 1970), 9; Arthur N. Gilbert, 'The Nature of Mutiny in the British Navy in the Eighteenth Century' in Daniel Masterson (ed.), *Naval History: The Sixth Symposium of the U.S. Naval Academy* (Wilmington, Del., 1987), 111–21; G.E. Mainwaring and Bonamy Dobree, *Mutiny: The Floating Republic: The Mutinies at Spithead and Nore, 1797* (London, 1935; reprint 1987); Joseph P. Moore, III, ' "The Greatest Enormity that Prevails": Direct Democracy and Workers' Self-Management in the British Naval Mutinies of 1797' in Colin Howell and Richard J. Twomey (eds), *Jack Tar in History: Essays in the History of Maritime Life and Labour* (Fredericton, New Brunswick, 1991), 76–104.

56. Morton, *The English Utopia*, ch. 1; F. Graus, 'Social Utopias in the Middle Ages' *Past and Present*, 38 (1967), 3–19.

CHAPTER 3

Living and Working Conditions in Chinese Pirate Communities, 1750–1850

Dian Murray

Introduction

Throughout history piracy on the South China coast has alternated between periods of quiet when the seas were, as the Chinese say, relatively free from 'foam' and periods in which great fleets ravaged the seaboard until they were finally brought to terms. During the fifteenth and sixteenth centuries, bands of Japanese pirates assisted by Chinese recruits forced the two governments into negotiations in which Japanese rulers undertook to stop the pillage in return for trading privileges in China. The presence of pirates around the provincial city of Shangchuan and the offer of Europeans to assist in their suppression led to the Portuguese settlement of Macao in the middle of the sixteenth century. A hundred years later, the pirate-patriot Cheng Ch'eng-kung so harried the mainland from his fortress on Taiwan that in 1660 a beleagered emperor ordered the coastal populations of 88 townships in Fujian and Kwangtung provinces to remove themselves inland 30 *li* and to remain there for 22 years. Between 1750 and 1850, the period under consideration here, similar patterns in the ebb and flow of piracy continued. The eighteenth century, until its final decade, was relatively quiet, and pirates, to the extent that they existed at all, did so in the form of a few struggling banditti who sheltered in the

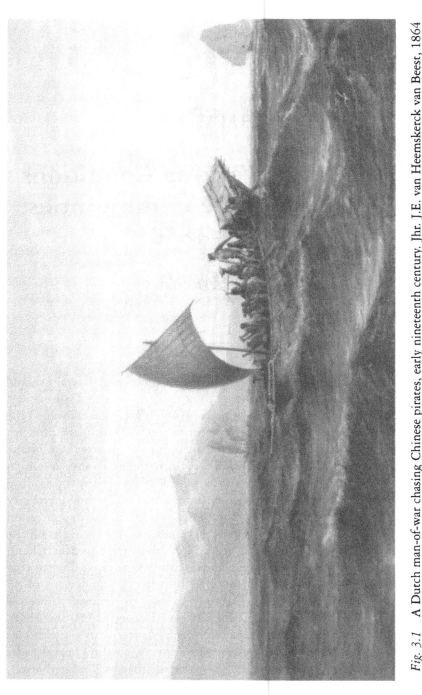

Fig. 3.1 A Dutch man-of-war chasing Chinese pirates, early nineteenth century. Jhr. J.E. van Heemskerck van Beest, 1864 (Netherlands Maritime Museum, Amsterdam)

offshore islands and carried out nocturnal depredations in shallow waters.[1]

Even Chinese officials themselves regarded piracy as little more than a coastal nuisance. However, between 1795 and 1810, piracy emerged again and forced government officials to deal with their most serious maritime threat in more than a century. Nowhere was the confrontation more intense than in Kwangtung province, where by 1805 a confederation of seven fleets, 2,000 junks, and between 50,000 and 70,000 pirates dominated the coasting trade and fishing industry. Scarcely a junk dared leave port without first paying the pirates protection money against attack. From the shore, the pirates next moved into the waterways of the interior, where they extorted considerable sums in the form of semi-annual payments from the villages and towns, burning with impunity those that refused to pay. On repeated occasions they severed communications between Canton and Macao, causing domestic prices to skyrocket and the bottom to drop out of the foreign market. Even Europeans were forced to negotiate with them for their safety, and in 1809 a confident pirate leader boasted to the Portuguese that in return for the loan of three or four men-of-war, he would give them two or three provinces after he had toppled the Ch'ing dynasty and conquered the mainland.[2]

Although great fleets of sea robbers were rare after 1810, instances of petty piracy were reported almost continuously and became even more intense with the outbreak of the Opium War in 1839. Persons of all descriptions armed by the Chinese government during the war retained their weapons for private use and swarmed into Hong Kong waters thereafter. As the principal opium distribution depot of the entire coast, Hong Kong attracted pirates and smugglers by the score. By 1844 pirates had once again assembled a fleet of 150 fighting vessels and were exacting blackmail from passing craft. In 1849 combined fleets from Great Britain and Vietnam destroyed 81 vessels and 2,100 of the forces under Chui-Apoo and Shap-ng-tsai, the two most notorious pirate leaders of the day.[3]

Given the manner in which piracy ebbed and flowed along the South China coast, any discussion of the living and working conditions in Chinese pirate communities must take into account the fact that differences in the size and longevity of their enterprise would have resulted in different living and working conditions for those who participated in them. This chapter will focus on the living and working conditions at either end of the spectrum: i.e. of those who, on the one hand, lived and operated as petty pirates in communities of part-time fishermen-pirates, and of those who, on the other hand, operated as professional pirates in the century's largest confederation. Although most of the data presented here are drawn from my study of Chinese piracy between 1780 and 1810, the relative constancy of both the physical environment and the operating technologies indicate that the piracy of this period typified that of the entire century between 1750 and 1850.

The Nature and Organization of Petty and Professional Pirate Gangs

The most striking aspect of petty piracy was its part-time and seasonal nature. Petty pirates were, above all, fishermen whose tendency to alternate careers of fishing and piracy was noted by Chinese officials as early as 1384.[4] Unable to discharge their financial obligations, fishermen throughout history were often compelled to supplement their incomes through small-scale trade. Yet, even then, the result was usually a livelihood so miserable that, for many, a successful pirate foray was the sole hope for a better life.[5] Thus, for fishermen pushed to the brink of survival and shut out from the other more prestigious careers ashore, piracy as a temporary survival strategy made sense. Like other secondary activities, piracy could be pursued on a part-time basis that accorded well with fishing, a seasonal pursuit that occupied only 120 or 150 days per year.[6]

During the summer when fishing was poor and dangerous, financially pressed fishermen could easily take advantage of the southerlies to sail north and plunder along the coast. Then, with the changing winds and the approach of autumn, they would sail south, return home, and resume their fishing. With almost predictable regularity, piracy along the South China coast increased dramatically during the third and fourth lunar months.[7]

Of the petty pirates encountered in this study, more than half were fishermen or sailors, and most were single men in the prime of life who hailed from the maritime regions of central and western Kwangtung.[8] So persistent was this tradition that as late as 1842, British and Chinese officials alike struggled to distinguish fisherman from pirate along the South China coast.[9]

By contrast, piracy within the confederation meant long-term, full-time employment for both leaders and followers to the point where by

1807 leaders refused to admit into their organizations individuals who did not agree to stay for at least eight or nine months.[10] Like petty pirates, many members of the confederation were fishermen, who joined 'by the hundreds', but in addition there were others who, in hoping to escape the tyranny and exactions of Ch'ing officials onshore, may have had somewhat more political reasons for signing up. At the same time, the confederation also included a few men of 'decent appearance' who joined with money in hand and one individual who, in mumbling a few words of English, even claimed to have visited Great Britain.[11]

The leaders of petty pirate gangs were almost always fishermen, who aside from possessing the major tool of the trade—a vessel—were relatively undifferentiated from their peers. By contrast, the leaders of the pirate confederation were men of prowess, individuals who stood out from the crowd because of their skills or experience. Prior to the founding of the confederation, six of its seven original leaders (and possibly even all seven) had fought in Vietnam and been commissioned by the Tay-son.[12] Confederation founder Cheng I was a pirate of pedigree whose ancestors dated from the seventeenth century. The first member of his branch of the family to have become a pirate was Cheng Chien, the son of an obscure farmer from Fukien who, in 1641, allied himself with Cheng Ch'eng-kung, better known as Koxinga. By the end of the Yung-cheng period (1723–35), two of Cheng Chien's great grandsons had become the pirate leaders of Hsin-an County, Kwangtung. One, who established his base atop Big Chicken Mountain (Ta-chi-shan) on Lantao Island, was the father of Cheng Ch'i, the family's major pirate leader of the Tay-son era, while the other, who built the sea goddess temple in the narrows of Li-yu-men at the eastern end of Victoria Harbour, was the father of confederation founder, Cheng I. Cheng I was five years younger than his cousin Cheng Ch'i and after serving with him in Vietnam, he returned to China in 1801, where, upon the latter's death, he gradually emerged as *primus inter pares* among the pirates of Kwangtung.[13]

Size and Composition of Pirate Gangs

The size and composition of petty and professional organizations differed as well. Those of the petty pirates were small, informal, *ad hoc* associations that took shape within hours or, at most, days of a given leader's decision to turn pirate. Would-be leaders, relying on networks of family, friends, and voluntary associations, seldom had trouble recruiting a dozen or so followers for a given mission.

Once at sea, such gangs often increased their effective manpower through the forced or voluntary labour of captives. Outstanding captives who found favour with gang leaders might even be catapulted into leadership positions themselves. Such promotions sometimes grew out of homosexual relations initiated by a gang leader, who would then reward the captive by commissioning him as the boss or skipper of a newly taken craft. The results of these endeavours were usually small gangs that consisted at most of between 10 and 30 men and a junk or two.[14] With the personal, patron–client associations of a given leader forming their nucleus, petty pirate bands existed as free agents, independent and autonomous with no overarching hierarchies of loyalty or command.

By contrast the confederation created in 1805 was predicated on concepts of hierarchy and inter-gang affiliation. It was initially composed of seven (and later six) great fleets (*ta-pang*). Consisting of between 70 and 300 vessels each, they were commonly referred to as the Red, Black, White, Green, Blue and Yellow Flag Fleets. The largest and most important Red Flag Fleet was composed of more than 300 junks and between 20,000 and 40,000 pirates.[15] Each large fleet, in turn, was composed of a number of squadrons (*ku* or *ta-ku*) of between 10 and 40 vessels each. These units were formed from the independent gangs (*huo*) that had once flourished at Chiang-p'ing and had later constituted the basis for the privateer fleets of the Tay-son. As intermediary units between the fleet and the individual junks, the squadrons were the major building blocks of the confederation. Although it is impossible to know exactly how many there were at any given time, one of the largest had 36 junks and a crew of 1,422 men and women.[16]

Below the squadrons were the individual junks, under bosses or skippers known as *lao-pan,* who at one time may have functioned as the commanders of petty pirate gangs. Each vessel also had a headman (*t'ou-mu* or *t'ou-jen*) who shared responsibility for its management with the *lao-pan.* The *t'ou-mu* were readily distinguishable from the rank and file by their better dress and fare. They also took active command of the ship during combat. Those appointed as *t'ou-mu* were men who had caught their superior's eye and were deemed capable of handling responsibility. As a result they possessed certain powers of appointment and frequently assigned tasks and rank to other crewmen.[17]

Next in importance to the *t'ou-mu* were the helmsmen (*to-kung*) who were charged with the general management of the sails and the steering. There were usually at least two helmsmen per vessel. They were sometimes selected from among the pirates themselves, but were more often hired from the outside as specialists. Under the helmsmen were three or four men (*huo-chang*) who manned the cannon, threw the anchors, and burned incense. Any remaining crew members were charged with hauling up the sails and sculling.[18]

Operating Procedures

Operating procedures within petty pirate gangs were simple, informal and *ad hoc* with little to bind members into long enduring units. Petty pirates tended to carry out short, swift missions. Allocation of their prizes was also straightforward: single shares for each of the crew members and double shares for the head of the gang and the provider of the vessel if they were not the same individual. Beyond that, codes of conduct, articles of co-operation, and mechanisms of punishment seem to have been scarcely specified.[19]

By contrast, procedures within the confederation were more complex. In the first instance, the confederation itself came into being as a result of a written agreement (*li-ho-yueh*) signed by Kwangtung's seven major pirate leaders in 1805. Its goal was to regularize the internal operating procedures of the member units, to prescribe methods of conduct and intra-group communication when at sea, and to stipulate how business transactions with outsiders were to be conducted.

In the name of order, each vessel was to be registered with one fleet only and clearly identified. Because the stability of the confederation as a whole would be threatened by individual junks switching affiliation or by fleet leaders encouraging them to do so, anyone caught tampering with the identification process would be subject to punishment. Provisions prohibiting pirates from fighting one another for prizes already taken or from undertaking unauthorizied activities on their own sought to prevent internal conflict. Because the leaders envisaged that much of their income would derive from the sale of protection to other members of waterworld society, their ability to extract protection fees would depend on all members honouring one another's contracts of sale. Harsh punishment was therefore prescribed for those who even passively allowed breaches to occur. Implicit in the document was also the pirates' view of their confederation as an ongoing organization with a future as well as a present. This view is evidenced by provisions allowing for deferred payments by confederation members lacking in cash for indemnities or other internal obligations. At the same time, the right to distribute confiscated property throughout the ranks and punish offenders was reserved for the confederation as a whole. The seven provisions of the pirates' articles of confederation were:

1. All junks must register and any one who does not will be confiscated.
2. Any junk which tries to 'fake' the flag or colour of another branch will become the property of the whole group.
3. If one of the vessels belonging to the confederation accosts an outside junk already under the confederation's protection, indemnification to the injured party must be made and the weapons and anchors of the offending junk confiscated. If the said boat is unable to make restitution, this amount will be deducted from its future shares.
4. In an attack, the cargo ship will become the property of the junk that strikes it first. Anyone who seizes such a junk from its original captors must return the vessel and booty along with a heavy indemnification.
5. Those who take measures to strike out against pirates wrongly attacking a protected junk will be rewarded with 100 silver dollars and if, in the process, any are wounded, the whole group will be responsible for their medical care. Anyone who witnesses such an event, but does not come forward to participate, will be punished as a co-conspirator.
6. Any vessels that sail out on their own to conduct unauthorized operations, will, when apprehended, be subject to seizure and confiscation. Their commanders will be executed.
7. If two flagships meet at sea with something to discuss, they should hoist a flag on their foremast, and the bosses should come to confer. If a branch leader has an order to transmit to his own fast boats, he should hoist a flag on the third mast, whereupon all junks must assemble and listen to the order.[20]

Within the individual squadrons and ships, operating procedures were also complicated. Among the ship's officers, regularly appointed pursers, designated by the pirates as 'fellows of the brush and ink' (*t'ung pi-mo*) or 'keepers of the treasury' (*sui-k'u*), were charged with keeping track of protection contracts and booty. All prizes taken were to be surrendered to the common fund for redistribution. No pirate could retain any goods taken as booty without first producing them for group inspection. Such goods were to be registered by the pirates' purser and distributed by the fleet leader. Customarily, 20 per cent of the booty would be returned to the original captor, and the remainder, referred to as the 'public fund', would be placed in a joint treasury or storehouse. Currency, too, was to be turned over to the squadron leader, who would remit a certain portion to the fleet leader and a small amount to the captor. The remainder was to be reserved for purchasing supplies and provisioning vessels that were unsuccessful in their own pursuits.[21]

In 1807, when the female pirate Cheng I Sao became the leader of the confederation, she issued a code of laws which further helped to transform the personal patron–client relationships that underpinned the confederation into more formal power relations (but whether or not these regulations were written is impossible to determine). The code was short and severe. Anyone caught giving commands on his own or disobeying those of a superior was to be immediately decapitated. Pilfering from the common treasury or public fund as well as stealing from villagers who regularly supplied the pirates were also capital offences. Desertion or absence without leave were to result in a man's ears being cut off and his being paraded through his squadron. Raping female captives was also a capital offence, and if there were fornication by mutual consent, the pirate was to be beheaded and the female captive cast overboard with a weight attached to her legs.[22]

On more than one occasion Westerners saw pirates who had violated the code flogged, put in irons, or quartered. According to one captive, the pirates' code was strictly enforced and transgressions punished with an efficiency that seemed 'almost incredible'. Such severity, he concluded, gave rise to a force that was intrepid in attack, desperate in defence and unyielding even when outnumbered.[23]

Not much is known about the presence of women in the petty pirate gangs of the late eighteenth and early nineteenth centuries, but they seem to have participated fully in the life of the confederation.[24] In theory, however, women were not allowed on board ship unless they were married to one of the men. Most pirate wives had no permanent residences onshore and lived with their children amidst the horribly cramped conditions afloat. Although it was not uncommon for pirate leaders to share their quarters with as many as five or six wives, the crews tended to be made up of mostly unmarried men. Western captives have also noted that despite the strictures against promiscuity, each vessel usually carried eight or ten women who were 'intended to please all the society indiscriminately and to do the work of their sex'. At the same time, they have also pointed out that the greater part of the crew seem to have been satisfied without women and to have committed 'almost publicly crimes against nature'.[25]

In principle, female captives were to be released, but Turner has indicated that the pirates customarily took their most beautiful captives as concubines or wives, returned the ugliest to shore, and ransomed the rest. Turner has also stated, however, that once a pirate had chosen a wife from among the captives, he was supposed to remain loyal to her thereafter.[26] On board ship, the women worked as hard as the men and, in keeping with the traditions of South China, took charge of handling the sampans. With unbound feet, they were active, mobile and able to hold rank within the confederation. In the heat of battle, they sometimes even fought side by side with their husbands. During an engagement in 1809, one pirate wife managed to wound several assailants while holding fast to the helm and defending herself with a cutlass.[27]

Living conditions on board ship were always crowded. Space was at such a premium that sometimes a pirate and his family had to share a small berth about four feet square. Captives and recruits usually bedded down on the deck, unsheltered from wind or rain. The galley consisted of a small wooden shed on the afterdeck, where the wooden casks for storing fresh water were also kept. The pirates' diet, except when they seized cargoes of pork or poultry, usually consisted of coarse red rice and fish. In times of scarcity they sometimes lived for weeks on caterpillars boiled in rice or on the rats encouraged to breed in the vermin-infested conditions of the hold. Leisure hours were spent gambling, playing cards and smoking opium.[28] Vessels on which Westerners were sometimes held captive possessed all the 'conveniences for opium smoking' and cabins that accommodated two persons '[who] might indulge in that luxury until they insensibly fell into a death-like sleep'.[29]

Like other boat dwellers of the South China Sea, neither petty nor professional pirates ever set sail without praying to their gods. Before each foray the joss was faithfully consulted, and if the omens were bad, the pirates would not go forth. To facilitate these practices, pirate leaders sometimes ordered the construction of temples aboard their largest ships on which the fleet's most important leaders would assemble before each major undertaking to burn incense and inquire about their chances for success. In the company of their men, pirate leaders frequently visited the temples onshore and made donations to the priests. Seldom, if ever, did they destroy a temple or harm a bonze.[30]

The Headquarters of Petty and Professional Pirates

Since water-based activity ultimately depends on the land for supply and shelter, continental headquarters were necessary to the success of both petty and professional pirates. Throughout most of the eighteenth and early nineteenth centuries, petty pirates made their headquarters on the periphery of the Chinese empire: around the island of Hainan or just across the border in Vietnamese coastal cities such as Nghe An, Doan Mien and Hue. But most important of all was the fishing mart Chiang-p'ing. Located almost on the border in An Quang province at the side of a small watercourse on the Van Ninh Chau peninsula, Chiang-p'ing was technically a part of Vietnam until 1885. However, it functioned as a market to which Chinese in all facets of the fishing industry flocked.

Accessible to fishermen but remote by any other standards, Chiang-p'ing was a rough and ready frontier town from which pirates could operate with little fear of detection. Far from strong administrative centres in either Vietnam or China, Chiang-p'ing was scarcely reached by the arm of the law, and so successful were Chinese pirates in playing borderland hide-and-seek that by 1790 piracy, rather than fishing, was the mainstay of Chiang-p'ing's economy. Most of the residents of the town's 2,000 households were eager to sell them provisions and market their prizes. Once on sale in Chiang-p'ing, pirate booty often found its way into the hands of Chinese merchants who came there to purchase it. Moreover, at any given moment pirate leaders also found in these border towns a pool of potential pirates in the form of the urban failures, social misfits and criminals who gathered there by the score. Such individuals eagerly rounded out the pirate gangs that formed in their vicinity.

Later, during the nineteenth century, as Chinese control of the coast weakened, Hong Kong itself gradually seems to have supplanted Chiang-p'ing as the premier headquarters of petty piracy. There, too, the island's native entrepreneurs supplied pirates with arms and ammunition, disposed of their booty, and informed them 'as to the movements of police and British gunboats'.[31]

While petty pirates confined themselves to short, swift raids conducted out of borderland towns, the pirates of the confederation dominated the entire coast of the Sino-Vietnamese waterworld and set up their headquarters much closer to its core at Canton. At the same time, they allocated specific operating territory to each of their constituent fleets.

Upon returning to China from Vietnam in 1802, the pirates, who would later collaborate, set up their first base of operation in the Lei-chou peninsula, whose relative isolation rendered it, like Chiang-p'ing, far from strong administrative centres. In rounding out this stronghold, they next took possession of Nao-chou and Wei-chou, two little-frequented islands which flanked the peninsula and gave them easy access to both the salt fleets of T'ien-pai and the vessels passing through the narrow strait of Hainan.[32]

From there, the pirates moved east along the coast to establish a second headquarters on Lantao Island which stretched from Victoria Harbour to the mouth of the Pearl River and provided access to the major seaways of Kwangtung. From Lantao, the pirates soon extended their operations into the small unfortified islands along the coast, as well as the two major passages of the Pearl River itself.[33]

The first, known as the 'Outer Passage', was the principal route to Canton. It ran east of Macao, through the Bogue, past the first and second bars to Whampoa. In covering it, Cheng I's anchorages included San-men, just south of Lantao, and Lung-hseh and San-chiao in the middle of the river north-west of Lintin. The second route, known as the 'Inner Passage', was more frequently used by small craft and was guarded by Cheng I from Chu-chou, P'ing-shan and Mo-tao. It followed the channel of the Pearl River that ran west of Macao through the broadway and flats to Hsiang-shan where it was fed by a host of tributaries that led to Canton.

After joining forces, a major consideration in the allocation of territory to confederation leaders seems to have been the fleet leader's native place. The leaders of the Blue, Yellow and White Flag Fleets who were natives of western Kwangtung made their headquarters in Lei-chou peninsula, while the leaders of the Red, Black and White fleets operated farther east in the region nearer Canton.[34]

Not only was the territorial sphere of professional pirates more extensive than that of petty pirates, but so were their supply networks. Instead of relying solely on one city or base, professional pirates had accomplices throughout the entire province. From agents in Fang-ch'eng, T'ien-pai, Tung-hai, Nao-chou, Lei-chou, Sui-ch'i, Wu-ch'uan, Hsin-an, Hai-k'ang, Jao-p'ing and Hsin-ning, the pirates obtained rice, wine, tung oil and wood; while from others in Hsiang-shan, P'an-yu, Lien-chou, Hai-k'ang, Hai-yang, Hainan, Kao-chou and Wu-ch'uan, they obtained iron, cannon and ammunition. So pervasive was their network that the arrest of 500 suppliers in 1805 scarcely affected their operations at all.[35]

Arms and Equipment

With regard to arms and equipment, petty piracy was a low overhead operation that could be conducted with implements at hand. In addition to the standard fishing vessels that often doubled as pirate craft, the knives, pointed bamboo pikes and cutting blades that completed the pirates' arsenal would have been standard equipment on most South China junks. Outfitting an expedition thus amounted to little more than recruiting accomplices, readying weapons, and procuring provisions.

In contrast to the petty pirates, professional pirates possessed a variety of craft and armaments. Their vessels included everything from ocean-going junks to row boats. In 1809, at the peak of its strength, 200 of the confederation's craft were ocean junks (yang-ch'uan), capable of carrying between 300 and 400 men and mounting 20–30 cannon. These were comparable in size to the British country ships that sailed between India and China. More numerous than the ocean junks were the seagoing craft (hai-ch'uan) which allowed pirates to carry out operations in coastal waters. Most vessels in this category consisted of captured merchant junks approximately 40 ft long and 14 ft wide which carried at most 200 men and between 12 and 25 cannon. Altogether the confederation boasted between 600 and 800 of these vessels which would have been most comparable to the American schooners or the Portuguese brigs (two masted ships of less than 200 tons displacement) then on the scene.[36]

Professional pirates also possessed a fleet of river junks to ply the empire's 'inner waters'. Foremost among them were the small rowboats of one or two sails, 14–20 oars, and crews of 18–30 men. They were armed with six to ten wall-pieces and well-stocked with boarding pikes and swords. Such vessels were used for communicating between ships and for going ashore at night to destroy villages that were delinquent in the payment of protection fees.[37]

Professional pirates also protected their fleets with an impressive array of armaments. In 1806 the flagship of the Red Flag Fleet mounted ten cannon (two long 18-pounders and eight small 6-pounders), but by 1809 the number of cannon had been increased to 38 on one deck alone. Two fired 24-pound shot while eight fired 18-pound shot.[38] Pirate cannon generally weighed between 60 and 3,000 catties. Some were wooden, with an iron bore, but the majority were smelted from varying grades of raw and scrap iron.[39] Stocks of other arms included crudely built wall-pieces commonly known as gingalls or Chinese blunderbusses. With a barrel 7 ft long and a weight of 12 lb, the gingall resembled the European wall-piece of the early eighteenth century or the elephant gun of the nineteenth.[40] Besides gingalls, the pirates possessed a miscellany of old match-locks and fowling pieces. Many of these, however, were of doubtful value since their owners knew little about their care and operation.[41]

The pirates' most deadly weapon, however, was a long bamboo pike with a sharp, sabre-like blade used in the hand to hand combat at which they so excelled. The majority of the pikes were between 14 and 18 ft long and were hurled like javelins. The pirates also had shorter pikes with shafts of wood and slightly curved blades that were sometimes sharpened on both edges. In addition, they wielded knives of all sorts and rounded out their arsenal with bows and arrows.[42] Professional pirates were also well-supplied with gunpowder and shot. Their ammunition was usually obtained from captured ships or stolen from government forts and smuggled to them by agents in Canton or Macao.

With no want of weapons, well-armed fleets looked like floating fortresses. In 1805 an 11 junk squadron of 301 men possessed an arsenal of 62 cannon, 40 lead shells, two fowling pieces, 36 catties of gunpowder, 27 catties of iron bullets, 216 knives, 180 bamboo spears, 134 short knives, 23 rattan shields and 10 iron chains.[43]

The Operation of Piracy

For petty pirates, piracy served as an economic survival strategy which, when resorted to periodically, enabled them to make ends meet. The object was the heist, a short, swift, lightning-fast attack, levelled against a single craft at sea where an individual's compensation depended directly upon what he could seize. Captives or junks could often be ransomed for silver *yuan,* while such everyday items as bean bran, dried fish, clothing, wine, betel nuts, vegetables, oil, rice, firewood, porcelain, iron nails, tea leaves and sugar, in constant circulation along the coast, could be sold for cash in home bases. Although the remuneration from such ventures was usually modest, an average strike seems nevertheless to have yielded most participants somewhere between 10 and 15 silver *yuan* or a sum equivalent to about 3½ months' salary for an agricultural labourer. Therefore, even at this level, piracy seems to have paid.[44]

The duration of petty pirate enterprises was, however, very short. Their guerrilla-like tactics consisted of striking swift blows and then retreating before stunned victims could recover their senses or offer resistance. By the time constabulary forces reached the water, striking pirates had usually vanished. Petty pirates typically remained at sea only a few days before returning to Chiang-p'ing or their home base to dispose of booty and divide the proceeds. After a successful mission, many gangs dispersed, never to come together again, but some carried out sporadic activities over a period of several months.

In contrast to the petty pirates for whom piracy was an economic survival strategy, piracy for the professionals was a form of economic entrepreneurship characterized by sophisticated financial operations. Thus, the pirates of the confederation differed most strikingly from those at Chiang-p'ing in the breadth of their financial undertakings. With small *ad hoc* groups, petty pirates were always dependent on the chance seizure of vessels at sea. In an organization of thousands, however, survival required more than chance encounters. Thus professional pirates were forced by sheer necessity to develop more dependable sources of income.

With the creation of the confederation, piracy in the waterworld became a big business within which the heist was but one dimension. In contrast to the uncoordinated assaults of petty pirates, attacks by the professionals were planned in advance and systematically executed. Confederation made it possible for professional pirates to overpower even large ocean-going junks by force and to operate freely in the inner waters of the coastal strip. It also made possible attacks on the shore whose objects were the plunder of villages, markets, rice fields, and small forts.[45] With confederation, the ransoming of captives, vessels, and even villages became more systematic and extended even to foreigners who were no longer exempt from attack. Vessels of no use to the pirates were ransomed at standard rates of 50 silver *yuan* for fishing junks and 130 *yuan* for cargo carriers. Human captives were seldom released for less than 90 *taels* each, while for foreigners the sum might go as high as 7,000 Spanish dollars.[46]

It was in the sale of protection, however, that the pirates most successfully regularized their financial operation. With the help of secret societies, the pirates first turned their attention to the salt trade whose merchants soon found it more expedient to negotiate directly or to hand over large sums for the safe passage of their junks than to pay high prices after a strike. By 1805 professional pirates so successfully dominated the salt trade that nearly every vessel setting out for Canton found it necessary to purchase protection which was sold at such standard rates as 50 *yuan* of silver for each 100 *pao* (packages) of salt. Sometimes the pirates even provided escort services, as in 1805 when a fleet of salt junks paid 200 Spanish dollars apiece for a pirate convoy to Canton.[47]

Through the collection of set fees, the pirates established a system that yielded predictable profits from season to season. They reached the pinnacle of their power when they were able to extend their system to every vessel afloat and a significant number of villages on land. In return for specified sums, merchants, junk owners, pilots and fishermen received documents signed by the pirate leaders. Usually these fees were collected annually, although temporary certificates could be purchased for specified periods. In some areas merchant junks were assessed by the value of their cargoes at rates ranging from 50 to 500 *yuan* of silver per trip. In other areas the price for an ocean-going merchant junk was 400 Spanish dollars upon leaving port and 800 upon return.[48]

Protection documents were widely available from pirate leaders aboard ship and from their agents onshore. As their activities expanded, members of the confederation established financial outposts along the coast and even set up a tax office in Canton as a collection point for fees. The overall headquarters of their operation, however, appear to have been at Macao where assistants sold protection and supplied them with weapons and ammunition. Pirate leaders were scrupulous in abiding by the terms of their protection documents which were universally respected throughout the confederation. On being intercepted, vessels had merely to produce their documents as proof of payment and were then to be allowed to proceed.[49]

Thanks to success in these endeavours, the confederation had little want of money, and its flagships often carried sums of between 50,000 and 100,000 dollars cash.[50] More than anything else, the pirates' ability to regularize their finances facilitated their transformation into true professionals.

The Ultimate Goal or Inspiration of Piracy

Western authors and scholars such as Daniel Defoe, Christopher Hill and Marcus Rediker have portrayed various Western pirates as creators of new social orders that stood in marked contrast to the regimes from which they had fled onshore. In his *History of the Pyrates*, Daniel Defoe dwelt in considerable detail on Libertalia, the democratic (and utopian) pirate community founded by Captain Misson on Madagascar. Christopher Hill has suggested that 'radical' Englishmen after their defeat in 1660 fled to the West Indies, where they may have infused privateer and buccaneer communities with ideas that 'originated in revolutionary England'.[51] Marcus Rediker has portrayed the social relations of Anglo-American pirates of the eighteenth century as having been marked by vigorous antipathy toward traditional authority and has asserted that the pirates constructed their world 'in defiant contradistinction to the . . . [one] they had left behind, in particular to its salient figures of power, the merchant captain and the royal official, and to the system of authority those figures represented and enforced'.[52]

Petty pirates in China seem to have been little influenced by ideological considerations or concerns other than those of economic survival. For confederation members, the attribution of motive becomes more difficult, though Chinese pirates seem to have experienced nothing like the rough egalitarianism that placed authority among some Western pirates in collective hands. Nor does there seem to have been much attempt to remake a world left behind. Instead, the preoccupation of Chinese pirates with large-scale organization and hierarchy seems to mirror, rather than revile, the society onshore.

In China, the question that comes most readily to mind with regard to most collective action, including piracy, is: were the actors rebels? Despite the fact that pirates, like rebels, dated their documents, which in this case consisted of an articles of confederation, with a reign title, and although visions of himself as emperor seem to have fired the imagination of the pirate leader mentioned in the introduction, the pirates' articles provide no reasons other than those of economic gain for the founding of their confederation and manifest no interest in ideology or politics. In couching their rhetoric in the convention of rebellion, the question that arises is: were pirates intending to challenge the state or were they merely speaking in the only voice available to the non-elite when at last they wanted to be heard?

Evidence for regarding pirates as something other than rebels is seen in their interest in collaborating with the state whenever possible. In selling protection and escort services to salt fleets, fishing vessels and riverine villages, pirates seem content to have trod on certain official prerogatives without manifesting any real desire to overthrow the state in the process. In the end, when its forces proved unable to defeat the pirates militarily, officials of the state finally cajoled confederation leaders into joining forces with them in a final pacification of the seas. From this perspective, the pirates' ultimate return to 'allegiance' as military officials should probably be regarded more as evidence of their willingness to profit from yet another opportunity for advancement than as capitulation or defeat. As a group primarily concerned with financial gain, the pirate confederation must call into question the assumption that the primary motivation for large-scale collective action in China is necessarily ideological and that its ultimate goal is inevitably rebellion.

Conclusion

From the foregoing discussion it should be clear that the living and working conditions in Chinese pirate communities between 1750 and 1850 would have varied greatly depending upon the kind of organization of which a member was a part. At the least professional end of the scale, petty pirates would have found themselves afloat in organizations with little structure or staying power, organizations in which their identity as pirates would probably have been as serendipitous as their livelihood as fishermen was precarious. Although small-scale by any standards, the pettiness of petty pirates may have afforded its practitioners one advantage: the ability to disappear, the ability to escape detection and hence apprehension by blending back unnoticed into the communities from which they sprang. Given that theirs was a small-scale phenomenon that posed little threat to maritime commerce as a whole, petty pirates, provided they did not become too ambitious or greedy, probably ran little risk of detection. Most of their activity has probably eluded both Chinese authorities and the historical record. Participation in this relatively risk-free piracy may have enabled individuals to experience economic survival, but their lives as pirates would have opened few doors to new lives ashore.

By contrast, the more professional the organization in which a pirate participated, the more structured and ordered his life afloat would have been, and the more differentiated from local communities he would have become. In one sense the more outside local communities a pirate became, the more at risk he was, for it was not so easy for pirates of the confederation to disappear unseen into their surrounding milieu. Yet in another sense, an individual's identity as a pirate was probably more secure, for he would have held a recognizable position in a relatively stable organization which would have concerned itself, at least to some extent, with his well-being and viability. In return, he, as an individual, would have been accountable to the organization for his actions. Within such organizations the risk of apprehension from the outside would have been inversely proportional to the degree of military prowess and negotiating ability demonstrated by the organization itself. In the case of the confederation, military strength, entrepeneurial cleverness and diplomatic finesse rendered the unit relatively invulnerable to assault from without. Thus, with its hands forced, the government had little alternative to negotiating a favourable settlement with pirates who could literally 'blow the imperial forces out of the water'. For such individuals, participation in well-ordered pirate communities may have served as stepping stones to new lives and military careers on shore. However, the risks associated with piracy would never have completely disappeared and the reward for the unlucky would have been apprehension and decapitation, regardless of whether they were petty or professional pirates.

Notes

1. Alexander Dalrymple, *Memoir Concerning the Pirates on the Coast of China Drawn up at the Desire of Hon. William Fullarton Elphinstone, Chr. Court of Directors of E. I. C.* (London, 1806), 2.
2. The Portuguese translation of the letter in which this boast appears is in Judice Biker and Julio Firmino, *Collção de tratados e concertos de pazes que o estado da India Portugueza fez com os reis e senhores com quem teve relações nas partes da Asia e Africa e Oriental, desde o principio da conquista até ao fim do seculo XVIII* (Lisboa, 1886), 253–5. The document is dated 26 Dec. 1809.
3. For a general survey of the vicissitudes of piracy along the South China coast, see Grace E. Fox, *British Admirals and Chinese Pirates 1832–1869* (London, 1940).
4. *Kuang-chou fu-chih* [Gazetteer of Kuang-shou prefecture], 1879; ed. Tai Chao-ch'en, 163 vols, (Taiwan reprint, 1966), 74: 10.

5. For examples of the poverty of the Tanka, see Charles Toogood Downing, *The Fan-Qui in China in 1836–7*, 3 vols (London, 1838), 1: 106, 144, 210, and 2: 222 and 223.

6. Kani Hiroaki, *A General Survey of the Boat People in Hong Kong* (Hong Kong, 1967), 70.

7. *Kuang-tung hai-fang hui-lan* [An Examination of Kwangtung's sea defence], ed. Lu K'un and Ch'eng Hung-ch'ih, 42 vols, (n.d.), 2: 17–17b; 23: 30, 25: 7; Wang Chih-i, 'I hai-k'ou ch'ing-hsing shu' [Discussion of the seaport situation], in Ho Ch'ang-ling, *Huang-ch'ao ching-shih wen-pien* [Statecraft writings of the Ch'ing period] 120 vols, (1827), 36.

8. For more information see Dian Murray, *Pirates of the South China Coast 1790–1810* (Stanford, 1987), 6.

9. Fox, *British Admirals*, 97–8.

10. J. Turner, 'Account of the Captivity of J. Turner, Chief Mate of the ship *Tay*, Amongst the Ladrones: Accompanied by some Observations Respecting Those Pirates' in Alexander Dalrymple (ed.), *Further Statement of the Ladrones on the Coast of China Intended as a Contribution of the Accounts Published by Mr. Dalrymple* (London, 1812), 66.

11. French, Russian and British observers have uniformly identified 'mandarin oppression' as a major cause of piracy. Carloman Louis Francois Felix Renouard de Sainte-Croix, *Voyage commercial et politique aux Indes Orientales, aux îles Philippines, à la China, avec des notions sür la Cochinchine et le Tonquin, pendant les annees 1803–1804 . . .*, 2 vols (Paris, 1810), 2: 53; Adam Johann Von Krusenstern, *Voyage Round the World in the Years 1803, 1804, 1805, and 1806 By the Order of His Imperial Majesty Alexander the First, on Board the ships Nadeshda and Neva*, transl. A.B. Hoppner, 2 vols (London, 1813), 281; Richard Glasspoole, 'A Brief Narrative of My Captivity and Treatment Amongst the Ladrones', in Karl Friedrich Neumann, *History of the Pirates Who Infested the China Sea from 1807 to 1810* (London, 1831), 103, 126; and Turner, 'Account', 66.

12. 'Tay-son' was the name of the rebellion that wracked Vietnam between 1771 and 1802. The name derived from the native village of the three rebel leaders Nguyen Van Lu, Nguyen Van Nhac and Nguyen Van Hui. By 1785 the Tay-son had conquered the south and were ready to turn their attention to the north where they drove the Trinh from Hue. Next, they moved on to Hanoi at which point the emperor requested aid from China, and in 1788 three Ch'ing armies entered Vietnam to restore his throne. After being soundly repulsed, the Chinese emperor acknowledged the suzerainty of the Tay-son over Vietnam and invested Nguyen Van Hue as the Emperor Quang Trung. In 1802, however, the defeat of the Tay-son brought an end to their rule

13. Hsü Chien-ping, 'Shih-tzu-ling yü Ch'ing-ch'u Hsiang-kang Chiu-lung, Hsin-chieh chih ch'ien-hai yü fu-chieh' [The Lion Rock and the abandonment of the coastal strip and its subsequent reoccupation during early Manchu rule], in Lo Hsiang-lin (ed.), *I-pa-ssu-erh nien i-ch'ien Hsiang-kang chi ch'i-tui wai-chiao-t'ung* [Hong Kong and its external communications before 1842] (Hong Kong, 1959), 133, 139, 1140; Hu Chieh-yü, 'Hsi-Ying-P'an yü Chang Pao-tsai huo-luan chih p'ing-ting' [Hsi-Ying-P'an and the end of the ravages of the pirate Chang Pao-tsai], in Lo Hsiang-lin, *I-pa-ssu-erh*, 152–61; Hsiao Wan-om, 'Research in the

History of the Pirates on the China Sea, 1140–1950', unpublished mss. in Chinese, Sept. 1976, fols 23, 25, 27; *Kuang-tung hai-fang hui-lan*, 42: 26–26b. CC 15/1.

14. Murray, *Pirates*, 24–6.

15. *Ching hai-fen chi* 1: 2b-3; Hu Chieh-yü, 151; Na-yen-ch'eng, *Na-wen i-kung tsou-i* [The collected memorials of Na-yen-ch'eng] (hereafter NYC) (1838, reprint Taipei, 1968), 12: 47, CC10/7/1.

16. Squadron commanders were referred to by Westerners as 'inferior chiefs', by pirates as 'great heads' (*ta-t'ou-mu*), and by government officials as 'robber heads' (*ta-shou* or *tsei-shou*). NYC 13: 57, CC10/11/6.

17. Turner, 'Account', 68; Kung-chang-tang [Palace Memorial archive] (hereafter KCT), National Palace Museum, Taipei. KCT 003611, CC3/1/13; KCT 003728, CC3/2/19; KCT 004602, CC4/5/29.

18. Turner, 'Account', 68; KCT 002531, CC2/5/29; KCT 003728, CC3/2/19, *Ching hai-fen chi* 1: 6b.

19. Murray, *Pirates*, 26, 27.

20. The original document may be found in Chu-p'i tsou-che [Rescripted Memorial Collection], First Historical Archives, Peking, CP 1058/2.

21. *Ching hai-fen chi* 1: 5b, 6b and Philip Maughan, 'An Account of the Ladrones Who Infested the Coast of China', in Dalrymple, *Further Statement*, 29.

22. *Ching hai-fen chi* 1: 5b-6b; Turner, 'Account', 71; Maughan, 'Account', 29.

23. Richard Glasspoole, 'Substance of Mr. Glasspoole's Relation, upon His Return to England Respecting the Ladrones', in Dalrymple, *Further Statement*, 44–5.

24. Captive Edward Brown wrote in 1857 that women were not even allowed to visit the vessel on which he was held or any other pirate craft. Edward Brown, *Cochin-China and My Experience of It* (Taipei reprint, 1971), 52.

25. The comment was made by Sainte-Croix but based on an interview with Turner. See Sainte-Croix, *Voyage*, 2: 57–8 and Turner, 'Account', 71.

26. Turner, 'Account', 71.

27. *Ching hai-fen chi* 1: 10b.

28. Maughan, 'Account', 26; Glasspoole, 'Brief Narrative', 107, 128; Turner, 'Account', 61–2.

29. Brown, *Cochin-China*, 41.

30. Maughan, 'Account', 29. In describing some of the ritual on the ship in which he was held captive, Edward Brown wrote:
    the steward lighted two tapers and some incense sticks, and placed them before a small gilded idol, which was located in a recess at the end of the cabin. He also set some small cakes before it, not as a sacrifice, for they [the pirates] always ate them afterwards; he then finished the ceremony by making several reverences before it [for the pirates believed that] as long as they apply a small portion of their stolen treasures in the purchase of gilt paper, incense sticks, and other articles used in . . . worship, they receive a remission of their crimes. (Brown, *Cochin-China*, 46).

31. Fox, *British Admirals*, 94–5.

32. *Ching hia-fen chi* 1: 4b; *Kuang-tung hai-fang hui-lan* 42: 32–3; Maughan, 'Account', 12.

33. Murray, *Pirates*, 68–9.

34. *Ching hai-fen chi* 1: 14–14b; Turner, 'Account', 67, NYC 13: 1b, CC10/9/4.

35. NYC 12: 51–52b, CC10/7/1; 12: 67b–68a, CC10/7/25.

36. C.A. Montalto de Jesus, *Historic Macao: International Traits in China Old and New* (2nd edn Macao, 1926), 231; Turner, 'Account', 63, 65; Maughan, 'Account', 24–5.

37. Turner, 'Account', 65.

38. Turner, p. 49; Glasspoole, 'Glasspoole's Letter to the President of the East India Company's Factory', 8 Dec. 1809, in Dalrymple, *Further Statement*, 33.

39. NYC 12: 81b, CC10/8/28; Sainte-Croix, *Voyage*, 2: 56.

40. Turner, 'Account', 63; G.R.G. Worcester, *Sail and Sweep in China: The History and Development of the Chinese Junk as Illustrated by the Collection of Junk Models in the Science Museum* (London, 1966), 44; Brown, *Cochin-China*, 79.

41. Glasspoole, 'Brief Narrative', 112.

42. Turner, 'Account', 63–4; Maughan, 'Account', 25; Sainte-Croix, *Voyage*, 2: 56; NYC 12: 53, CC10/7/1.

43. NYC 12: 81b–82, CC10/8/28; 13: 35b–36, CC10/10/2.

44. Murray, *Pirates*, 26–7.

45. Murray, *Pirates*, 80–1.

46. KCT 000981, CC1/7/29; NYC 12: 41, CC10/7/1; Sainte-Croix, *Voyage*, 2: 54; NYC 14: 23, CC10/4/20; Turner, 'Account', 49–61.

47. NYC 12: 31b–32, CC10/6/15; Canton consultations, 4 April 1805.

48. Maughan, 'Account', 30, 69; Von Krusenstern, *Voyage*, 2: 310; NYC 12: 32, CC10/6/15.

49. Turner, 'Account', 69; Von Krusenstern, *Voyage*, 2: 310.

50. Maughan, 'Account', 30; Turner, 'Account', 72.

51. Daniel Defoe, *A General History of the Pyrates*, ed. Manuel Schonhorn (Columbia, S.C., 1972), 383–418; Christopher Hill, 'Radical Pirates?' in Christopher Hill (ed.), *The Collected Essays of Christopher Hill* (Amherst, Mass., 1985), vol. 1, 161-87.

52. Marcus Rediker, *Between the Devil and the Deep Blue Sea* (Cambridge, 1987), 267, and his chapter in this volume.

CHAPTER 4

Living and Working Conditions in Philippine Pirate Communities, 1750–1850

Ghislaine Loyré

Introduction

Piracy can be said to be one of the enduring economic activities of the Malay world. Throughout the course of history it has taken various forms and been practised to various degrees in the Philippines. To illustrate this phenomenon, this chapter will examine the way in which raiding was organized by the Muslim ethnic groups in the southern islands, in particular the island of Mindanao and the Sulu Archipelago. It must be admitted, though, that Mindanao rulers obtained more income from the trade they had established with non-Muslim neighbouring tribes than from the selling of plundered goods.

Basically the 'pirates' were coastal raiders, destroying and pillaging coastal villages and capturing the inhabitants. Occasionally, they attacked native ships. Embroiled in a war of succession, the rulers of Mindanao and their followers had to stop the raiding by necessity. Consequently the raiders, either native or mixed groups of maritime ethnic communities, moved to the sultanate of Sulu which remained more active and had developed into a central trading place. Here Asian and Western traders met. The opportunities for the sale of booty from expeditions were very favourable as many types of goods were available in exchange.

In Sulu, the sultan kept aloof from raids; the *datus*, however, increasingly engaged in these enterprises. In the last decade of the eighteenth century *datu* Camsa, the son-in-law of the sultan of Sulu, led pillaging expeditions in the Philippines selling the captives in Jolo, Borneo, Makassar and Batavia.[1] Whether the sultan favoured these expeditions or not is another question, but we can almost be sure that he knew about them. Camsa's raiding expeditions were notorious. Generally speaking, even if in his discussions with the Spanish the sultan claimed non-involvement, he was still getting a share of the price of the goods sold, which made him an accessory after the fact. For example, in 1775, when *datu* Teteng destroyed the British warehouse in Balambangan, the sultan received a share amounting to 45 pieces of artillery, powder and, as a voluntary contribution, 2,000 pesos.

These local *datus* also took advantage of the activities of the pirates, since they were instrumental in bringing more goods to the market at Jolo, the centre of the Archipelago. Consequently, they did not need to lead expeditions themselves. This meant that piracy was concentrated in the hands of smaller communities, who were less politically developed, transforming them into what can be called professional pirates. Nonetheless, it does not seem that their 'piratical' activities scared potential customers away from the market at Jolo.

Even so, pirates did reside in the territory of a leading sultan. In the wake of Mindanao, Sulu became the main pirate base. Although the inhabitants were subjects of the sultan, they grew more and more independent, undertaking voyages on their own account. These people included the Samals and the Iranuns and, by implication, the Tirun of Borneo who were part of the Sulu sultanate at that time. These links were of a political nature because the sultanates provided a structured setting, but also had a social and economic basis. Moreover, the sultan, or the *datus*, probably intervened in the settling of some particularly difficult conflicts within these communities. In doing so, they assumed the role of a sort of supreme court. Sultanate and pirates had to co-operate in the face of a common threat, the Spaniards. Piracy in the Philippines peaked in the eighteenth century, and simultaneously its character changed.

The Communities

'Communities' is a rather general expression to describe the various ethnic groups scattered throughout a number of islands where piracy was practised in the 1750–1850 period. Three of the main groups can

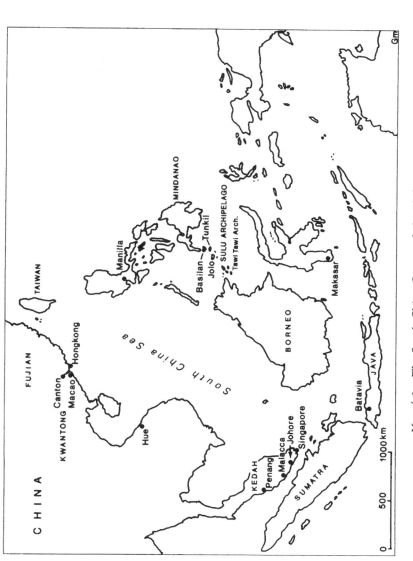

Map 4.1 The South China Coast and the Philippines

be identified ethnically. Let me hasten to add that Western sources were confused in their attempts to distinguish them from one another. Indeed, when strangers were sighted at sea, the immediate reaction in the villages was simply to shout 'Moros'. Moreover, when scores or even hundreds of men were seen shouting and fighting, there was really no time to look for distinguishing marks. In the early eighteenth century, Iranun, Magindanao and Balangingi had all become synonyms for pirates.

The communities which were mainly active in Philippine waters were the Samals, who inhabited the islands between Jolo and Borneo; Iranuns (or Ilanuns) originally from Mindanao but slowly settling in the same area; and Tiruns, who were established on the east coast of Borneo. In the eighteenth century, they all inhabited the territory of the Sulu sultanate. All belonged to different ethnic groups and in spite of common economic activity and the same type of environment, they maintained their own culture. Iranun pirates had left Minandao, their native island, and their communities were later joined by outsiders: outlaws (*renegados*) from the Christian areas and runaway criminals. They had the advantage of knowing the waters and areas where they had previously lived.

The piratical ethnic groups were generally called *Moros* by the Spaniards. Religion was not the main reason for this, for the Iranuns may not all have been Muslims; many of them must have had little notion of Islamic precepts. Nor had Samals been systematically converted. Consequently, when Cesar Majul calls the battles between the Muslims and the Spaniards the 'Moro Wars' we may assume that, with some exceptions, these were forays with an economic purpose. Even though the raids on Spanish forts appeared to be of a more strategic nature, it seems that the overall aim was to procure loot. We cannot exclude the possibility that occasionally the religious war (*jihad*) was used as an excuse, but it seems probable that such an excuse was superfluous.[2]

The Iranuns

Iranuns belonging to the Maranao group were the coastal inhabitants of Mindanao, and the immediate neighbours of the Mindanao sultanate. It took some time for them to emerge as an entity in contemporary writings for they usually raided along with—or under—the Mindanao sultanate. This changed when some of them decided to move away from Mindanao. One reason for this may have been the rigidity of the social structures in the sultanate. Another probable cause was the inability of the Maguindanao to lead the expeditions properly or to sell the booty successfully. What is certain is that this sedentary group, who lived on fertile land, sometimes chose to migrate to less welcoming islands and to rely entirely on piracy. We may assume that this had consequences not only for their way of life, but for their social organization as well.

Settled on the eastern shore of a southern bay, called the Moro Gulf, at the centre of the southern coast of Mindanao, some of them moved to the north and east coasts of the Sulu Archipelago and to Basilan.[3] There they placed themselves under the leadership of the lord of Sulu. We assume that their chiefs changed their allegiance. Although we cannot date these movements nor determine the extent of the migrant population, we know that in 1790 they were powerful enough to chase the Tausugs, who belonged to the Sulu sultanate, out of Tempasok.[4] Some of these Iranun communities were integrated into the Tausug population, while others refused to do so, even as late as the twentieth century.[5] The arrival of the Iranuns in the Sulu sultanate meant an influx of considerable supplementary skill. The sultanate became even more powerful from its accumulation of wealth and its market was better provided with goods.

The Samals or Samals-Balangingi

Not all Samals engaged in piracy. The Samals were people of the sea; they lived off the sea. They used to bring all types of marine produce to the market of Jolo, where these were mainly purchased by the Chinese. Later on, piracy enabled them to put their knowledge of the sea to use and increase their income. We may assume that the Tausug *datus* progressively initiated them into raiding, integrating them as a fighting force on their raiding expeditions. They became sedentary during the period under discussion.

Little historical and anthropological work has been done on them and the work by James Warren is mainly based on Western sources. Located in the islands of Balangingi and Tunkil, Samals can be readily identified ethnographically.[6] They are a group of people, including integrated slaves, who emerged in that area and were attracted to raiding. It was only at the beginning of the nineteenth century that the Samals appear in the sources. They started by being tributaries of the

Tausugs who appointed one of them to be their local representative. So, whatever their situation, they were under the authority of a Tausug *datu*.

The authority of the Tausug *datu* even extended to giving permission to raid through an intermediary of the local representative (*panglima*), who acted as organizer, choosing the heads of boats and obtaining the necessary equipment from the Tausug himself. On return, the Samals would repay their debt in slaves.[7] The leader of each boat would recruit his crew himself. The representative and the boat leaders (*nakodah*), who sometimes originated from the Visayas Islands (the group of central islands of the Philippines), determined the route. Each boat carried one person who was in charge of the crew and one pilot. Slaves also participated as rowers and in some cases they were even more numerous than the fighting force. This leads us to assume a combination of strong coercion and obvious personal interest. Though they were not allowed to carry arms, they were able to do all kinds of jobs for their masters. Apparently a religious man who read from the Koran would accompany the expedition as well as an experienced old man who would give advice.[8] It seems reasonable to assume that the religious men may have been provided, if not chosen, by the Tausugs, but we do not think that this was systematic.

As they became more powerful the Samals tended to follow a more independent line and started to raid without waiting for permission. The local representative then felt powerful enough to follow his own course. The year 1848 marked a turning point when the Spaniards destroyed the forts of Balangingi forcing the Samals to disperse and reconstitute themselves elsewhere. It is amazing how long the Spaniards bided their time before striking. The settlement was almost completely destroyed. Those who escaped needed three years to reorganize themselves. They resettled in Palawan, near Jolo, in the Tawi-Tawi Archipelago. Upon learning of their whereabouts, the Spaniards again attacked, this time almost immediately.

The Tiruns

Though during the period under consideration the Tiruns lived in the coastal area of the eastern part of Borneo between the Sibuko River and the Tapeadurian, thus outside Philippine waters, they belonged to Sulu territory. Moreover, they carried out their raids within the Philippines, more often on their own initiative rather than under the direction of the Tausugs. If the conversion of the Samals is doubtful, the Tiruns were certainly not Islamized. We suggest that this situation may have been the result of an attempt to keep these inferior subjects of the sultan fully under control. It also enabled the sultan to collect tribute among them. In order to dominate them better, Tausug *datus* lived with them in Borneo in the name of the sultan of Sulu. Obviously, the Tausug felt that their personal presence was necessary and did not choose a local representative. In spite of this, or in order to keep them under tighter control, or simply because of a personal attraction, the father of Sultan Badarud-Din of Sulu married a Tirun woman from the family of their chief.

In 1757, in order to comply with the insistent demands of the Spaniards, the Tausugs assisted them in retaliating against the Tiruns in their own lands for their raids in the Philippines.[9] The Sulu sultan had first excused their expeditions and told the Spaniards that, although the Tiruns were his subjects, they acted without his permission. No doubt, in spite of the reasons given, the sultan did not mind this since he probably also gained a share of the booty.

Social Conditions and Systems of Grouping

Whoever these ethnic groups were, it seems appropriate to say that the political point of reference was given by the Tausug sultanate of Sulu. At any rate the sultan of Sulu was at the apex of the hierarchy. The Tausug *datus* would regulate the communities either directly or through a representative, which allowed for at least one or two social strata. These were sought-after alliances. Among the communities we may suppose that the pirate leaders (*nakoda*) must have represented the top local social level, unless their power was limited to when they were at sea. In Mindanao there were titles which distinguished those functions related to the sea according the period: *raja laut, capitan laut*. We assume that these started off as expeditionary leaders, before getting a position within a sultanate.

A larger percentage of the loot was given to the chiefs, making it possible for them to maintain a higher standard of living and to demand a bride-price for their daughters corresponding to the status of their birth. We cannot be sure that hereditary leadership continued, since some Iranuns may have left Mindanao because the social divisions were too rigid, preventing anyone of lower birth from rising in the society. Away from Mindanao the Iranun communities were free from dominance from home, although some ties were probably maintained. The Iranuns also claimed a consanguineal relationship with the royal lineage of the Maguindanao, so moving away also constituted a break away from the sultanate of the Magindanaon which had begun to lose its influence.

Iranuns claimed the same descent from Sarip Kabunsuan, and therefore from the Prophet, as did the Maguindanao. This first official Muslim missionary provides the essential genealogical link to the sultanate of Johore and thence to the Prophet Mohammed. Both groups claimed that Sahip Kabunsuan arrived in their territory first. The point is that there were several marriages between the ruling house of Mindanao and that of Sulu. This provided some Iranuns with a claim to kinship with some Tausug *datus*, using genealogies as proofs. Consequently, some of the Iranun leaders, supposing they were themselves of royal descent, could claim a link to the Jolo sultanate. Obviously they would be considered as country cousins, but surely this must still have affected the relationship between the two ethnic groups. There are no documents to establish that new alliances were forged through marriages but it is not improbable that this happened. By taking such wives the Tausug *datus* would have ensured themselves all the more strongly of the loyalty of these pirates. Be that as it may, the Iranuns had a way of getting a foothold on the social ladder of the Tausugs.

Another point is that those Iranun communities which were attracted to Sulu would have moved with their own *datus*. Consequently the old order would have been preserved, in view of the fact that these populations were likely to have been raiders before moving from Mindanao to the Sulu Archipelago. Whatever the circumstances, it seems reasonable to suppose that the ability to raid was more important than blood for successful leadership. It is more than probable that some skilled pirates did become chiefs and achieved power which was later only justified by blood-ties.

Socially speaking, Samals must be distinguished from the Iranuns. They were an alien group scattered throughout the islands. Some Tausug *datus* must have married Samal women, or taken them as concubines, yet it is unlikely that a Tausug woman would have condescended to marry a Samal, as this group was considered inferior. On raids the Iranuns must have assumed a similar attitude towards their companions and this must have affected their raiding. One can even imagine that some Iranuns commanded the Samal pirates who joined them. The Samals did turn to Islam but only very slowly and their interest in genealogies was not based on a Muslim ancestor. Thus, we suppose that their social classes were not divided between those who were descended from the Prophet and those who were not. So the social divisions may not have been as numerous or as rigid. The chiefs were most probably the leaders of raids. The slaves of the pirate communities were at the lowest level: people who could not link themselves to any genealogy and could not claim a knowledge of the customs.

The constitution of a community destroyed after the intervention of the Spaniards enables us to study one example of it at a later stage. After the destruction of the four forts of Balangingi, and in spite of the severe punishment inflicted by the colonial power and the refusal of the sultan of Sulu to acknowledge their intentions, one chief still decided to go on raiding. Returning to one of the islands of Balangingi, he proclaimed himself an independent sultan. He built 40 houses, gathered 400 armed men and started constructing a fort. Sources do not say what followers he had kept with him, but we can assume that he gathered some people who had been isolated by the intervention of the Spaniards.[10] The situation is peculiar but it shows that the decisions of one man could be enough to start a community of raiders. From then on the pirate leader would bypass the decision of the sultan of Sulu to go raiding. In this case, he met with immediate failure because, for once, the Spaniards reacted immediately and destroyed the new settlement.

Communities differed considerably in size. We have an approximate idea of the number of people through the figures given by the Spaniards when they destroyed the Samals' lairs. More than a hundred Samals died in Balangingi in 1848. The same year, in Sipak, 340 Samals died; there were 150 prisoners, plus those who escaped and those who perished in the swamps, which means an estimated total population of between 600 and 700 persons.[11] In Tonkil, there were 960 houses indicating a population of 4,000–16,000 people, an average of four to six persons per house.[12] So, as far as the Samals are concerned, they can be counted either by the hundred or by the thousand. Hunt has made a survey of pirate communities: ten communities have been located representing a male population of over 4,000 and a fleet of 30 boats at most for each community, a total crew of a hundred per boat.[13] Figures suggest that raiding fleets were temporary and flexible. They would assemble to achieve a certain objective and then disperse.

Cooperation between communities was based on personal alliances between chiefs. Alliances were probably confirmed by marriage ties but, on the whole, they were very temporary, for the duration of one or two raiding seasons. Only on rare occasions would these alliances lead to a geographical move and physical regrouping. External battles necessitated the gathering of a number of normally independent communities.

Living and Working Conditions

Living conditions were very precarious. Water was the key to every settlement. There had to be an island with a supply of fresh water and with a river which would obviate living directly on the coast, thus allowing shelter from bad weather and from enemies, but at the same time providing very easy access to the sea. Mangroves or swamps, like those at Balangingi and Tunkil where the Samals-Balangingi were settled, were another defensive asset. Using the protection offered by rocks in shallow water and currents was another strategy adopted against surprise attacks. Some communities simply lived on boats.

The Samals had four forts: Balangingi, Sipac, Gucotingal and Sangap. The fort of Sipac was made of wood, had a three-tier compound and was surrounded by a moat, marshes, and the sea.[14] It was destroyed by Spanish cannons. Generally speaking, these forts were 'situated on raised ground and protected by coral reefs on three sides, were surrounded by stockades of two, three, and four tiers of stout tree trunks, packed with earth and coral to a height of twenty feet, and defended with heavy cannon'.[15]

The raiding season was regulated by the prevailing weather conditions: the north-west monsoon from December to February brought them to Celebes, Borneo, East Sumatra and the Straits of Malacca, and the August–October south-east winds took them to the Philippines. Balangingi-Samals went to the northern islands of the Philippines in March and October. The Southern Palawan would also cut off the maritime route of the Borneo traders. In the same way, others would cut the route to the Mindanao sultanate. Navigation was not risky because the ships would follow the coasts. They usually used native boats which were too small to face rough seas. These boats would not carry more than the bare essentials: men, arms, sometimes some swivel guns, and a minimum of cargo, but very little food and water. The pirates usually lived off the place they were attacking. The objective was to leave with almost nothing in order to bring back as much booty as possible, captives in particular. Anyway, the coast was never too far away to get the food they needed. At times, these raiders really were 'pirates' attacking fishermen, local trading boats, or Chinese junks bound for Manila. In 1770 the galleon *San Juan* plying between Manila and Acapulco had to leave without her full complement of cargo because the Chinese goods had not yet arrived due to the activities of the 'pirates'.[16] But in general they preferred to attack quiet villagers living on the coast.

Methods of Fighting

The fighting prowess of the *Moros* was often criticized by the Spaniards. None the less, they could be brave if they had no time to flee, as in Balangingi in 1848: 100 Samals died but the Spaniards had 50 wounded and seven dead. It was unusual for Spaniards to have more than a few casualties in encounters with the *Moros*.[17] In Sipac, it was even worse, for there were 16 Spaniards dead, 124 wounded and 22 people disappeared.[18]

Spanish sources stigmatize the pirates as cruel because of the harsh treatment meted out to their captives, and treacherous because often they took Western ships by surprise or by the use of ploys. As an example we could mention the *goleta San José* which was taken by surprise in 1798 in Philippine waters where it had anchored due to the protection offered by the presence of the brother and the nephew of the sultan of Sulu.[19] Under other circumstances they would have been unable to attack these towering ships, as these communities were pirates and not an organized army. They calculated the risk involved and fought only if they had a chance of gaining something. If not, they would run away and disappear rather than risk their lives. Moreover, if they were followed too closely they would dispose of all that was in their boats, including booty and captives. These pirates would only fight if they had no way of escaping, but then they would fight fiercely as if their homes were being attacked.[20] In Balangingi the Samals must have been taken by surprise, for all too often the Spanish expeditions to Jolo and especially to Mindanao would find the so-called 'pirate lairs' empty. The population had gone, leaving everything behind.

In order to facilitate their activities, the *Moros* would have bases closer to their targets, mainly in the Visayas, the islands in the centre of the Philippine Archipelago: Masbate, Burias and Mindoro. From there they could make more raids for they had only a short distance to sail and could make the most of the winds. Moreover, they could return home to offload prisoners and goods to avoid accumulation aboard ship. Pirates took special precautions too. They even used code names for some islands so that they could not be betrayed by runaway slaves.[21]

Ships

The size of the ships, their number, and the loot they could bring back can be studied from some examples which provide us with many details. Average numbers can be deduced from a chronological list of all expeditions which we have been able to compile from archives and published materials in English and Spanish.[22] Let us consider one example: in 1798 25 boats (*pancos*) attacked various places in the Visayas. They carried 500 *Moros* plus 800 slaves as oarsmen. They enslaved 450 persons, including three priests, one of whom was sold for 2,500 pesos (no identification is given of who these pirates were).[23] One can deduce various things from this example: slaves used as oarsmen; a total of 1,750 persons on 25 boats, meaning 70 persons per vessel. These pirates had been established for four years in Burias where they had stayed with no apparent intervention on the part of the Spaniards throughout that period. In 1752 there was another case of *Moros* from Tuboc, comprising 300 persons on only two local ships (*joangas*).[24] Sometimes the pirates could number as many as 3,000, as in 1849.[25]

The size of the ships varied in carrying capacity from 30 to 200 men. Some had a double tier of rowers with as many as 250 crossed-legged rowers and another level above for the warriors.[26] A ship could be 26 m long and 10 m at the beam and have a capacity of 60 tons, to provide a picture of some measurements. Generally, the ships of the Balangingi could accommodate from 50 to 80 warriors plus 100 oarsmen. But after their destruction by the Spaniards in 1848, the ships became smaller and carried at most 100 men, fighters and rowers included.[27] Another question which remains to be answered is how many ships assembled for raids. The Balangingi from various communities had to join together so that their ships would number between 30 and 50. Expeditions would rarely surpass a total of 75 ships of various sizes.

Arms

The pirate ships were well armed. Pirates could purchase arms at the market of Jolo, but often they would seize them from victims. During the expedition against the four forts of the Balangingi, the Spaniards took 124 pieces of artillery, some made of bronze and some of iron, including obus of 6 lb, cannon of 1–24 lb, culverin of 2 lb, falconet of 4 and 2 lb, *lantaca*, and four useless cannon. This does not mean that the Samals actually used all these arms, but they were the fruit of plunder.[28] In fact, in spite of this, the *Moros* did not resort much to arms. Either they were not well versed in the art of firing them or they did not maintain firearms properly. They relied mostly on the light, 6–24 lb culverins at the stern of their ships. Locally, these were called *lantaca*. The Spaniards believed that the slave trade financed the purchase of arms and ammunition from the Dutch. The analysis of Dutch sources, however, proves this was mistaken.[29] The *Moros* did not buy their arms from the Dutch; rather, their loot supplied them with most of their firearms. If some raids were carried out only by a very small number of ships and on a very small scale, other ships could be well equipped with a compass or even with a brass telescope.[30]

Piracy and Colonialism

Piracy in the Philippines was not a response to colonialism for it had existed before the arrival in the area of Western empires. However, colonialism altered the rules of political and economic life in several ways.

When the Spaniards arrived in the Philippines, there were no sultanates; instead petty chiefs engaged in piracy with their followers. The influence of Islam, the presence of an enemy, and increasing facilities for piracy enabled the inhabitants to prosper and to organize themselves into sultanates based on piracy. Missionaries gathered the people into villages, not allowing them any defence for fear they might rebel. Thus targets were 'offered' more easily to the pirates. Spanish sources of this period constantly complain about the raids which destroyed, sometimes more than once, almost all the villages of the central islands of the Philippines and the northern coast of Mindanao. The Spaniards had to exempt the inhabitants from paying taxes because so many people were taken away and some areas were totally devastated.

The Spaniards could barely defend their colony against foreign attacks and were even incapable of preventing the pirates from coming close to the capital and, for instance, from destroying a gun foundry, which was supposed to be the best protected place. It was the same with forts which lacked men, arms and munitions. In 1751 a decree was passed which authorized all corsairs to keep the booty they had obtained for themselves, in order to improve the fight against piracy. But this did not seem to work any better in the Philippines than anywhere else.

Colonial powers, especially the Dutch in Indonesia with their trading monopoly, disrupted traditional trade and consequently the political, religious, and marriage unions between islands in the Philippines and the nearby islands of the Indonesian Archipelago.

Before rigorously fighting piracy, the Westerners had indirectly encouraged it. The Dutch bought slaves from Sulu to obtain labour for Indonesia. The British bought all types of commodities from them to sell to the Chinese in exchange for tea. Opium also became a means of buying birds' nests, tortoise-shells, shark-fins, and tripangs. This enabled them to save the silver which would normally have served for this purchase. In fact, the Chinese did not want any of the goods the English sold in the area. These factors caused piracy to boom.

Economic Life: Food Production and Booty

Any economic activity outside of raiding was reduced to a minimum. The communities did have coconut palms but no subsistence agriculture was practised. They were said to have relied on the Tausugs who themselves obtained their rice supply from Mindanao. Some must have carried out enough agriculture for the minimum of food subsistence when the men were away. Others might have traded to a small extent and fished, including fish-drying, which sometimes supplemented the irregular income provided by raiding (which occurred at certain seasons, once or twice a year). These activities were mostly carried out by the women, children, older people, and probably slaves for most of the year while the men were out on raids. The most essential activity was probably the fish-drying which satisfied basic nutritional requirements.

In 1762, in the *Moros* base in the island of Mindoro, where they had been settled for several years, the Spaniards took 10,000 spears, some carriages, and one small swivel culverin representing in all a value of

31,026 pesos. This is more than the cost of the expedition, which was 25,260 pesos for no less than 1,252 men. Though Mindoro is close to Manila and was consequently less expensive than southerly expeditions, the comparison of these figures offers a perspective on some of the goods accumulated by the pirates. Besides, they regularly sent slaves, as well as some other goods, to the markets.[31]

The booty mainly consisted of slaves but, at the height of their power, also gold coins, jewels and arms. Whatever their prey, everything had its price in the busy market of Jolo. Slaves were more than mere slaves, or just goods for exchange, because some of them would accompany the *Moros* on expeditions. These slave oarsmen must have been fully trusted because by their sheer numbers, even if un-armed, they could be very dangerous. They could stab the *Moros* in the back while they were raiding villages. Consequently, one can assume that these slaves obtained a share of the booty. They might have considered that they were better off with the pirates than if they had been returned to the village-missions. Moreover, the involvement of the slaves had become absolutely necessary because the native popu-lation in Jolo would have been insufficient to go raiding: 50 per cent of the population of the island were slaves.[32]

At the end of the eighteenth century, some 500 persons a year would have been captured and enslaved.[33] This constituted a severe haemorrhage for the islands of the Philippines but it is estimated that it did not represent more than one or two per raider. From an economic point of view, though, this shows that the loss to the Spanish colony was more than the gain for the pirates. Both the Sulu Archipelago as well as the Dutch in Indonesia had need of extra labour.

The sharing of the slaves among the Balangingi has been described very precisely. The chief of the ship and his two right-hand men had the biggest share: six or ten slaves for the former and around two slaves for the next two in rank. The men, divided into warriors and navi-gators, received less than the leaders. Part of the booty was always reserved for the head of the village and for the owner of the ship, and in some cases for the person providing the arms and the ammunition.[34] After such a distribution, we may well wonder what was left for the crew in spite of these apparently clearly defined rules.

In another context, some raiders borrowed ships and guns, and had to pay upon returning with part of the booty including interest. They would have to yield as much as one-third of the booty in payment,[35] but this was seldom enough to end the vicious circle of indebtedness once started.[36] Borrowing entailed interest payments, which were too crippling to repay. Accordingly, the debt would double,[37] or in the southern Philippines it could treble, and people would therefore be tied for life.

Slaves provided the scale for barter. Among the Balangingi one slave was equivalent to 200–300 *gantans* (3.1 kg) of rice in 1850. One local ship was worth six to eight slaves and the hire of these ships was estimated at two or three slaves. Borrowing was thus very expensive at one-third of the total purchase price. A portable cannon was loaned for the price of one slave.[38] Cloth was also used as a yardstick of value in exchange.

Various types of what we usually call 'slaves' existed. People brought in from outside were the lowest class and were tied to a master for life. People of the same kin 'enslaved' for misbehaviour, or for their inability to pay a fine or repay a debt, were a higher class and were tied to a master for a temporary period until the debt or fine were paid.

Conclusion

Whatever scale or form it took, piracy thus existed as a way of life for several centuries in the southern Philippines. It was extremely important for the development of the various political entities of the region and for their relationship to the colonial powers. Piracy enabled communities not only to escape outside control but also to live according to their own choice. Their culture and their religion were not altered by the colonial regime. At a later stage, piracy enabled the communities to achieve some degree of independence from the sultanate of Sulu. It also enabled the inhabitants of the southern Philippines to avoid the Spanish administrative patterns of trading, paying taxes, and identification papers. The notions of piracy and trading must not be placed in opposition to one another. Whereas a weaker opponent could always be attacked, a stronger party was better approached by trade. As we have already seen, Islam did not form a motive for raiding. These communities were not Islamized to any great extent, if at all. But Islam provided a structure for the sultanates, without which those communities would not have expanded in terms of population numbers and raids. The year 1850 saw the introduction of steam in the struggle between the Spaniards and the pirates. So dominance started to shift from the *Moros* to the colonial powers. This was the beginning of the end of the pirate communities. Then, by 1890, the efforts of the

Spaniards, the Dutch and the British considerably limited piracy to small-scale targets. It appears that before this period the Western powers had not been fully conscious of their losses through piracy or were not alert enough to make concerted efforts to eradicate it. After 1890, however, communities had to convert to fishing, collecting sea products, or tilling a little land and growing coconuts. But sailors continued plying the seas between the southern tip of the western Philippines and Borneo to bring back goods from Singapore. All of this still feeds today's trade, called the 'barter trade', of Zamboanga (the extreme south-west tip of Mindanao) and it is carried out with full legal sanctions.

Notes

1. José Montero y Vidal, *Historia de la piratería Malayo-mahometana en Mindanao, Joló y Borneo desde el descubrimiento de dichas islas hasta Junio de 1888*, 2 vol, (Madrid, 1888), 361.
2. Ghislaine Loyré, 'Une histoire des Maguindanaon est-elle possible? Contribution à l'étude d'une ethnie musulmane aux Philippines dans les temps modernes' (unpublished Ph.D., Paris, 1992), 370.
3. James F. Warren, *The Sulu Zone 1768–1890. The Dynamics of External Trade, Slavery, and Ethnicity in the Transformation of a Southeast Asian Maritime State* (Singapore, 1981), 248–54); Ghislaine Loyré , *A la recherche de l'Islam Philippin. La communauté maranao* (Paris, 1989), 56.
4. Warren, *The Sulu Zone*, 261.
5. Warren, *The Sulu Zone*, 255.
6. Warren, *The Sulu Zone*, 301.
7. Warren, *The Sulu Zone*, 307.
8. Warren, *The Sulu Zone*, 309.
9. Cesar Adib Majul, *Muslims in the Philippines* (Manila, 1978), 202.
10. Montero y Vidal, *Historia*, 419.
11. Montero y Vidal, *Historia*, 411.
12. Montero y Vidal, *Historia*, 430.
13. J. Hunt, 'Some particulars relating to Sulo in the Archipelago of Felicia', in J. H. Moor (ed.) *Notices of the Indian Archipelago and Adjacent Countries* (London, 1967), 31–60; Warren, *The Sulu Zone*, 255.
14. Emilio Bernaldez, *Reseña historica de la guerra al sur de Filipinas, sostenida por las armas Espanolas contra los piratas de aquel archipielago desde la conquista hasta nuestros dias* (Madrid, 1857), 150; Majul, *Muslims*, 274.
15. Warren, *The Sulu Zone*, 301.
16. Warren, *The Sulu Zone*, 278.
17. Montero y Vidal, *Historia*, 409.
18. Montero y Vidal, *Historia*, 411.
19. Montero y Vidal, *Historia*, 366.

20. Ghislaine Loyré, 'Les Moros, barbaresques des Mers Orientales' (with A. Rey), *Hérodote*, 52 (1989), 106.
21. Warren, *The Sulu Zone*, 305–6.
22. Ghislaine Loyré, *Sultanats et Piraterie dans les Philippines du Sud* (Paris, 1978), 400–15.
23. Montero y Vidal, *Historia*, 365.
24. Montero y Vidal, *Historia*, 303.
25. Montero y Vidal, *Historia*, 424.
26. M. de Pagés, *Voyage autour du monde et vers les deux pôles par terre et par mer pendant les années 1767, 1768, 1769, 1770, 1771, 1773, 1774 et 1776* (Paris, 1782), 178.
27. Warren, *The Sulu Zone*, 310.
28. Montero y Vidal, *Historia*, 415.
29. Ruurdje Laarhoven-Casino, *From Ship to Shore: Maguindanao in the Seventeenth Century* (Quezon City, 1985), 144.
30. Warren, *The Sulu Zone*, 257.
31. Montero y Vidal, *Historia*, 334.
32. Warren, *The Sulu Zone*, 345.
33. Montero y Vidal, *Historia*, 358.
34. Warren, *The Sulu Zone*, 397–8.
35. Thomas Forrest, *A Voyage to New Guinea and the Moluccas from Balambangan*, 1779 (Manila, 1971), 331.
36. Loyré, *Sultanats*, 106.
37. Vicentes Barrantes, *Guerras piràticas de Filipinas contra mindanaos y joloanos corregidas é ilustradas* (Madrid, 1878), 266.
38. Warren, *The Sulu Zone*, 306.

CHAPTER 5

Piracy in the Eastern Seas, 1750–1850: Some Economic Implications

J.L. Anderson

Introduction: Three Types of Piracy

Piracy by its character is a business enterprise. Privateers, who sailed under letter of marque or with a commission, could claim that patriotic motives were paramount, or at least mingled with calculations of profit and loss. Pirates could make no such claim; when men (or women) went 'on the account' it was on their own account. Being a business, piracy is in principle amenable to economic analysis in terms of its nature, causes and effects. In this chapter these aspects of piracy are considered, the focus being on the waters of the Malay Archipelago and the South China Sea in the first half of the nineteenth century. In particular, the direct and indirect costs to the affected communities will be analysed.

Precise definitions of piracy are not necessary for economic analysis. In general historical works, or those dealing with the interplay of law, politics and commercial navigation in areas and times of limited state development, the shading between privateering and piracy is a legitimate object of inquiry. In the Bronze Age Aegean Sea, around the coasts of medieval Europe, in the early modern Mediterranean Sea and in nineteenth-century Malaysian waters, the line between piracy and reprisal often cannot easily be drawn by scholars in an objective way. However, the economic implications of arbitrary and indiscriminate seizure of vessels, goods and persons at sea and along coasts can be analysed without reference to fine distinctions of motive.

Piracy may be classified under three headings: parasitic, episodic and intrinsic. The character of any particular armed foray against sea-borne commerce or littoral dwellers may have elements of all three forms but it is useful for the purposes of analysis to distinguish them as they have different causes and effects.

The extent of parasitic piracy is a function of trade. The function is parabolic rather than linear, for although initially piracy will increase with an increase in trade, after a point piracy may be expected to decline. Initially, expanding sea-borne commerce means more vessels and goods are at hazard and there is more profit in piracy. Existing pirate 'firms' increase their size and improve their efficiency, and additional 'firms' are drawn into the 'industry'. However, there are economies of scale in the provision of protection, so the increased volume of trade can be protected at a lower cost per unit. At some point, instead of merchant vessels carrying expensive guns and soldiers, it will be cost-effective for specialized warships to provide protection for a convoy. With further increases in trade, a government can be persuaded to provide naval patrols to hunt pirates or even mount expeditions to destroy pirate bases. Each of these steps will tend to increase the costs and decrease the returns to piracy, and pirate 'firms' will exit the industry. Parasitic piracy, feeding directly or indirectly on increasing European trade and ultimately suppressed by European naval power, was a characteristic of much of the piracy in the century 1750–1850.

A variant of parasitic piracy emanated from the Sulu Archipelago. The late eighteenth-century expansion of European trade in the eastern seas, particularly in tea, led to an increase in demand for the maritime and forest products of the Southeast Asian region which were accept-able in the China trade. In order to obtain these products, and more importantly the labour required for their collection, the Sulu sultanate became a centre for piracy and slave-raiding on an increasing scale.[1] The Iranun and Balangingi, striking out in all directions from their bases in the Sulu area, became by the mid-nineteenth century the most powerful and feared raiders in the waters of the Malay world.

Episodic piracy may for simplicity be expressed as an inverse function of trade or more generally of employment opportunities for labour, capital and enterprise in sea-going activities. When this source of income fails, otherwise idle seamen can be driven for survival to use their vessels and skills for illegal purposes. The decline in employment opportunities for mariners may be fortuitous, the result of demobilization after a war or a downturn in the business cycle, or it may be the consequence of a third party achieving a monopoly position in the carriage of goods. The Dutch East India Company, by systematically monopolizing the trade of the East Indies, seems to have intensified the problem of piracy in the area. Episodic piracy may be expected to wane with the passing of the economic hardship or political circumstances that created it. Bugis piracy appears to be an example.[2]

In some instances, piracy was neither a peripheral nor occasional activity, but was an integral part of public finance: in short, it was intrinsic to the functioning of the state. This situation arose when small, insular or littoral states, hardly more than port towns, lacked the resource base from which regular taxes could be raised, leading rulers to rely at best on tribute levied on passers-by and at worst on outright piracy. Examples can be drawn from a variety of places and times: the Bronze Age Greeks of Homeric verse, the Vikings that harassed Dark Age Europeans, the corsairs of the North African coast and many of the rulers and retainers in the small states of the Malay world.

Piracy in the Malay World

Many of the characteristically small political units of much of the Malay Peninsula and Indonesian Archipelago were located at or near river mouths. Lacking extensive, revenue-producing lands, the rulers of those states had to rely for their finances on tribute exacted from dwellers in the remoter areas, levies on water-borne goods, and on piracy. The *orang laut*, or sea people, who made up about one-third of the clients of the sultan of Johore, spent much of their time cruising local waters to protect Johore's traders and to harass other shipping.[3] A similar exercise of force was important in the rise of Malacca.[4] Less reputable rulers were still more deeply involved in piracy and its usual adjunct, slave-raiding and trading. In 1830 Rear Admiral Owen observed that piracy was 'as important a buttress of state or tribal exchequers as are certain national lotteries of our own day'.[5]

Recourse to piracy, and to the warfare of which it was often an expression, was a rational economic strategy for individual rulers. War and piracy were conducted in such a manner as to acquire labour as well as goods. In the labour-scarce economies of the Southeast Asia region, men and women in various degrees of dependency were valued as contributions to the prestige, power and productivity of a small state, and slaves were highly marketable commodities. However, this approach to the problem of public finance and of augmenting the labour supply regardless of cost to the labourers was not a zero-sum activity: as will be shown, losses were not balanced by gains. Furthermore, economic growth was lessened as a consequence of uncertainty and of the high costs of protection against pirates.

In Europe, a necessary part of the process of economic development was the coalescence of feudal principalities to form nation-states that possessed a monopoly of violence: the nation-state became the sole provider of law and order and defence. Insular or peninsular Southeast Asian states could seldom enjoy a similar monopoly of violence within a substantial and defined area. The states' political structure was fragile, some states were ephemeral, and their size and location made them vulnerable to attack: the sea was a highway, not a barrier. As in medieval Europe, rulers had little choice other than to engage in forms of warfare, but whereas in Europe stability could come with the establishment of large states able to defend delineated frontiers, in Southeast Asia the topography and maritime nature of the region contributed substantially to the difficulty of achieving stability.

Lack of stability in the foregoing sense not only kept protection costs high per capita, but created uncertainty which reduces investment and economic activity. With arbitrary confiscation, as with prevalent piracy, 'no man is certain of his property or of the fruits of his labour'.[6] A reasonable certainty in that respect is necessary to induce producers to postpone consumption or to forego leisure, and to allocate their time and resources to create productive assets; in short, to invest. Uncertainty, to which piracy contributed, can explain the limited use of capital in manufacturing in the region better than lack of resources or an assumption of indigenous idleness. In Southeast Asia, production was to order, without the accumulation of stocks and perhaps equipment that would be vulnerable to seizure.[7]

Piracy: Economic Effects

Turning to the more immediate effects of piracy, the lack of records makes the task of quantification impossible, and judgements made on direct evidence are fraught with difficulty. For example, the few notations of European vessels thought to have been taken by pirates could in some cases simply reflect the perils of the sea.[8] The losses of the far more numerous and vulnerable native craft often went unrecorded. Trends in trade figures reflect not only the activities of pirates but also a complex of other causes operating within and beyond the region. Because trade flourished in the eastern seas in the nineteenth century, some doubt has been expressed about whether piracy could have caused significant harm.[9] However, the issue is not what was, but what might have been; that is to say what the trade figures would have been in a hypothetical absence of piracy. Of course a counterfactual proposition cannot be directly tested by reference to the documents, but some verification may be obtained by the use of market theory, and by a reconsideration of some of the trade statistics.

A generalized illustration of losses due to piracy can be given by taking the diversion of goods to pirates as a form of tax on producers, or more realistically as tribute. In that case, piracy would add to the costs of production. Any given quantity on the market would become more expensive, or, at a given price, less would be available. Prices would be higher to buyers, but producers would receive less, the difference representing the value of goods taken by the pirates. Producers, receiving less return, would contract production, and in time only the lower-cost firms would remain within the industry. Unfortunately, this winnowing of firms would not necessarily represent a gain in efficiency if transport costs were significant. Piracy would raise transport costs disproportionately to other costs. If the probability of pirate attack were a function of the distance over which the goods were transported, producers remote from the nodal port would be penalized while producers located nearby, whether efficient in production or not, would suffer little imposition.

Altering assumptions in this general model can show shifts in the incidence of losses due to piracy, but the losses are not eliminated. For example, if pirates were to place their loot on the market, prices would not rise and the loss would be borne wholly by the producers, with the consequent reduction in output analysed above.

Even if pirates place their loot on the market, and leaving aside the effects of their depredations on production and on producers' incentive, there would not be a simple transfer of goods between producers and traders, having no effect on society. Pirates acquire goods to the value of those lost to the producers, but the process is not costless to the pirates; they must use their labour, capital and enterprise for the purpose. If those factors of production were used to create goods rather than merely transferring ownership of them, there would be a benefit to the wider society. If the pirates genuinely have no alternative employment, then their depredations might be seen at best as a grossly arbitrary and economically inefficient form of out-door relief.[10]

The existence of pirates involves a further form of loss in that producers must allocate some of their resources to defend themselves and their property. In this category of costs are those associated with insurance, load splitting, the delays of convoy, purchase of weaponry, and the carriage of soldiers on board vessels or sailors above the number necessary to work the ship. A contemporary observed of the eastern seas that 'the Malay depredations are a serious injury to our commerce. They raise the rate of insurance and the expense of equipment, by compelling the merchants to arm their vessels . . .'.[11] Falling ocean freight rates on the North Atlantic in the eighteenth century have been ascribed in large part to the reduced levels of manning made possible by a diminished threat of attack by pirates.[12]

Up to this point the analysis has been conducted as if piratical action were predictable and quantifiable by producers in terms of monetary cost, as is a systematic tax. However, this underestimates the deleterious effect. Piracy increases the riskiness of production and distribution, and so discourages activity in those pursuits. The consequences of piratical attack could include not just the loss of the vessel and cargo, but the loss of life or liberty of the crew, this last being a particular risk in the eastern seas and in the Mediterranean. The stakes were surely high enough to move all but the most desperate or resolute traders into risk-averse behaviour. Trade by sea and production would for that reason be further inhibited.

These theoretical considerations show the ways in which a trading community can sustain losses, in terms of current welfare and economic growth, as a consequence of piracy. In relation to nineteenth-century trade in the eastern seas, the conclusions are supported by con-temporary comment and indirectly by trade statistics. One comment in particular neatly encapsulates the reality behind the theory: 'piracy raises the cost of all native produce brought to Singapore; it gives the bold a monopoly of carriage; and obliges them to go in larger numbers and with more expensive equipment than would otherwise be necessary'.[13]

Piracy was endemic in the waters of Southeast Asia from earliest recorded times. It was often an acceptable adjunct to an adventurer's attempt to establish or to overthrow a state, or a ruler's attempt to preserve one. Well before their regular navigation of those seas in the

Sung dynasty, Chinese voyagers remarked on the hazard that pirates presented to merchants.[14] However, piracy seems to have entered an epidemic phase in the seventeenth and eighteenth centuries, arguably as a result of European penetration of this area at a time when local empires were in decline. The Portuguese inserted themselves aggressively into the local trade patterns and the Dutch diverted and monopolized trade flows, in each case to the net detriment of local traders. In these cases, the European presence reduced the returns to legitimate native activity and by increasing maritime traffic provided more opportunities for piracy.[15]

In the Malay world, because of the terrain and the jungle, travellers and goods had generally to move by sea. Traffic was heavy, with watercraft 'always passing and re-passing'.[16] This trade was small-scale, the consequence of limited resources and sparse population, and was carried in small boats. These were vulnerable to attack, as they could not prudently venture far from the coast and could seldom gather in sufficient numbers to provide mutual support: 'the unprotected trade languishes from the natural dread of the better disposed natives of undertaking a coastal voyage'.[17]

The prey of pirates in these waters was seldom European shipping. Native craft individually carried less cargo, probably of a less valuable nature, but there were many of them, and it was less risky and costly to attack them than to attack a large, possibly well-armed and probably resolutely defended European sailing ship. Piracy, as already noted, was a business: costs and benefits seem to have been carefully weighed. Pirate warriors were reportedly courageous, but rather than seek glory or riches by making an attempt on a European vessel they generally preferred, like cautious bourgeois businessmen, to maximize long-term profit (and chances of survival) by accepting the low profit margins with high turnover that attacks on native boats offered. 'They harassed the trading *prahus* incessantly, cutting them off and murdering or making slaves of the crews.'[18] This had secondary effects on the native inhabitants: 'the shackles which piracy imposed on trade and navigation impeded the development of their industry and stifled in them all desire to labour'.[19]

Consideration of the nature of the pirates' prey allows some insight to be gained about the effects of piracy. As explained earlier, these effects cannot be discovered directly from the trade statistics as it is necessary to compare what was, with what might have been. However, given that the burden of piracy fell primarily on native trade, it would be expected that during periods of intense pirate activity the volume of goods carried in native *prahus* would decline relative to that carried in square-rigged ships, almost exclusively European. Such a change in relativities is discernible in the trade figures for Singapore, the most important entrepôt in the western area of the Indonesian seas in the nineteenth century.

Pirate activity affecting Singapore appears to have intensified in the late 1820s and early 1830s. The merchant community became increasingly vociferous in its complaints about piracy, in 1833 petitioning the governor and in 1835 memorializing the governor-general and petitioning the king in council, claiming that the extent of piracy was such as 'to threaten native trade with total annihilation'.[20] The governor wrote of his fear in similar terms.[21] Bugis traders in Singapore in 1831 threatened to go elsewhere unless they were given more protection.[22] Table 5.1 shows the number of *prahus* and the tonnage carried by them in this period; the tonnage declined from 45,082 in 1827–8 to a low of 28,714 in 1832–3.

There was of course a connection between the activities of square-rigged vessels and the *prahus*, as the latter carried local products to Singapore for reshipment to Europe and China, and distributed goods from those countries to small ports on the peninsula and throughout the archipelago. However, it does not appear that the square-rigged ships were simply taking over the local carrying trade at this time: as the number of *prahus* and the tonnage they carried declined, the growth in the number of square-rigged ships in trade slowed and that of tonnage was arrested.

A different view is presented by Trocki, who argues that trade was not noticeably affected by piracy.[24] He observes that piracy expanded with trade, and that there are no statistics showing destruction of trade. Both issues have been dealt with above. On the first point, his conclusion does not follow from the premise, given the nature of parasitic piracy. On the second, an implicit counterfactual proposition is involved, and in any case the nature of piracy in the eastern seas was such as to leave few witnesses and little direct, quantitative evidence.

The only quantitative estimate available on the effect of piracy is of very doubtful value. In their petition to the governor, a number of Chinese merchants estimated their losses through piracy, principally in the east coast trade, to be $15,000 to $20,000 per annum, or less than 2 per cent of the total.[25] Although the sum would represent a considerably higher proportion of net revenue or profit, it hardly

Table 5.1
Number and Tonnage of Square-rigged Vessels and Native Craft
Importing into Singapore[23]

| | Square-rigged | | Native Craft | |
	No.	Tonnage	No.	Tonnage
1822	139	51,076	1,454	15,892
1823	166	56,740	1,519	20,193
1824	168	48,749	1,459	27,076
1825	190	58,810	1,886	32,522
1826	234	72,172	1,614	36,653
1827–8	370	101,878	2,856	45,082
1828–9	378	121,717	2,149	41,437
1829–30	367	117,527	1,705	37,921
1830–1	406	120,676	1,743	38,887
1831–2	413	124,835	1,466	32,372
1832–3	420	120,443	1,566	28,714
1833–4	475	137,298	1,599	34,927
1834–5	517	156,518	1,484	37,521

supports claims of 'severe' losses, or the forecast that piracy would 'annihilate' the native trade of the port. Furthermore, the estimate seems incredibly low, when, in the year of the petition, a single *sampan-pukat* (a small native vessel) taken by pirates carried property reportedly valued at $10,000.[26] Several similar boats that were blockaded by pirates at Pahang at about that time had 'property on board to the amount of upwards of 200,000 dollars'. One of these, later attacked by pirates, was said to be carrying cargo to the value of $14,000.[27] In this context, it is significant that the petition was not signed by European merchants 'for fear that the cost of government action against pirates might bring increased taxes'.[28] The government could well have argued, with impeccable economic logic, that for the eradication of piracy the petitioners should pay a sum up to the value of their losses. There was a clear incentive for the petitioners to complain that piracy caused loss, but to conceal the real value of that loss. They emphasized instead the expansion of trade that could occur if piracy were eliminated.

Trocki further suggests that the anti-piracy campaigns themselves destroyed native trade. He cites in support an item in the *Singapore Free Press* of 1846 which makes that assertion and states that 'this trade [with the Borneo area] which was steadily augmenting is now all but annihilated'.[29] However, the journalist's perception is not supported by the trade statistics. After a dip in the number of *prahus* arriving from and departing for Borneo around the middle of the 1830s and between 1838–9 and 1841–2, the trend rose and remained high until the 1860s.[30] The expeditions of Brooke, Keppel, Cochrane and others against the Borneo pirates between 1843 and 1849 appear to have been singularly successful in freeing legitimate native trade with Borneo from the constraints imposed by the fear of and loss from piracy.

By the 1860s, as Trocki indicates, square-rigged vessels were indeed replacing native craft. The reason was, as a contemporary observed, that 'these square rigged vessels are apparently not generally subject to the attacks of pirates who appear to respect their supposed means of defence'.[31] This shift in carriers itself indicates that piracy had some effect. The change would have reduced some of the risks borne by native traders, but as the change was made for reasons of security rather than efficiency it would have carried its own cost.

The Suppression of Piracy

Lacking adequate protection from the East India Company and the British government, merchants in Singapore tried to reduce their losses to pirates by incurring the expense of acquiring, arming and manning their own cruisers. In 1832 the Chinese merchants sent four *sampan-pukats*, equipped with swivel guns and each carrying 30 well-armed men, to drive the pirates from the approaches to Singapore.[32] The following year they negotiated to arm a brig so as to provide an escort for some of their boats that were blockaded by pirates in the port of Pahang.[33] However, efforts on this scale could have only political significance. Economies of scale in the provision of protection that make it cost-effective can rest only on the resources of governments; and the legal power of governments is usually necessary to compel 'free riders'[34] to contribute to a purpose of common benefit. A longer-term problem of the provision of protection by private enterprise is that the protectors may find more profit in piracy.

To pay for the suppression of piracy, the government proposed a levy on sea-borne exports and imports of the Straits Settlements, of which Singapore was the most significant. This was rejected with the 'greatest alarm' by the merchants.[35] The proposal was of course against free-trade philosophy, but its rejection is likely to have been based more firmly on self-interest. As a port, Singapore had close competitors, actual or potential: Malacca, Penang, Makassar, Batavia and nearby Rhio. Accordingly, the demand for port services at Singapore would have been (and still is) highly sensitive to price change, such as would have been occasioned by the proposed levy. On the other side of the cost/benefit calculation, it was unlikely that piracy would have been significantly affected by the limited action that the government was inclined to undertake.[36] The cost of diversion of trade that might be expected to result from a levy no doubt appeared greater than the benefits expected from government action.

The methods adopted for the suppression of piracy were common to the European powers with major interests in the area. All recognized that cruising, even with steam gun-vessels, was a palliative rather than a cure. A number of observers urged that expeditions be mounted against pirate strongholds. This military solution to the problem can be specified in economic terms: it raised the cost of piracy relative to its return. Brooke made this explicit: 'when these communities lose more than they gain by piracy . . . then, and only then, will they discontinue it'.[37] Application of this policy met with some success. A pirate base was destroyed on the island of Galang near Singapore in 1836, and Brooke's expeditions against pirates in Borneo broke the power of the coastal sultans, gaining and retaining the allegiance of the Sea-Dyaks.

Political domination, together with more effective cruisers and weaponry, brought an end to significant piracy in Southeast Asian waters. However, to suppress piracy effectively, the political domination had to be comprehensive, not piecemeal. When the British East India Company established a base on Penang Island and the adjacent mainland, which was part of the state of Kedah, it simply increased the intensity of piracy in the area. Trade was diverted from local ports to the free, safe port at Penang, impoverishing the state of Kedah.[38] At a stroke, the East India Company had concentrated a wealth of targets for piracy and created a host of impoverished Malay retainers and traders. The pirate problem in Malaysian waters was not solved until in 1874 the British, feeling their interests in tin were threatened by disturbances in peninsular Malaya, ended their policy of non-intervention in local politics and administration. The new policy of 'paramountcy', according to Rubin, 'lay in a world order that exalted rights of property, of goods in transit or in warehouses, to be free from interference'.[39] Whatever the morality of the matter, the economics were sound.

Chinese Piracy

The Chinese experience of piracy between 1750 and 1850 contrasted with that of Southeast Asia. In the latter, piracy was associated with a multiplicity of small, contending states. Piracy in South China was geographically and economically peripheral to a great but declining empire. The extent of decline was such that for a brief period in the early nineteenth century the pirates aped the empire's nature and usurped some of its functions. Pirates, initially a minor irritant along the China coast, became numerous and powerful as auxiliaries of the Vietnamese Tay-son emperor. When after 1801 the Tay-son collapsed and that patronage ceased, the Chinese pirates were sufficiently organized, skilled and experienced in warfare to dominate the South China Sea. In the first decade of the nineteenth century, many thousands of pirates in hundreds of junks formed a confederacy, based on the fundamental Chinese structures of family, clan and place. The confederacy enforced discipline within its ranks, sold safe conduct passes, defeated Chinese naval forces and defied European cruisers.[40]

Although competition in economic matters is usually beneficial, the creation by the pirates of an organization competitive with the state was not. Economies of scale in the provision of protection are such that it is a 'natural monopoly', that is, the service is provided more cheaply if there are no competitors. The costs of having competing groups in the protection industry are not confined to economic losses, as is demonstrated by the wretched lot of any people who have been trapped between the demands of government forces and powerful insurgent groups.

Even if the pirates had a complete monopoly in the provision of protection, permitting them to reduce costs, it is highly unlikely that they would choose to do so.[41] When, as in this case, the owners of the 'firm' providing protection are also the employees, there is no incentive on the part of producers to reduce their costs which are in effect their rewards. Indeed, there is incentive to increase the size of the enterprise beyond an economic optimum for reasons of power and prestige. Furthermore, the costs of protection would be less for an established government as legitimacy reduces enforcement costs. If rules are accepted as being in some sense 'fair', people will generally abide by them even though it be in their immediate interest not to do so.[42] The Chinese state invested an enormous effort in establishing its legitimacy; a primary function of scholar-officials was to inculcate the

Confucian virtues of filial piety and respect for traditional authority. The pirates offered no moral or philosophical equivalent.[43]

A monopoly of protection, implying as it does a monopoly of violence, is a special kind of monopoly that can extract from consumers a higher price than can a conventional monopolist. In a market, even when confronted with a monopolist seller, consumers can decline to buy. When dealing with a monopolist of violence, such behaviour may well attract the violence feared. Consumer choice is constrained. One can envisage a demand schedule that relates the price that will be paid for protection to the quantity of the service provided; there is likely to be a separate demand schedule and a higher price for security from those who control violence if they are able to exercise that violence for their own purposes. Records of the period are replete with accounts of villages burnt and inhabitants slaughtered when the pirates were defied or payment of tribute withheld.[44]

If the protection firm is owned by a third party rather than its employees, it will be in the interest of the owner to minimize costs so as to maximize the net revenue. Resources so acquired by a legitimate government may be used in unproductive ways—conspicuous consumption is the generic term—but some may be used for productive purposes besides protection. Chinese examples are flood control, evernormal granaries and the maintenance of transport links. Payment to pirates simply supports pirates; and the protection they offer is protection only from themselves.

The inability of the Chinese officials to deal with large-scale piracy was due to inadequacy of resources, itself the result of political problems and attitudes. At the turn of the century, rebellions in China had drawn the attention and resources of the government away from the problems of the coast. Rural disturbances claimed priority: any interruption to production in that sector could seriously damage the economy and threaten the dynasty. Sea-borne trade was by contrast peripheral in every sense, insignificant to the empire both economically and politically. This scale of priorities saw coastal defence neglected at the best of times; and the early nineteenth century was not the best of times in China. The dynasty was in decline, and population was increasingly pressing on land resources.

The effect of governmental neglect of the maritime realm was compounded by policies designed to prevent the concentration of military or naval power in the hands of Chinese officials and commanders remote from the central Manchu authority in Peking. Naval forces were little more than prefectural water-police, scattered among the many coastal jurisdictions, poorly equipped and led, with an inefficient command structure.[45]

Attempts to suppress piracy having failed, Chinese officials in 1809 placed an embargo on shipping, to deprive the pirates of the trade on which they subsisted. This was a traditional and quintessentially bureaucratic approach to the problem: if piracy is costly to suppress and it thrives on trade, then prohibit trade.[46] The cost to the treasury in foregone taxes would be no more than the cost of suppression as the treasury bears the full cost of the latter, but taxes collected are only part of the benefit that a society would enjoy from a trade unimpeded by piracy.[47] With trade prohibited, officials can have a quieter life, but merchants and consumers lose. However, in the Confucian schema, merchants were of little political account, and, short of rebellion, consumers had not the means to make their dissatisfaction felt. Despite its negative nature, the policy had a useful indirect effect: to secure provisions, the pirates attacked towns and villages, and the peasants' reaction ultimately contributed to ending the pirate menace.[48]

Although the pirate confederacy fragmented in 1810, piracy continued and grew with trade. The problem was largely ignored by the British, the chief traders in the region. This may have been due to the delicacy of usurping the police powers of a sensitive sovereign state. More probably it was because much of British trade was in opium, and as the carriers of that commodity could provide their clippers with adequate weaponry there was little moral or material reason for them to press for the effective policing of Chinese waters.

The First Opium War (1839–42) aggravated the problem of piracy. Political disturbance in the fragile, overpopulated Chinese economy reduced the chances of survival for many Chinese, while the expansion in sea-borne traffic consequent upon the opening of the five 'treaty ports' to Western trade increased the opportunities for predation. The course of the war had weakened and demoralized the Imperial navy. Hong Kong island was ceded to Britain and became an entrepôt for the opium trade. Traditionally a pirate lair, it became a base for the disposal of loot and the acquisition of supplies and intelligence. British attempts to deal with the problem by registering junks and com-missioning a gunboat were inadequate and ineffective.[49]

The British policy of avoiding involvement in the policing of Chinese waters may have been politically prudent, but after the Opium War it became increasingly costly. By 1849, intervention could no

Fig. 5.1 The *Jolly Bachelor* engaging pirates
(National Maritime Museum, Greenwich)

longer be avoided; the pirates had again become organized, levying tribute on their victims ashore and afloat. Destruction of the pirate fleets in a series of engagements gave only temporary respite. In 1852, the assistant Chinese secretary at Hong Kong wrote of piracy in a memorandum: 'the extent of its effect upon the Junk Trade of this Colony it would not be easy to ascertain, but it must suffer much from the insecurity of the seas between Hong Kong and the petty towns with which all its native trade is carried on'.[50] By 1854, with the T'ai P'ing rebellion adding to lawlessness, trade had virtually ceased between Hong Kong and Canton. Conditions were similar on the central China coast.[51]

In the preceding decade and a half, masters of Chinese junks sought protection by sailing with armed European vessels, 'for which they paid heavily'.[52] The payment could be even heavier than expected: the protector would sometimes plunder the vessels he was engaged to protect. This was a fundamental problem of 'private enterprise' protection, in which behaviour would almost by definition be guided by the profit motive rather than duty and the law. Even the provision of monetary incentives and rewards to British naval personnel created problems turning on conflict of interests.

The spectacularly successful engagements in which steam gunboats were instrumental in destroying large pirate fleets increased the risk to pirates, but it did not suppress piracy. Pirate crews could be readily replaced from the desperate or the coerced, while trading junks and fishing boats could be easily equipped for piracy. It was necessary to attack the economic foundations of piracy by reducing poverty and raising the costs and reducing the returns of piracy over the long term. The first of these was beyond the capacity of any government as things were in China at that time, but, for the waters around Hong Kong, the British were able to take effective measures to achieve the latter objectives by law.

The 'Ordinance for the Suppression of Piracy (H.K.) 1866' prescribed severe penalties for having any dealings with a pirate, whether to receive stolen goods or to provide vessels, arms or supplies.[53] This had the effect of reducing the demand for the products of piracy, while raising the cost of the enterprise. Caught between rising costs and falling returns, many pirate 'firms' would choose to leave the industry. Those remaining, ill-equipped and desperate, could be eliminated by cruising gunboats which were both active and successful in this period.[54] The suppression of piracy in Chinese waters in general is a longer story, involving co-operation between Chinese and Western authorities.

Conclusion

In sum, the economic effects of piracy on the productive community were negative and seem in the instances considered to have been substantial. The random violence of piracy is of course distinct from the purposeful exercise of armed force at sea by some who might be perceived by their victims to be pirates. The economic implications can be quite different, at least in the long run. Would there have been a 'Golden Century' in the Netherlands, or even an accelerated pace of economic development in early modern Europe, without the *Watergeuzen?*

Notes

1. This analysis is drawn from James Francis Warren's *The Sulu Zone, 1768–1890. The Dynamics of External Trade, Slavery, and Ethnicity in the Transformation of a Southeast Asian Maritime State* (Singapore, 1981).
2. L.A. Mills, *British Malaya 1824–1867* (Kuala Lumpur, 1966), 231; Philip Gosse, *The History of Piracy* (New York, 1934), 284.
3. Leonard Y. Andaya, 'The Structure of Power in Seventeenth Century Johore' in Anthony Reid and Lance Castles (eds), *Pre-Colonial State Systems in Southeast Asia: the Malay Peninsula, Sumatra, Bali-Lombok, South Celebes* (Kuala Lumpur, 1975), 7.
4. William H. McNeill, *The Pursuit of Power. Technology, Armed Force and Society since AD 1000* (Oxford, 1983), 51.
5. Gerald S. Graham, *Great Britain and the Indian Ocean. A Study in Maritime Enterprise 1810–1850* (Oxford, 1967), 364.
6. G.F. De Bruyn Kops, 'Sketch of the Rhio-Lingga Archipelago' *Journal of the Indian Archipelago and Eastern Asia,* IX (1855), 107. This journal (sometimes cited as Logan's Journal) is referred to hereafter as *JIA.*
7. Anthony Reid, *Southeast Asia in The Age of Commerce 1450–1680. Volume One. The Lands Below the Winds* (New Haven, 1988), 102.
8. For example, *British Parliamentary Papers, Accounts & Papers* (1850) LV, 9, 'Return of British Vessels Attacked or Plundered by Malay or Dyak Pirates off the Coast of Borneo, August 1839–1849'.
9. Carl A. Trocki, *Prince of Pirates: The Temenggongs and the Development of Johor and Singapore 1784–1885* (Singapore, 1979), 86–7. Concern about this point is also expressed by Christopher Hooi, 'Piracy and its Suppression in Malayan Waters 1800–1867', Academic Exercise, University of Singapore (Singapore, 1957), 66.
10. It seems likely that alternative employment would have been available. In general, land was not the limiting factor of production in the archipelago. The Dutch settled 400 pirates as agriculturists; Charles Hill, 'Notes on Piracy in

Eastern Waters' *The Indian Antiquary*, 51 (June 1928), 215. Also Spenser St. John, 'Piracy in the Indian Archipelago' *JIA*, III (1849), 260.

11. Anon., 'The Malay Pirates, with a Sketch of their System and Territory' *United Services Journal and Naval and Military Magazine*, (1 April 1838), 464.

12. Douglass C. North, 'Sources of Productivity Change in Ocean Shipping 1600–1850' *Journal of Political Economy*, 76 (1968).

13. Anon., 'Malay Amoks and Piracies', *JIA* III (1849), 464.

14. Paul Wheatley, *The Golden Khersonese: Studies in the Historical Geography of the Malay Peninsular before AD 1500* (Kuala Lumpur, 1966) 38, 57, 82, 91.

15. D.G.E. Hall, *A History of South-East Asia* (London, 1964), 498ff. As observed above, the depredations of the Balangingi and Iranun were indirectly stimulated by the growth of European trade in the eastern seas.

16. George Windsor Earl, *The Eastern Seas, or Voyages and Adventures in the Indian Archipelago in 1832–33–34 . . . etc.* (London, 1837), 38.

17. Sir James Brooke, 'Memorandum on the Suppression of Piracy and the Extension of Commerce in the Eastern Archipelago' *British Parliamentary Papers, Accounts & Papers* (1851), LVI, 134.

18. Anon., 'The Piracy and Slave Trade of the Indian Archipelago' *JIA*, III (1849), 632.

19. Anon., 'Piracy', 634. See also Mills, *British Malaya*, 220.

20. 'The Piracy and Slave trade of the Indian Archipelago' *JIA*, IV (1850), 159–60.

21. C.M. Turnbull, *The Straits Settlements 1826–1867: Indian Presidency to Crown Colony* (London, 1972), 246.

22. 'The Piracy . . .' *JIA*, IV (1850), 146.

23. See T.J. Newbold, *Political and Statistical Account of the British Settlements in the Straits of Malacca, etc.,* vol. 1 (London, 1839), 369.

24. Trocki, *Prince of Pirates*, 86–7.

25. Mills, *British Malaya*, 238. 'Petition of the undersigned Inhabitants of Singapore', B.L. (India Office Library), Bengal Public Consultations, 5 August to 30 September 1833.

26. 'The Piracy . . .' *JIA*, IV (1850), 149–50.

27. *Ibid.*

28. Turnbull, *The Straits*, 245. In forwarding the petition to the governor-general, the governor indeed recommended the imposition of a 'moderate Custom duty'. B.L. (India Office Library), Bengal Public Consultations, 5 August to 30 September 1833.

29. Trocki, *Prince*, 86–7.

30. Wong Lin Ken, 'The Trade of Singapore, 1819–1869' *Journal of The Malay Branch of the Royal Asiatic Society*, XXIII, Part 4, (1960), Table IXb, 283.

31. Commodore Hay, quoted by Nicholas Tarling, *Piracy and Politics in the Malay World: A Study of British Imperialism in Nineteenth-Century South-East Asia* (Nendeln, 1978), 173.

32. 'The Piracy . . .' *JIA*, IV (1850), 147.

33. 'The Piracy . . .' *JIA*, IV (1850), 150.

34. 'Free-riding' exists when a consumer enjoys the benefit of a service or acquires a commodity without having contributed to its cost. It would be unlikely that a member of a convoy would be a free-rider; a merchant navigating seas kept free

from piracy could be. The difference is the ease with which fees for service can be collected and the ability to exclude the potential free-rider from the service offered.

35. 'The Piracy . . .' *JIA*, IV (1850), 400.

36. British policy of non-intervention in the affairs of the Malay political units restricted suppression of piracy in so far as it was intrinsic to the operation of those units. There were, in addition, legal problems of definition and prosecution, and physical difficulties of detection and capture. Moreover, the British East India Company was reluctant to involve itself in the problems and expense of a vigorous trade protection, when it was largely the profits of Chinese merchants and the persons and property of Malay traders that it would have been protecting.

37. John C. Templer (ed.) *The Private Letters of Sir James Brooke, K.C.B., Rajah of Sarawak, Narrating the Events of his Life from 1838 to the Present Time* vol. II (ed.) (London, 1853), 110.

38. Tarling, *Piracy and Politics*, 12.

39. Alfred P. Rubin, *Piracy, Paramountcy and Protectorates* (Kuala Lumpur, 1974), 54.

40. Dian H. Murray, *Pirates of the South China Coast 1790–1810* (Stanford, 1987), 86, 137, and her contribution in this volume.

41. The economic model of protection used in this section was developed by F.C. Lane in the context of Venetian trade. See Lane, 'Economic Consequences of Organized Violence' *Journal of Economic History*, XVIII (1958), no. 4.

42. Douglass C. North, *Structure and Change in Economic History* (New York, 1981), 45ff.

43. The notion that these pirates were social or political revolutionaries is disposed of in Chang Thomas Chung-Shen, *Ts'ai Ch'ien the Pirate King who Dominates the Seas: A Study of Coastal Piracy in China 1795–1810* (Ann Arbor, 1986), 208–9.

44. Murray, *Pirates*, 88, 127–31.

45. Murray, *Pirates*, 100–1.

46. The expedient was adopted to deal with 'Japanese' pirates in the sixteenth century, and with the Ming loyalist 'pirate' Cheng Ch'eng-Kung (Koxinga) in the seventeenth century. John K. Fairbank, Edwin O. Reischauer and Albert M. Craig, *East Asia: The Modern Transformation* (London, 1965), 118–19; John K. Fairbank and Edwin O. Reischauer, *East Asia: The Great Tradition* (London, 1960), 331.

47. Theoretically, piracy will be suppressed up to the point at which the marginal costs of suppression equal the marginal benefits. The costs are paid by the government, the benefits shared by the government, the merchants and the consumers.

48. Murray, *Pirates*, 123, 146.

49. Grace E. Fox, *British Admirals and Chinese Pirates 1832–1869* (London, 1940), 99ff.

50. Fox, *British Admirals*, 120.

51. Fox, *British Admirals*, 123.

52. Fox, *British Admirals*, 106.

53. Fox, *British Admirals*, 159.

54. Antony Preston and John Major, *Send a Gunboat! A Study of the Gunboat and its Role in British Policy* (London, 1967), 69.

CHAPTER 6

Mediterranean Privateering between the Treaties of Utrecht and Paris, 1715–1856: First Reflections

Gonçal López Nadal

Introduction

Over a long period of time privateering in the Mediterranean made its presence felt in both the economic and military spheres. As an institutionalized maritime activity based on pillage it occupied human endeavour in varying degrees from its origins right up to its final abolition as a legitimate means of commerce and warfare at sea. Nevertheless, strange though it may seem, it is still difficult to establish precisely its chronological boundaries, especially with regard to its earlier forms as an organized system of navigation during the centuries leading up to the first international maritime code, as represented, for example, in the case of the *Mare Nostrum*, by *El Llibre del Consolat de la Mar i dels Fets Marítims*.[1] As for the disappearance of privateering as a legitimate form of activity, one would be hard put to point to a single date which would have world-wide validity. Even in the case of the *Mare Nostrum* not all the countries involved recognized the points laid down by the Declaration of Paris in 1856. One may cite the case of Spain, which would not adhere to the Declaration until the Second Peace Conference held in 1907.[2]

Privateering in the Mediterranean performed many different roles in the societies which practised it during the period stretching from the

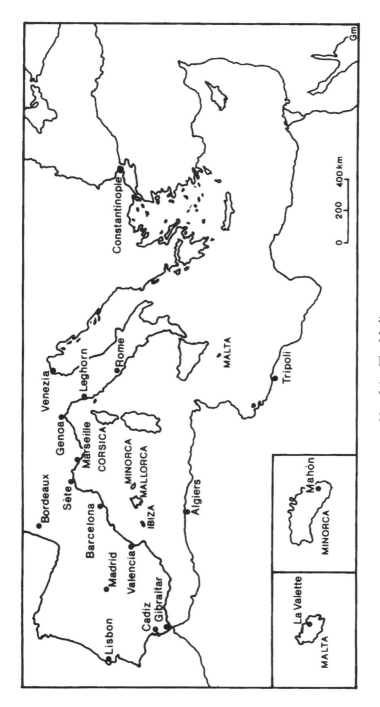

Map 6.1   The Mediterranean

fourteenth to the nineteenth centuries. One such role, probably the most noteworthy, was as a recourse, or an alternative, to the carrying out of military, economic or even ideological tasks. This may be the reason why this form of privateering acquired a specific rank that marks it out from that which evolved in Western societies, or—with the exception of the Barbary corsairs—in non-European ones. We are speaking of the configuration of the *corso* as a specific institution, which was not entirely the same as what was understood by the French and English terms applied to Atlantic activities, namely *guerre de course* and/or privateering. The important distinction implied in *fare il corso*— a term presumably taken from the Italian—indicates something characteristic, inherent in its own milieu, and which achieves the status of an institution in certain societies which Michel Fontenay and Alberto Tenenti classify as *Etats-Corsaires*.[3]

My aim is not to present a comparative study between the Mediterranean *corso* and Atlantic *privateering* because, among other reasons, the former term should be reserved predominantly for the part played by this type of enterprise in what has been called 'the Golden Age of Mediterranean privateering', that is to say the period between Lepanto (1581) and Utrecht (1715).[4] In consequence, while we still await a specific monograph dealing with the resemblances and differences between these two activities, it would be worthwhile to consider the Proceedings of the San Francisco International Congress (*Privateering and Piracy*) of 1975, as well as those at Naples (*Le Genti di Mare*) of 1981, and at Athens (*Economies Méditerranéennes*) of 1983 and—though not of the same standing precisely—that in Palma de Mallorca (*El Comerç Alternatiu*) of 1989.[5] In this chapter I shall attempt to give a general picture of Mediterranean privateering during the eighteenth century, or more precisely, its evolution between the Treaty of Utrecht and the Treaty of Paris. Both events mark, on the one hand, the high point of the phenomenon we call *corso* and the beginning of its slow decline, as a result of the progressive weakening of those factors that had made it possible; and on the other hand, its derogation from being a legitimate system of activity at sea. We are dealing, therefore, with privateering (*corsarismo*)—and not with the *corso*—in the Mediterranean during its last phase, a period during which, according to Fontenay and Tenenti, a degree of geographical extension in northern privateering was in evidence,[6] a parallel process that would continue up to the dismantling of its structures halfway through the following century.

Mediterranean Privateering up to the War of the Spanish Succession

Up to the present time the only general and solidly based study of Mediterranean privateering has been, and still is, the paper by Michel Fontenay and Alberto Tenenti presented at the San Francisco International Congress in 1975.[7] Although some of the arguments have fortunately been complemented by new studies, such as those on the specific cases of Majorca[8] and Minorca,[9] and others on Barbary[10] and Malta,[11] their work, in general terms, remains the best starting point for the examination of this type of navigation during the process of decline that led to its final extinction.

As is well known, for most European countries the eighteenth century represented a period of general recovery. In such a context the link that existed between privateering and crisis—in their various political and economic structures—placed the former in an exceedingly delicate position. To judge by what had happened in the Mediterranean up to that time, privateering had signified an alternative system of trade which evolved because of critical circumstances, more particularly from the time when the ports and cities of the North began to attract political and economic power to themselves. The shifting of the centre northwards forced the South to look for other means and to find a new way by which to pursue its maritime trade. And, in a parallel process, the decline of certain long-established powers—namely, Spain, and even the Ottoman Empire—made it advisable to use private navies, which proved highly convenient in the business of carrying out and winning battles at sea. Paradoxically, the battle of Lepanto, a 'land-battle at sea' in which neither side triumphed, proved to be the crucial moment as far as the above-mentioned changes are concerned.

From the end of the sixteenth century the navies of the North, especially those of England and the United Provinces, entered the Mediterranean to impose their political and economic power on the area. Their presence had repercussions on the revival of the activities of the Barbary corsairs, particularly when groups of Dutch seamen established themselves in some of the seaboard cities of the Magreb. These immigrants modernized the corsairs' system of operation, even sailing their new vessels as *rais*.[12] As a result Algiers, and to a lesser extent Tunis and Tripoli, developed into the principal foci of North African privateering. Moreover, while privateering was the means by which these Ottoman states carried out their merchant and military operations, at the same time it became the best instrument by which the *Jihad* could be prosecuted.[13]

In the face of the danger posed by the Barbary corsairs, Christendom adopted a corresponding attitude and fervently justified its prosecution of war at sea by invoking the name of Crusade. During the first half of the seventeenth century the Knights of St John and those of St Stephen undertook the task of keeping the Muslim privateers at bay. These knights were Tuscan and Maltese privateers, mostly of a military character, but in both cases imbued with a powerful ideological outlook.[14] The Majorcans were to join them in their mission during the second half of the century, thus contributing forcefully to the downfall of the 'infidel'.[15] During this period, which fell between 1652 and 1703/15, a new element was added to to the *raison d'être* of the *corso*; this was the seizure of merchant ships flying the enemy flag. This was no mere confrontation, however, between the Cross and the Crescent, but something much more important, namely the use of the *corso* as an auxiliary fleet, which could, and did, take part in wars between European powers. It was in response to such a development that this form of privateering was taken up by the many and varied subjects of the Catholic king—Valencians, Majorcans, people from Ibiza and Sardinia, as well as from Naples and Sicily—all took part in practically uninterrupted conflict with *Sa Majesté Très Chrétienne*. Nevertheless, political rivalry alone cannot explain the transformation of a number of these *corsos* (e.g. the Majorcan) into real commercial enterprises. This came about as a result of the prospect of controlling certain maritime routes and of attacking and taking French vessels carrying rich cargoes from the key centres of Mediterranean trade, especially from the Levant and en route to Lacydon.[16]

Over and above the calls to the eternal crusade against the Moors, the high level of growth achieved by the Mediterranean corsairs was due to the interrelationship between war and commerce. This link, so clearly favourable to the exercise of such activity, was used to full advantage by the privateers from the North, especially by the Zeelanders from Vlissingen (Flushing), who were known in this part of the world as *peschelingues*.[17] The Tuscan port of Leghorn, an excellent operational centre for such activities in the Mediterranean, was put to full use by the Atlantic corsairs, as well as by the English navy.[18] This being the situation, we should not be surprised that the Majorcans— the main privateering force of 'Spain'—together with those of Flushing, and the already powerful Royal Navy, managed to inflict the greatest disruption upon French trade in the Mediterranean in the course of the closing years of the century, during the Nine Years War (1688–97), by greatly exceeding the number of seizures made by other Spaniards, as well as those made by the Dutch, Italian, and even by the notorious and feared corsairs of Barbary.[19]

Mediterranean Privateering in the Eighteenth Century

Mediterranean privateering was to undergo a serious transformation in the course of the following century and a half, especially for the European nations. The forces which had caused privateering to flourish and reach its climax would begin to waver one by one—without there being any necessary relation of cause and effect between the two processes. In reality, the political, along with the economic and ideological, forces which had once sustained privateering changed drastically, leaving this alternative system without its *raison d'être*.

The War of the Spanish Succession gave Spain a Bourbon dynasty. Consequently, the French were no longer considered to be enemies of the Catholic Monarchy. The Family Pacts deprived Spanish privateers of some of their richest booty. The new adversaries—people who mostly operated in other areas—hardly constituted a worthwhile target to ensure the future success of privateering activity in the *Mare Nostrum*. Neither could the now weakened forces of the Magreb be placed in that category. Official naval forces increased their operational strength, thus enabling them to do without auxiliary help almost completely. The structure of mercantile trade witnessed an intensive growth of companies that could guarantee the successful transportation of their cargoes. In addition, commercial treaties between Christian and Muslim states now took the place of those confrontations that had earlier marked the relation between them. This being the case, the *corso* had no choice but to continue its existence simply as a legal institution, and await new circumstances that might lead to renewed activities in the economic and military spheres. And as we shall see, such circumstances would arise in certain nations only.

One of the most surprising features to come to light in the evolution of Mediterranean privateering in its final phase is the profusion of *ad hoc* regulations, quite disproportionate to the much reduced part it now played. During the seventeenth century Spanish privateering was governed—allowing for variations from time to time—by the General Ordinance for Privateering (*La Ordenanza General del Corso*) issued on

24 December 1621, and the Supplementary Additional Royal Commands (*los Reales Despachos*) made on 27 August 1623 and 27 September 1624.[20] Between the introduction of these rules and their abolition at the beginning of the present century, stretched a long series of new ordinances, instructions and addenda, which focused directly on the regulation of this seafaring practice. There are at least eight new dispositions, dated respectively 17 January 1718 (and reformed by means of the Supplement of 30 August 1739); 1 February 1762; 1 July 1779 (this being supplemented with an *Adición* in that same year); 13 March 1780 (Royal Declaration);[21] 23 September 1794; 12 October 1796; 20 June 1801 (later reprinted, accompanied by the corresponding Additions (*Adiciones*) made on 14 February 1805),[22] and 27 December 1837.[23] And it is worth noting that between 1805 and 1837 two instructions concerning privateering were promulgated in 1810 during the brief rule of Joseph Napoleon I.[24] These frequent modifications in the rules and code of practice reveal the increasing desire of the new administration, installed in 1715, to exercise control.

At first glance, the French case seems little different. The ancient *Ordonnances* of 1596 were rewritten at least three times during the second half of the following century, in the Regulations of 1673 and 1694, and the 'General Ordinance' of 1681, sponsored by Colbert. A new Regulation dates from the beginning of the eighteenth century (25 July 1704); and from that time until the law of 28 March 1778 was promulgated we find a long list of observations, reports and instructions concerning very specific aspects of privateering, particularly regarding the procedures to be adopted in the case of seizures (court actions, payment of 10 per cent into public funds, and so forth).[25]

An examination of these regulations gives the impression that they applied to privateering in the Atlantic, though naturally they did not exclude that which was carried out in the Mediterranean. To cite an instance, there is a reference of 14 November 1798 to the application in Cartagena de Indias (America) of the *Spanish Ordenanza de Corso* of 1796, covering the procedures to be adopted after the capture of the English schooner *Polly*.[26] Nevertheless, the impression given is that such regulations had more to do with military aspects than economic ones, and even less connection with ideological considerations. Two instances support this conclusion. First, the intense involvement of the royal naval forces themselves—that is, if we follow Marina Alfonso Mola's argument, a public and official form of privateering[27]—was not an altogether new situation during the second half of the seventeenth century when official Spanish and French galleys, the British Royal Navy and the navy of the Papal States[28] had made interventions of this nature. However, there is some difficulty in establishing the actual privateering character of such an expedition. Proof may perhaps be sought in the fact that some of the most eminent admirals in the respective navies—for example, the Majorcan Antoni Barceló—were considered to be corsairs.

Second, it is worth noting that the main targets of the Mediterranean privateers' attacks—if we except the Minorcans and some of the Barbary states—were the English, whose presence was backed up by their own considerable war machine. There are some interesting instructions signed by the Queen of Spain and dated 5 August 1702. These constituted a new series of regulations, 42 in all, instructing 'the vessels of the dominions of France and Spain . . . to take part in privateering'. They bring together the procedures in force under both Crowns.[29] I cannot judge the exact limits of these instructions—which were excluded from those set out above—but it seems fair to attribute their validity to the circumstances then obtaining, under which one portion of Spain served the Bourbon cause, and another—precisely that which focused on the Mediterranean area—served the Austrian dynasty. Whatever the case, even supposing a rapid return to independence of action by both Spanish and French privateers, everything points to the idea that most privateering interventions in the Mediterranean were probably more military than commercial in character. This would confirm, therefore, Michel Fontenay and Alberto Tenenti's thesis of the Atlanticization of Mediterranean privateering during its last phase.

The fact that the prey to despoil would now be outsiders becomes a key factor in the decline of Mediterranean privateering. This is clearly reflected in the substitution that occurs in the main participants. Without actually disappearing, but nonetheless suffering a certain degree of ostracism, Italian and Spanish privateers—the latter no longer divided into regional groupings of Majorcan, Valencian and Catalan—together with those from the small ports of French *Midi*, those of the Orders of St John and St Stephen, and even the Barbary corsairs themselves in the first part of century, cede ground to those who for the most part sailed under the British flag: namely, the Minorcans. These constituted the only group possessing the ideal requirements to conduct the *corso*, excepting, of course, the crusading factor. And to the activities carried out by the people of the Mediterranean, one must add the seizures made by the Western naval powers, in particular the Royal Navy.

At the present time the information we possess concerning the operational capability of Spanish corsairs in the Mediterranean points to the existence of actions specifically of a defensive nature, generally carried out on an individual basis rather than in squadrons, such as had been the case during the second half of the previous century. Such a restriction was a consequence of privateering no longer being an economically sound venture, due to the conjunction of circumstances referred to earlier; as a result, it was hardly worthwhile investing constantly in armaments, nor maintaining a complicated infrastructure with a view to mid-term or long-term returns. Faced with such a situation, corsairs would only undertake expeditions that had very concrete and limited objectives on a private basis. This is especially reflected in the privateering actions carried out by the Majorcans, and at the beginning of the nineteenth century by corsairs from the island of Ibiza. In the case of the former, a good instance is the expedition that took place between 20 September 1739 and 4 May 1740, in which two xabeks (*jabeques*) took part under the respective command of Antoni Portell and Jaume Santandreu.[30] And in the latter case, there are the successive captures attributed to the Riquer family—e.g. of the English vessel *Felicity*, under the command of the Roman captain Michelle Novelli, better known as 'The Pope' (*El Papa*), by Juan Riquer de Francisco (better known as *El Vives*) captain of the xabek *San Antonio de Padua y Santa Isabel*.[31]

Restricting the business of privateering to carrying out tasks of a basically defensive character—that is, a return to what it had been in early times—is very much a feature of the Catalan case. As has been pointed out by Eloy Martín Corrales and Carlos Martínez Shaw,[32] privateering hardly attracted the attention of Catalan bourgeoisie. It evolved as an instrument in the fight against North African privateers, who had been attracted by the high volume of the Catalan traffic.[33] Between 1730 and 1789 over a thousand natives of this region were taken hostage on board their vessels, or in the coastal villages.[34] In less than two years—November 1759 to February 1761—the Muslims managed to capture 96 Catalan vessels, valued at 708,000 pesos.[35] Such incidents, and others similar to them, prompted the setting up of private expeditions at the request of the institutions of the former Principality. Their deployment, nevertheless, was not limited to coastal defence, since during the American War of Independence the Catalans chose to apprehend English vessels, and even some flying a neutral flag, such as Venetian and Danish ships, this being the only circumstance favourable to the exercise of this form of maritime commerce.[36] The dearth of experienced seamen, the bureaucratic restrictions on armaments and on voyages imposed by the administration, and the recapture of Port Mahon by the Spaniards in 1782, resulted in the dismantling of what might have been an outstanding Catalan privateering business.[37]

As in the previous century, the French littoral of the Mediterranean did not engage to any extent in privateering. On the contrary, and in concert with the developments that had occurred, the merchants of the port of Marseilles were the principal targets for enemy forces. According to Paul Masson's calculations, if the War of the Spanish Succession had cost them 1,755 vessels lost,[38] the War of the Austrian Succession occasioned the further loss of 708 at the very least; and to these must be added another 790 seizures during the Seven Years War.[39] These figures are very high—too high, if glanced at cursorily— being far higher than the seizures made by Provençal corsairs, to whom 150 captures are attributed in the last conflict mentioned, of which the majority would probably have been English.[40] The disproportion is striking. For that reason, we should not be surprised at the variety of steps taken by the Chambre de Commerce in Marseilles to combat enemy privateering. If during the seventeenth century, taking advantage of treaties established with the Magreb, this institution had called upon the assistance of the Barbary states, so the Chambre de Commerce was now quick to entice West European privateers, especially those from St Malo, to come and instruct the people of the South in how to practise this type of seafaring. Gaston Rambert points out that the financing, *in toto* or in part, of more than one hundred vessels from Brittany was carried out with capital from Marseilles. All the same, it was the Royal Navy itself that was to exercise the task of defending French trade most efficiently, as is demonstrated by the reduction in losses during the years of the American War of Independence.

The religious orders of St John of Jerusalem and St Stephen went on performing their role as first line of defence against the Barbary corsairs. Michel Fontenay, making perhaps exaggerated a claim, has dubbed Malta the *Alger chrétienne*, where over a considerable period privateering on a large scale would be the main, if not indeed the only, maritime activity.[41] During the eighteenth century the total number of privateering interventions carried out by the Maltese fell to the same degree as did those of their opponents. Michel Fontenay has traced a graph representing private armaments carried out under the flag of 'Religion' or 'The Grand Master' during the seventeenth and eighteenth centuries. This reveals a clear fall in the number of letters of marque, especially from the five-year period 1640–5 onwards. Nevertheless, during the years 1760–4 and 1780–4, there was a significant recovery, due almost certainly to the increase of North African privateering during the second half of the eighteenth century.[42] Tuscan privateering, which began in 1561 with the creation of the order of St Stephen by the Grand Duke Cosimo I,[43] continued in its sacred task of combatting the infidel. However, its activities hardly merit attention during the period that concerns us, given the change in its relations with the Muslim world after the imposition of the Austrian dynasty in 1737.[44]

These two cases—the Maltese and the Tuscan—represent, in effect, the very opposite to the situation in the southern French ports. If the latter continued to be the main victims of the privateering marauders in the Mediterranean, the ports of Leghorn and La Vallette, in contrast, profited greatly, given their excellent relations with all the European powers, setting themselves up as markets for seizures, and in consequence for slaves. Furthermore, Leghorn, in particular, was a base of great importance for the seafaring activities of the people of northern Europe.[45]

The 'Age of Enlightenment' brought few benefits to the Barbary corsairs. In contrast to the intense activity that had marked the end of the sixteenth century and the first half of the seventeenth, their principal cities experienced successive punitive attacks by the European powers in the last decades of the latter century. The constant effort of the 'privateering orders' and of others with more worldly motivation—for example, the Majorcans—would force them into a state of recession from which they would, nevertheless, recover progressively throughout the second half of the eighteenth century. This is what emerges from Albert Devoulx's important study of the registers of Algerian seizures between 1737 and 1826.[46] The resurgence of the Barbary peril can be traced more to the technical factors—especially the reinforcement of their firepower—than to any increase in the number of privateering vessels.[47] Another contributory factor was probably the intensification of mercantile traffic, which presented a considerable attraction as targets for seizure; and yet another factor was their own fluctuating political relations with the Mediterranean states, more particularly Spain and France. Eloy Martín Corrales has studied the consequences of this for Catalan coastal trade, placing the rhythm of Barbary activities on a par with the latent presence of plague as serious obstacles to the development of this particular commerce.[48] This was the time when the Barbary privateers became one of the most feared threats to the lives of those who dwelt along the eastern seaboard of the Iberian peninsula, as may be judged by the part they represented in popular folklore tradition.[49] The reason for this is easy to grasp: their interest in maintaining their market in captives because of its very high profitability through the redemption of those captured and/or the status accorded them in the social and professional world of these republics. It is possible here that we find the authentic reason which obliged prisoners who had become victims of Barbary corsairs to renounce their faith.[50]

As was pointed out earlier, the Minorcans were best prepared to carry out privateering in the Mediterranean. The island, after its capture by the English during the War of the Spanish Succession, would remain under their suzerainty until 1802, although during two intervening periods it experienced French (1756–63) and Spanish (1782–98) domination. The slight activity that had marked the Minorcan privateers in the previous century contrasts with its intensity during the one that followed, especially the second half of the century.[51] In the course of *la Guerra de l'any Quarenta* (the War of the Austrian Succession) the Minorcans made a minimum of 79 seizures,[52] most of then Spanish and French. Nevertheless, it was during the second English domination, and more particularly during the extension of the North American conflict to Europe, that the Minorcans displayed what they could really do as privateers. Amador Marí Puig indicated that between 1778 and 1781, 55 Minorcan ships made 225 seizures from various nationalities (French, Spanish, Genoese, Neapolitan, Swedish and Danish) to the value of close on 2 million pieces of eight.[53] We should not be surprised at the description 'nest of thieves' which the Marquis of Sollerich, a Majorcan aristocrat, used when exhorting the Count of Floridablanca to put an end to this state of things, since 'the whole of the Mediterranean is infested, its commerce destroyed and our navigation no longer free'.[54] All the same, and come what may, Majorcan, Genoese and Greek merchants came to Port Mahon to buy the booty for re-sale elsewhere. In this way the *corso* was transformed into a huge business in which people of diverse origin and social class (businessmen, nobles, clerics, British, Jewish immigrants, Italians, etc.) would invest their money. Again, their status as citizens of His Britannic Majesty meant that the Minorcans enjoyed a privileged relationship with North African cities, especially with Tripoli, a situation that would be entirely reversed when the political status of the island changed, since during the years of French and Spanish occupation Minorca again suffered from the attacks of the Barbary corsairs.[55]

The actions of corsairs in the Mediterranean were complemented by the presence and activity of fleets from the North, especially the English. Continuing the process initiated at the beginning of the previous century—and indeed, a little earlier—the Dutch (from Flushing) carried out their patrols from their centre of operations in Leghorn, effecting several captures during the 1740s. The English were more incisive, taking advantage of their bases in Gibraltar and Port Mahon, as they would make use of Malta after 1800. Nevertheless, even before this occupation the Royal Navy had successfully plied the waters of the Eastern Mediterranean, drawing the local people into English service—thus, during the Seven Years War Greek sailors from Cythera and Crete actively collaborated under the British flag, intercepting the movements of French ships in the most strategic points of the Mediterranean Levant.[56]

Conclusions

During the eighteenth century and up to the 1850s, privateering gradually adapted itself to the systems of navigation—both military and commercial—which the new European powers imposed. Particular attention must be paid to the way in which, during that development, privateering showed an ability to adapt which allowed some ports to re-assert their former role of *corso*. These, however, formed a minority (for instance, Port Mahon) since the majority had to assume functions that were less profitable. In these cases the response consisted in the employment of the same arms—*corso* against *corso*—reminiscent of similar situations from an earlier age, when privateering had hardly begun to assert itself as a small-scale artisan activity to which all the seaboard communities of the Mediterranean had been drawn. We are, therefore, witnessing a final phase, the epilogue to a story that refuses to lie down and die. It is not, however, just that. The ever-present menace of the Barbary corsairs was still around,[57] but the danger no longer stemmed primarily from their interminable attacks. Now instead the main threat came from the official fleets of the principal European countries. As Robert Paris has been able to demonstrate, the kingdom of the marauders fell prey in its turn to an intense rivalry between the great maritime and trading powers, a fact that substantiates the author's final and justified perovation: *les vrais corsaires remplacèrent les pirates.*[58]

Notes

I would like to express my gratitude to Marina Alfonso Mola, Carles Manera, Amador Marí Puig and, especially, to Eloy Martín Corrales for their help. And, of course, to Gareth Alban Davies, for his translation from Spanish.

1. It is quite possible that the old Rodhian Laws, of uncertain date, mentioned privateering as applied to Phoenician and Greek navigation. On the other hand we should not consider les *Jugements d'Oléron* (1150/1180) as a maritime code of direct influence on Mediterranean navigation The *Llibre del Consolat de Mar* was written between the second half of the thirteenth century and the beginning of the fourteenth. On the maritime rules and their previous laws, see J.L. de Azcarraga y Bustamante, *El corso marítimo* (Madrid, 1950); A. de Capmany y de Montpalau, *El Llibre del Consolat del Mar* (Barcelona, 1965); P.F. Feraud, 'Les Jugements d'Oléron ou Róles d'Oléron' *Neptunia,* 162 (1986), 1–9.

2. During the Spanish–American War of 1898, the Spanish government issued some orders—on 23 of April of that same year—recognizing the legitimate intervention of its privateers. See Azcarraga y Bustamante, *El corso,* 25 and 379; G. López Nadal, 'La course et les societés méditerranéennes: une voie alternative', in *Perception de la Méditerranée d'après les cartes et les racits des voyageurs* (forthcoming).

3. 'Elevé au rang d'institution par certains Etats-corsaires où le public le disputait au particulier dans une sainte et profitable émulation, il permettait sous couvert d'une lutte intransigeante et perpétuelle par la vraie foi de se livrer à des rapines continuelles, non seulement sur l'infidèle, mais encore sur tous ceux qui voulaient practiser avec lui'. M. Fontenay and A. Tententi, 'Course et piraterie méditerranéenne de la fin du Moyen Age au début du XIXème siècle' in M. Mollat (ed.), *Course et Piraterie,* (Paris, 1975), [Abstracts of Papers, 15].

4. I do not agree completely with M. Fontenay and A. Tenenti when they consider that the beginning of the decline of the Mediterranean privateering starts in the second half of the seventeenth century ('Aprés Lépante, commence une troisième et dernière période qui voit l'apogée du phénoméne, vers 1580–1640, puis son déclin et au cours de laquelle le *corso* après avoir rélayé la guerre d'escadres, dégénére de plus en plus vers une semipiraterie' in Mollat (ed.) *Course et Piraterie* [Abstract 16]). I think that the intense privateering activities of the Majorcans and the seafarers from the North, especially those from Vlissingen (Flushing), allows the extension of this 'golden age' to 1715, after the Spanish Succession War ended. See G. López Nadal, *El corsarisme mallorquí a la Mediterrània Occidental, 1652–1698: un comerç forçat* (Barcelona, 1986).

5. The proceedings have been published respectively in Paris 'cyclostyled' in 1975; Napoli in 1981; Athens (*Equilibres et Intercommunications, XIIe-XIXe siècles*) in 1986; and Palma de Mallorca (*Corsarisme i Contraban*, ss. XV-XVIII) in 1990.

6. Fontenay and Tenenti in Mollat (ed.) *Course et Piraterie*, 78–9.

7. See notes 3 and 5. Its main contributions are in A. Toussaint, *Histoire des corsaires* (Paris, 1985).

8. López Nadal, *El corsarisme mallorquí*; 'La course et les societés'; and 'Corsarismo y abastecimiento de grano en Mallorca durante la segunda mitad del siglo XVII' *Estudis d'Història Econòmica*, (1991–2), 27–50.

9. J.F. Pons Vila, 'Contribuciòn al estudio del corsarismo menorquín en el Setecientos. El viaje del jabeque "San Antonio de Padua" a las órdenes del capitèn Francesc Maspoch (1780)' *Mayurqa*, 7 (1985), 233–45; and A. Marí Puig, 'Cors i comerç a Menorca. La comercialització de les preses (1778–1781)' in *El comerç alternatiu* (Palma de Mallorca, 1990), 201–16.

10. C. Manca, *Il modelo di sviluppo economico delle città barbaresche dopo Lepanto* (Napoli, 1982); R. Pennell, 'Tripoli in the Late Seventeenth Century: the Economics of Corsairing in a "Sterile Country"' *Lybian Studies*, 16 (1985), 101–12. S. Boubaker, *La Régence de Tunis au XVIIe siècle: ses relations commerciales avec les ports de l'Europe méditerranéenne, (Marseille et Livourne)* (Zaghouan, 1987); Karray Kossentini, 'La course maghrébine et les pouvoirs locaux avant Lépante', and S. Bono, 'Guerra corsara e commercio nel Maghreb barbaresco', both in *El comerç alternatiu*, 117–31 and 133–44. I should also mention two works by R. Pennell, 'John Drummond-Hay: Tangiers as the Centre of a Spider's Web' (conference paper read in Tangiers in October 1990), and 'Piracy of the North Moroccan Coasts in the First Half of the Nineteenth Century'. Public lecture given to the British Society for Moroccan Studies. University of London, May 1991 (both texts provided by the author).

11. M. Fontenay, 'L'empire ottoman et le risque corsaire au XVIIe siécle', in *Economies Méditerranéennes*, vol. I, 429–59; 'La place de la course dans l'économie portuaire: l'exemple de Malte et des ports barbaresques', in *I porti come impresa economica* (Firenze, 1988), 843–79; and 'Corsaires de la Foi ou rentiers du sol? Les Chevaliers de Malte dans le corso méditerranéen' *Revue d'Histoire Moderne et Contemporaine*, XXV (1988), 361–84; S. Bono, 'Corsari cristiani sulle coste di Palestina' *Islam, Storia e Civiltà*, 34 (1911), 37–49.

12. Especially Simon de Danser and Jan Jansz, called afterwards Simon Rais and Mourad Rais. P. Gosse, *The History of Piracy* (London, 1932); S. Bono, *I corsari barbareschi* (Torino, 1964). Also the British Captain John Ward deserves to be mentioned: see C. Lloyd, *English corsairs on the Barbary coast* (London, 1981).

13. A. Djeghloul, 'La formation sociale algerienne à la veille de la colonisation' *La Pensée*, 185 (1976), 61–81; J. Weiner, 'New Approaches to the Study of the Barbary Corsairs' *Revue d'Histoire Maghrébine*, 13/14 (1979), 204–8. Similar criteria have been previously expressed by British historians such as G.N. Clark, 'The Barbary Corsairs in the Seventeenth Century' *Cambridge Historical Journal*, VIII (1944), 22–5; S.G. Fisher, *Barbary Legend: War, Trade and Piracy in North Africa (1415–1830)* (Oxford, 1957); P. Earle, *Corsairs of Malta and Barbary* (London, 1970); and J. de Courcy Ireland, 'The Corsairs of North Africa' *Mariner's Mirror*, 66 (1980), 271–83. On the ideological use of privateering and its insertion in the various form of 'spiritual' action (*crusade/jihad*), see M. Fontenay,

'Los fenòmenos corsarios en la periferizaciòn del Mediterráneo' in *Desigualdad y Dependencia:la periferización del Mediterràneo Occidental, ss. XII-XIX* (Murcia, 1986), 116–21; G. López Nadal, 'El corsarismo en las estructuras mercantiles: las fronteras del convencionalismo' in *El comerç alternatiu,* 267–76.

14. On Maltese privateering, in addition to the studies of Fontenay (n.11), Bono (n.11, 12), Lloyd (n.12), Earle (n.12) and Fontenay and Tenenti (n.2), we must mention J. Salva Riera, *La Orden de Malta y las acciones navales españolas contra Turcos y Berberiscos en los siglos XVI y XVII* (Madrid, 1944); J. Godechot, 'La course maltaise le long des côtes barbaresques à la fin du XVIIIe siècle' *Revue Africaine,* XCVII (1952), 105–13; J. Mathiex, 'Trafic et prix de l'homme en Méditerranée aux XVIIe et XVIIIe siècles', *Annales* IX (1954), 157–64; R. Cavaliero, 'The decline of the Maltese corso in the XVIII Century' *Melita Historica,* 2/4 (1959), 224–38; *The Last of the Crusaders. The Knight of St John and Malta in the Eighteenth Century* (London, 1960); P. Cassar, 'The Maltese corsairs and the Order of St John of Jerusalem' *Catholic Historical Review,* XLVI (1960), 137–56; B. Blouet, *The Story of Malta* (Malta, 1967); V. Mori Ubaldini, *La marina del sovrano militare ordine di San Giovanni di Gerusalemme di Rodi e di Malta* (Rome, 1971); P. Caruana Curran, 'The Maltese Corsair Courts' *Law Journal,* 5 (1975), 1–10. There is less literature on Tuscan privateering: in addition to the above mentioned studies of Bono (n.11 and 12), Lloyd (n.12) and Fontenay and Tenenti (n.2), we must mention G. Guarnieri, *I cavalieri di St Stefano nella storia della marina italiana (1566–1859)* (Pisa, 1960); *L'ordine nei suoi aspetti organizzativi interni soto il Grande Magistero Mediceo* (Pisa, 1965–66); and *Livorno Medicea, 1577–1737* (Livorno, 1970). See also G. Finazzo, 'La corsa nel Mediterraneo nel XVII secolo', in *L'Universo* (1972), 1135–57; C. Piazza, 'Datti sulla navigazione Stefaniana del 1678 al 1716', in *Livorno e il Mediterraneo nell'Età Medicea* (Livorno, 1978), 405–11.

15. López Nadal, *El corsarisme mallorquí,* 339–444; and 'Els enemics de la Fe: un cas més de discriminaciò històrica', in *Estudis de Prehistòria d'Història de Mayurqa i d'Història de Mallorca. Homenatge a Guillem Rosselló Bordoy* (Palma, 1982).

16. P. Masson, *Histoire du commerce français dans le Levant au XVIIe siècle* (Paris, 1986); R. Paris, *Histoire du commerce de Marseille. V. Le Levant de 1660 à 1789* (Paris, 1957); J. Mathiex 'Sur la marine marchande barbaresque', *Annales,* XIII (1958), 87–93. See also López Nadal, *El corsarisme mallorquí* 41–238; M. Fontenay, 'Interlope et violence dans l'économie d'échanges:l'exemple des eaux grecques de l'empire ottoman aux XVIe et XVIIe siècles', in *El comerç alternatiu,* 279–89.

17. 'J'ay eu advis quil est passé en ces mers deux navires corsaires de Flessingue qu'on appelle *Peschelingues'*. Letter written by the French consul in Leghorn, François Cotolendi, to the Marquis of Seignelay of 8 April 1678. López Nadal, *El corsarisme mallorquí,* 70.

18. There is no monograph on Dutch privateering in the Mediterranean; some references are found in López Nadal, *El corsarisme mallorquí.* On the expeditions against the Barbary States I should mention J.K. Oudendijk, 'The Dutch Republic and Algiers 1662–1664', in Mollat (ed.), *Course et Piraterie* I, 146–60. On its presence in Italian ports, A. Bicci, 'Gli Olandesi nel Mediterraneo: Amsterdam e Italia (sec. XVII)' in *Economies Méditerranéennes,* vol. I, 39–76. As to the British presence in Leghorn we must mention the Proceedings of the

Congress *Gli inglesi a Livorno e all'isole d'Elba* (Livorno, 1980); see also H.A. Haywards, 'Gli inglesi a Livorno al tempo di Medici'; C. Ciano, 'Uno sguardo tra Livorno e l'Europa del Nord verso la metà del Seicento'; and M. Morviducci, 'Lo scontro anglo-olandese avvenuto nel porto di Livorno il 14 Marzo 1563 nella relazioni di Francesco Feroni', all in *Livorno e il Mediterraneo*, 268–73, 149–68 and 395–404.

19. Of a total of 329 seizures made in the Mediterranean between 1689 and 1697, 56 were attributed to the British, 54 to the Majorcans, 41 to the seamen from Flushing (+ the Peschelingues), 41 to the Turkish and Barbary corsairs, 30 to the 'Spanish', 22 to the Sicilians, 14 to the Neapolitans, 14 to those from Finale—a Spanish port on the Italian Riviera—12 to those from Ibiza, 9 to the Dutch, 6 to those from Ceuta, 5 to the Catalans, and so forth. López Nadal *El corsarisme mallorquí*, 184–6.

20. The Spanish *Ordenanza General de Corso* of 24 December 1621 stars as follows: 'La orden que han de guardar los Vassallos destos Reynos y Seyorios de Espaya que con licencia mia quisieren armar por su quenta Nauios de alto bordo para andar en la costa de la mar dellos en busca de Nauios de enemigos assi de Turcos y moros como de mis rebeldes de las islas de Olanda y Gelanda y hazerles la guerra y lo que por ello se les concede es lo siguiente . . .'. Archivo de la Corona de Aragon (Barcelona), Consejo de Aragcn, Negociado de Mallorca, Legajo 1008 (without foliate). [transcription in López Nadal, *El corsarisme mallorquí*, Documentary Appendix, n 1, 485–9]. Note the unique reference to the ships of the United Provinces ('Islas de Olanda y Gelanda') as being enemies of the Crown subject to seizure by the privateers of the Catholic king.

21. On Spanish legislation on privateering during the eighteenth century see especially Azcarraga y Bustamante, *El corso marítimo*, 95–124, 258–65, 291–305 and 308–71; M. Alfonso Mola, 'La procedencia de los barcos en la Carrera de Indias. El corso de la Armada (1778–1802)', in *El comerç alternatiu*, 231–3. See also J.F. Guillen, *Indice de los papeles de la sección 'Corso y Presas' del Archivo General de la Marina 'Don Alvaro de Bazán'* (Madrid, 1953) (especially 11–14).

22. '. . . así como los artículos VI, VII, VIII y IX de la Ordenanza de Matrículas de Mar de 1802 en las que se hace referencia explicita a las formalidades necesarias para armarse en corso'. Alfonso Mola, 'La procedencia', 232. On the reprinting of 14 February 1805, see Guillen, *Indice de los papeles*, 14 (no. 81).

23. Guillen, *Indice de los papeles*, 14 (no. 91).

24. 'Instrucciones de corso del Gobierno intruso (1810) y Instrucciones de corso de José Napoleón I 1810', Guillen, *Indice de los papeles*, 14 and 55 (no. 85 and no. 402).

25. Archives de France (AF), Paris, Fonds Publiques de l'Ancien Régime, G-5. 'Conseil des Prises', no. 211. The last maritime law 'Ordonnance du Roi concernant les prises faites par les Vaisseaux, Fregates & autres Batiments de Sa Majesté). Du 28 Mars 1778' is transcribed by Azcarraga y Bustamante, *El corso*, Doc. App. no. 18, 240–350. Alfonso Mola notes its influence on Spanish legislation, particularly in the *Adicional a la Ordenanza de Corso de 1779*, 'La procedencia', 233.

26. Guillen, *Indice de los papeles*, 13 (no. 72). On Spanish privateering in the American colonies ('Carrera de Indias') see M. Alfonso Mola, 'Corso y flota de Indias: los

convoys ingleses apresados entre 1780 y 1795' in *Actas de las IX Jornadas de Andalucía y América* (Sevilla, 1991), 197–222.

27. Mola, 'La procedencia', 233.

28. See A. Guglielmoti, *Storia della Marina Pontificia* (Firenze, 1847–77); and *La Guerra di pirati e la Marina Pontificia* (Firenze, 1876).

29. AF. Marine A-5. These Regulations are introduced by *El Rey y la Reina Governadora* and in their foreword we can read as follows: 'Por quanto considerando quan necesario y conveniente es que los vasallos de los dominios de Espaya y Francia se apliquen a interrumpir la navegacion asi de Turcos y Moros como de los demas enemigos y tienen al presente y pudieren tener en adelante ambas coronas solicitandoles todos los dayos posibles y haviendo tenido presentes las Ordenanzas que el Rey Xrmo mi Seyor y mi Abuelo tiene expedidas a este fin, como tambien las que estavan dadas por los Srs Reyes mis predecesores: He resuelto que los Espayoles y Franceses que de aqui en adelante se emplearen en el corso se arreglen a lo que se previene en los capitulos que siguen . . .'. Note the lack of reference to a particular nation compared to the previously mentioned Ordenanza dated in 1621 (See n.20).

30. 'Viaje en corso y Merc. del Xaveque del Patron Antoni Portell. Cuenta y Razon de el' and 'Viaje en corso y Merc. del Patron Juan Santandreu. Cuenta y Razon de el'. Archivo Privado de Antoni Marcel (Palma de Mallorca). Documents provided by Carles Manera.

31. See I. Macabich, *Historia de Ibiza* (Palma, 1967) vol. III, for a general consideration of privateering in Ibiza; on the capture of the vessel of *The Pope* (El Papa), widely mentioned, see pages 77–86.

32. E. Martín Corrales, 'Impulso de la actividad marítima catalana y corsarismo norteafricano (1680–1714)', in *XIII Congrès d'Història de la Corona d'Aragò* (Palma de Mallorca, 1990), vol. III, 1185–194; C. Martínez Shaw, 'Un mal negocio: el corso catalàn durante la guerra de las 13 Colonias', in *El comerç alternatiu,* 189–99.

33. E. Martín Corrales, 'La huella del corso norteafricano en la mentalidad colectiva catalana del siglo XVIII', in *El comerç alternatiu,* 219. Also, M. Barrio Gozalo, 'El corso norteafricano y su incidencia en el Principado de Cataluya durante el siglo XVIII' *Anals de l'Institut d'Estudis Gironins* XXVII (1985), 313–27; J.A. Asensio Bernalte and J. Fabreques Roig, 'Incidencias corsarias en la costa catalana durante el reinado de Carlos III (1759–1788) según la Gazeta de Madrid', in *I Congrès d'Història Moderna de Catalunya* (Barcelona, 1984), vol. I, 721–30.

34. Barrio Gozalo, 'El corso norteafricano', 326; Martín Corrales, 'La huella del corso', 219.

35. Martín Corrales, 'La huella del corso', 219.

36. Martínez Shaw, 'Un mal negocio', 189–99.

37. '. . . el cese de hostilidades permitiò la liquidaciòn de una empresa que no había sido más que instrumental, propiciada por una coyuntura muy concreta y por ello necesariamente efímera. Una vez garantizada con la paz la reanudaciòn del tráfico marítimo, la burguesía mercantil catalana perdiò todo interés por el armamento en corso, que no se había revelado como un negocio lo suficientemente atractivo como para conquistar su lugar en el complejo de la economía marítima del Principado', Martínez Shaw, 'Un mal negocio', 199.

38. L. Bergasse and G. Rambert, *Histoire du Commerce de Marseille. IV De 1599 à 1660/ de 1660 à 1789* (Paris, 1954), 601.

39. Bergasse and Rambert, *Histoire du Commerce,* 601.

40. Bergasse and Rambert, *Histoire du Commerce,* 602.

41. Fontenay and Tenenti, in Mollat (ed.), *Course et Piraterie,* 88.

42. Fontenay and Tenenti, in Mollat (ed.), *Course et Piraterie,* 89; see also Cavaliero, 'The decline'; and *The Last Crusaders.*

43. 'imité des Chevaliers de Malte, mais sur de bases purement italiennes, voire toscanes', Fontenay and Tenenti, in Mollat (ed.), *Course et Piraterie,* 90.

44. Fontenay and Tenenti, in Mollat (ed.), *Course et Piraterie,* 91. See also, G. Guarnieri, *Cavalieri di Sto Stefano* (Pisa, 1928); and *Cavalieri di Sto Stefano nella storia.*

45. See note 18.

46. A. Devoulx, 'Le régistre des prises maritimes' *Revue Africaine,* XV (1871), 326–74, 447–57 and XVI (1872), 70–7, 145–6, 233–40 and 293–303. Fontenay graphically structures these seizures in graphs in Fontenay and Tenenti, in Mollat (ed.), *Course et Piraterie,* 84, and S. Bono uses these *régistres* in his analysis on the captured goods, 'Guerra corsara e commercio', 135–40. On Barbary corsairs in the eighteenth century see A. Devoulx, 'La marine et la Régence d'Alger' *Revue Africaine,* XIII (1869), 384–420; L. Lacoste, 'La marine algérienne sous les Turcs' *Revue Maritime,* (1931/1932), 239–49.

47. 'On constate en effet une augmentation considérable des pièces (elles passent de 12 en moyenne par bateau au milieu du siècle à 25 vers la fin) et plus encore une amèlioration de celles-ci; Les pierriers, plus nombreux que les canons jusqu'en 1745 disparaissent totalement au profit de ces derniers à partir de 1760', Fontenay and Tenenti, in Mollat (ed.), *Course et Piraterie,* 108.

48. E. Martín Corrales, 'Dos obstáculos en las relaciones comerciales entre Cataluña y los países musulmanes en el siglo XVIII', in *Actes del I. Congrès d'Història,* vol. 1, 611–17. More recently, the same author has decided that these consequences were not so harmful for the Catalan trade; the North-African corsairs preferred to obtain more slaves (fishermen and coastal dwellers) and not to attack the reinforced vessels. E. Martín Corrales, 'Il commercio della Catalogna con il mondo islamico mediterraneo nel Settecento' *Islam. Storia e Civiltà,* 22 (1988), 35–51.

49. Martín Corrales, 'La huella del corso'.

50. B.L. Bennassar, *Les chrítiens d'Allah: L'histoire extraordinaire des renégats XVIe-XVIIIe siècles* (Paris, 1989).

51. López Nadal, *El corsarisme mallorquí,* 367–70.

52. Marí Puig, *Cors i comerç,* 201–3.

53. Marí Puig, *Cors i comerç,* 201–3. See also F. Hernandez Sanz, 'Un corsario menorquín', and 'Jornal del corsari St. Antony de Padua', in *Cultura i societat a Menorca* (Ferreries, 1987), 54–110 and 274–96.

54. J.L. Terron Ponce, 'La reconquista de Menorca por el Duque de Crillon' in *Museo Militar de San Felipe* (1981) (Doc. App. no. 3–4); Marí Puig, *Cors i comerç,* 203.

55. On North African privateering raids on Port Mahon and Ciudadela during the sixteenth and seventeenth centuries, see P. Ruidavets y Tuduri, *Historia de la Isla de Menorca* (Mahón, 1988).

56. Paris, *Histoire du Commerce*. On Eastern Mediterranean piracy and privateering, see D.A. Zakythinos, 'Corsaires et pirates dans les mers grecques au temps de la domination turque' *L'Hellanisme Contemporain*, 10/11 (1939), 695–738.

57. Fontenay and Tenenti, in Mollat (ed.), *Course et Piraterie*, 103.

58. Paris, *Histoire du Commerce*, 183.

CHAPTER 7

A Restless Spirit: British Privateering Enterprise, 1739–1815

David J. Starkey

'The Spirit of Enterprise'

Spirits of various kinds were associated with British privateering activity in the eighteenth century. Spiritous liquors were a prominent feature of the business, with brandy and wine forming a common and valuable prize cargo, as well as an important part of the diets of privateersmen like Captain Joseph Clapp, alleged to have spent six weeks of a cruise 'drinking and whoring' in the Azores, and John Johnson, a 22-year-old seaman 'addicted greatly to liquor'.[1] 'Spirited' defences were frequently offered by privateersmen in the face of superior enemy forces; 'spirits' were lifted in maritime communities by the arrival of rich prizes; there was even an occasion when mercantile, pro-privateering opinion conceded that 'the Administration had acted with spirit' in publishing the anti-Dutch Manifesto of 1780.[2] Darker spirits were held to afflict some privateering ventures; for instance, the morbid, doomed albatross which trailed the *Speedwell*—and inspired Coleridge's 'Ancient Mariner'—was seen as an ill omen by the crew, while rumours of the presence of supernatural forces undermined morale aboard the *Boscawen* on her second, ill-fated cruise in 1745.[3] Yet the true spirit of privateering in the eighteenth century is revealed in the Earl of Derby's speech to the House of Lords in 1778. Referring to the recent, remarkable successes of Liverpool's privateering venturers, he applauded 'the spirit of enterprise which had stimulated them to exert themselves so much against the enemy'.[4]

Thus, the spirit which moved individuals to risk their capital or their lives in privateering ventures was neither alcoholic, charismatic, nor evil. Rather it was the spirit of enterprise, the urge to accumulate capital, which persuaded investors and seafarers to attempt to exploit the predatory opportunities thrown up by wartime. As such, this was a restless spirit, for the prospects of earning profits from privateering, and therefore the scale of the business, varied considerably between localities, as well as over time. This chapter considers three central aspects of the mercurial spirit of privateering: the market forces which conditioned this unusual form of enterprise; the extent and nature of commerce-raiding operations; and the economic significance of the activity. In addressing these issues, it is hoped that this discussion will reveal something of the long-term trends which marked British privateering enterprise between 1739 and 1815.

Market Forces

Like other forms of British maritime enterprise, the privateering business operated within a legal and institutional framework erected by the state.[5] This regulatory apparatus was highly developed by the mid-eighteenth century as the state sought to supplement its naval power by encouraging, directing and controlling the energies of the private armed forces it sanctioned. Encouragement was manifest in the legislation of 1708, by which the Crown not only relinquished its right to share in the profits of privateering but also offered bounties to venturers engaged in the capture of enemy men-of-war and *corsaires*.[6] The privateering effort was directed at specific targets by the grant of letters of marque or privateer commissions designating the nationality of vessels and goods liable to condemnation as prize. Control was effected by the 'instructions to privateers', a well-defined set of rules governing the conduct of privateersmen at sea, and by the various Prize Acts which laid down the process by which captured properties were to be adjudicated in the High Court of Admiralty. Though some modification, such as the prohibition of the practice of ransoming prizes, took place in the second half of the eighteenth century, the system which regulated privateering activity in 1739 was still very much intact in 1815.

Within this framework, the scale and character of Britain's

privateering business were determined by a range of market forces. This was an unconventional market, however. On the supply side, privateering enterprise, as an impermanent feature of the maritime economy, was largely dependent on resources normally deployed in the mercantile marine. The capacity of the shipping industry therefore placed an important constraint on private commerce-raiding activity, fashioning the volume and the quality of inputs into the business in any given locality. Moreover, as capital and labour were required by other maritime services, privateering promoters were obliged to compete in the markets for funds, vessels and seafarers, rivalry being particularly intense at times when trade presented a profitable investment opportunity, and the Impress Service proved efficient in securing manpower for the Navy.[7] Other sources of supply were also tapped. Landmen were attracted in large numbers to serve in privateers, while redundant naval vessels were purchased and despatched on cruises, and, as wars proceeded, profits were ploughed back into the business and prize vessels re-fitted as commerce-raiders. Likewise, attempts were made to attract funds from beyond the maritime community; thus, privateering associations were established to mobilize the capital of the small investor, while one patriotic correspondent suggested that 'the spirit of privateering among the ladies should be encouraged by every husband, father and brother in the Kingdom. If a shilling only was subscribed by every petticoat, the Dons of Spain would not have a cloak to cover them.'[8]

Thus, by competing in, and broadening, the factor markets, commerce-raiding promoters generally obtained an adequate supply of productive resources. Essentially, however, privateering was a demand-led activity, in the sense that the perceived abundance and vulnerability of the prey conditioned the extent and the character of the predatory response. In turn, the number and type of prospective prizes—and, therefore, the number and type of privateers—depended upon a range of interrelated factors. At base, the nationality of the subjects against whom reprisals were permissible conditioned the size of the target facing privateering venturers. This target, moreover, might appear great or small according to the location of the would-be predator's home base in relation to the enemy's favoured shipping routes, while it might suffer absolute diminution as a result of the operations of rival commerce-raiders—naval vessels, or privateers belonging to other regions or allied powers. A further, more important influence was the balance of power in the naval war, for control of the seas might curtail the enemy's shipping operations, or at least impair his ability to protect his overseas and coastal trades. At the same time, such ascendancy generally rendered sea-borne trade a safer and more attractive proposition for investors at home. While these conditions normally entailed a subdued interest in private commerce-raiding, the reverse was often true. Accordingly, at times when the navy was stretched or on the defensive, the enemy's shipping was able to proceed and the spirit of privateering was active in many British ports.

Certain of the forces which shaped the British privateering response remained more or less constant over the 1739–1815 period. On the supply side, for instance, the spatial complexion of the privateering fleet, reflecting that of the shipping industry at large, changed little during the era. Typically, the smallest units of the licensed force were fitted out in the Channel Islands and the ports of the English Channel coast,[9] bases in which capital accumulation was limited and the shipping stock generally comprised diminutive coasting and short-sea vessels. At the other end of the scale, it was from the major ports—London, Bristol and, increasingly, Liverpool—where capital and labour were available in some abundance, that the larger elements of the fleet embarked.

The most obvious of the constant demand factors was the enmity of France. With the exception of the Anglo-Spanish War of 1739–44 and the early stages of the American Revolution, French ships and goods formed the principal target for British privateering venturers throughout the conflicts of the 1739–1815 period. However, the extent and conduct of France's overseas trade vacillated considerably, largely in line with the fluctuating course of the Anglo-French naval war. As Britain assumed a growing preponderance in this conflict, so the French were obliged to restrict their merchant shipping operations, relying increasingly on neutral carriers for the conveyance of colonial goods. This changing pattern had a pronounced impact on the British privateering response. Thus, the business tended to contract in certain respects over the long term, the successive peaks in activity which accompanied the naval defeats and retreats of 1756–7 and 1778–82 serving as notable exceptions which proved the general rule. At the same time, the shift to neutral carriers generally reduced the risks and the rewards associated with commerce-raiding activity, and therefore the scale of the typical venture declined, while significant organizational changes occurred. Accordingly, at both the macro and the micro level, British privateering enterprise in the Napoleonic era was very different from that of the 1740s and 1750s.

Changes in Scale and Organization

The British privateering business embraced various forms of activity in the eighteenth century. Common to all was the right to attack and seize the vessels and sea-borne goods of a specified nation, the power of reprisal vested in a letter of marque or privateer commission. Though each vessel carrying such an authorization possessed a predatory potential, many were set forth to engage in trade, so to these so-called 'letters of marque' commerce-raiding represented an incidental, opportunist facet of the venture. Such merchantmen were often 'runners', vessels which sailed without convoy in a risky attempt to corner a market, while a sizeable number were East Indiamen, transports, customs cutters or other vessels employed in specialist occupations. If such craft were numerically significant, and of no small importance in a military or commercial sense,[10] the spirit of privateering really prevailed in the main branch of the business, in the private men-of-war set out specifically to appropriate the enemy's sea-borne property. By identifying and considering these overtly predatory vessels, the true pattern of Britain's commerce-raiding enterprise in the 1739–1815 period can be discerned.

Such an examination is possible due to the survival of all of the declarations made by captains applying for letters of marque during the 'long' eighteenth century. Numerous problems arise in the analysis of this unique source, however, one of the most serious being the lack of distinction made between 'letters of marque' and private men-of-war. This difficulty can be overcome to some extent by the establishment of criteria relating to the declared tonnage and manning

Table 7.1

Private Men-of-War as a Proportion of the Privateering Fleet, 1739–1815

	Total PMW	Total Fleet	% PMW
1739–48	377	1,191	31.7
1756–62	478	1,679	28.5
1777–83	805	2,676	30.1
1793–1801	216	1,795	12.0
1803–15	175	1,810	9.7
	2,051	9,151	22.4

PMW = private men-of-war. See Table 7.2 for definition of these vessels.
Source: PRO, HCA 25, 26. Letter of Marque Declarations.

figures—private men-of-war were invariably heavily manned in relation to their size—and the application of these benchmarks to the stock of commissioned vessels. By such means, the number of 'Channel' privateers (comparatively small vessels, of limited firepower, operating in home waters) and 'deep-water' private ships-of-war (well-armed vessels despatched to cruise in the Bay of Biscay, the Western Approaches, or further afield) can be approximated.[11] Thus, as Table 7.1 indicates, some 2,051 private men-of-war set forth from British ports between 1739 and 1815, over 22 per cent of the total number of vessels licensed during the period. In absolute terms, the number of private men-of-war more than doubled between the War of the Austrian Succession and the American Revolutionary War, before declining appreciably in the French Revolutionary and Napoleonic Wars. As an element of the fleet commissioned in each conflict, however, private men-of-war were most significant, at 31.7 per cent in the 1739–48 war, the proportion falling slightly in the 1756–63 and 1777–83 conflicts, and considerably thereafter. In the long term, quite clearly, private men-of-war tended to form a diminishing part of Britain's privateering enterprise.

Further analysis of the letter of marque declarations permits a clearer view of the pattern of commerce-raiding activity within each war. The private men-of-war enumerated in Table 7.1 generally embarked on cruises of between two weeks and nine months in duration. As the declarations were dated and declarants were obliged to state the length of time for which their vessels were victualled, a good impression as to the start and end of each undertaking can be gained. Aggregating this data provides a guide to the ebb and flow of Britain's commerce-raiding enterprise, a guide which indicates that the business was prone to strong and sometimes sudden fluctuations.[12] A clear pattern can be detected in the vacillating rate of activity. Thus, during the wartime phases when reprisals were not permissible against France—from July 1739 to March 1744, and from April 1777 to August 1778—only a few, at most, private men-of-war were set forth.

In contrast, the early stages of each Anglo-French conflict witnessed a burst of predatory activity as venturers despatched their craft to cruise against an apparently abundant and poorly defended prey. Accordingly, as Table 7.2 shows, peaks in the activity rate occurred in September 1744, October 1757, May 1793 and July 1803. In each case, the number of private men-of-war in operation declined—though relatively high levels of activity were sustained between 1745 and

Table 7.2
Peak Monthly Activity Rates of Private Men-of-War,
1739–1815

	Month	'Channel' No.	Men	'Deep-Water' No.	Men	Total No.	Men
1739–1748	Sep. 1744	13	654	64	9,978	77	10,632
1756–1762	Oct. 1757	26	985	70	10,346	96	11,331
1777–1783	Feb. 1781	342	10,518	111	8,947	453	19,465
1793–1801	May 1793	42	1,332	27	2,200	69	3,532
1803–1815	Jul. 1803	91	2,708	10	565	101	3,273

'Channel'=vessels of 99 tons or less, manned in the ratio of 2.5 tons per man or less.
'Deep-water'=vessels of 100 tons or more, manned in the ratio of 2.5 tons per man
or less; vessels with crews of 100 men or more, excluding ships operated by the East
India Company.
Source: PRO, HCA 25, 26. Letter of Marque Declarations.

1748—as the conflict progressed and the navy gained the upper hand
in the sea war, obliging the French to transfer their colonial cargoes to
neutral holds. During the American Revolutionary War, however, the
level of commerce-raiding activity intensified as the conflict proceeded,
scaling new heights with the grant of reprisals against France in the
autumn of 1778, Spain in the summer of 1779, and the United
Provinces during the winter of 1780–1. At this latter juncture, with
some 453 private men-of-war and over 19,000 privateersmen active in
February 1781, Britain's eighteenth-century privateering effort reached
its zenith.

This opening phase of the Fourth Anglo-Dutch War was unusual in
other respects. From a British perspective the sudden onset of hostilities had, for the first time in the eighteenth century, altered the status
of Europe's chief carrying fleet from neutral to belligerent, thereby
exposing a vast array of vessels and cargoes to seizure and common,
uncontested condemnation. Contemporaries estimated that the Dutch
had 'full 16,000 traders employed . . . which from their imaginary
security must fall an easy conquest to our ships of war'.[13] Such an
opportunity precipitated a privateering response that was extraordinary
in its breadth as well as its intensity. Whereas predatory operations
during Anglo-French conflicts were generally concentrated in London,
Bristol, the Channel Islands, and at other bases (for instance,
Dartmouth in 1744–5, Liverpool in 1778–9, Plymouth in 1805–7)
visited briefly by the spirit of privateering, private men-of-war were

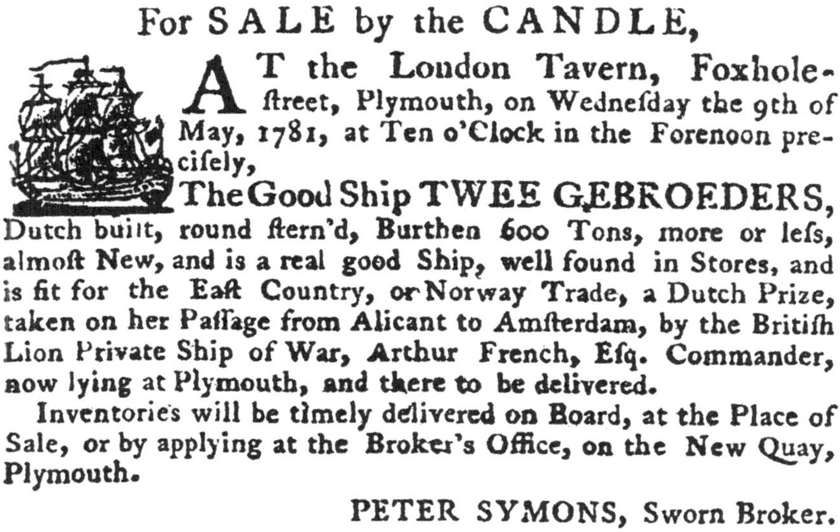

For S A L E by the C A N D L E,

A T the London Tavern, Foxhole-ftreet, Plymouth, on Wednefday the 9th of May, 1781, at Ten o'Clock in the Forenoon pre-cifely,

The Good Ship **TWEE GEBROEDERS,** Dutch built, round ftern'd, Burthen 600 Tons, more or lefs, almoft New, and is a real good Ship, well found in Stores, and is fit for the Eaft Country, or Norway Trade, a Dutch Prize, taken on her Paffage from Alicant to Amfterdam, by the Britifh Lion Private Ship of War, Arthur French, Efq. Commander, now lying at Plymouth, and there to be delivered.

Inventories will be tImely delivered on Board, at the Place of Sale, or by applying at the Broker's Office, on the New Quay, Plymouth.

PETER SYMONS, Sworn Broker.

Fig. 7.1   For Sale by the Candle, the Good Ship *Twee Gebroeders*

The sudden onset of war with the United Provinces in December 1780 stimulated a boom in British privateering enterprise as ventures sought to exploit the prize taking opportunities presented by the large and poorly protected Dutch merchant fleet. Advertised for sale in May 1780, the *Twee Gebroeders* was one of the Dutch prizes condemned to British private ships-of-war during the commerce-raiding mania of early 1781. [*Exeter Flying Post*, April 1781]

despatched from at least 80 ports throughout the British Isles during the first three months of the Dutch War. 'I suppose there never was such a general spirit for privateering in this or any other nation before', wrote one merchant in January 1781[14] as commerce-raiders were expeditiously fitted out in Scottish and Irish bases, along the North Sea coast, and in numerous small havens in southern England which were normally unmoved by the quest for prizes.

The participation of so many ports in the privateering war against the Dutch was related to the scale of predatory operations which, in turn, was a function of the nature of the prey. Embarking in peacetime as neutrals, Dutch carriers were protected by their flag and their papers rather than by cutlasses and carriage guns. Accordingly, they were vulnerable to the most diminutive of assailants, a factor reflected in the outset of an unprecedented number of small-scale predators from ports lacking the resources to equip the more substantial privateering ventures.[15]

Table 7.3
Private Men-of-War by Type and War, 1739–1815

| | 'Channel' | 'Deep Water' | | Total |
		40–149 men	150+ men	
1739–1748	160	122	95	377
1756–1762	256	152	70	478
1777–1783	517	269	19	805
1793–1801	153	63	0	216
1803–1815	133	42	0	175

See Table 7.2 for definition of 'Channel' and 'Deep-Water' vessels.
Source: PRO, HCA 25, 26. Letter of Marque Declarations.

In essence, this shift towards the less powerful form of private-man-of-war highlighted a long-term transition which had been occurring since the 1740s. Then, as Table 7.3 indicates, 'deep-water' private ships-of-war were the predominant form of commerce-raiding enterprise, accounting for nearly 60 per cent of the ventures undertaken, and a much higher proportion of the men engaged, during the Austrian Succession War. Prominent amongst this fleet were the great 'privateers of force', powerful ships of over 400 tons, equipped with at least 24 carriage guns and worked in quasi-naval fashion by complements of 150 or more men.[16] A combination of factors encouraged investors to fit out these substantial craft. As Britain failed to achieve the decisive naval superiority of later conflicts, the colonial trade of the Bourbon powers was able to proceed throughout the war. This commerce was both extensive and valuable, the Spaniards despatching rich cargoes of American bullion to Europe, while the French shipped ever-increasing quantities of tropical produce, notably sugar, from their Caribbean possessions. It was also defended by measures which proved to be inadequate. Thus, the Spaniards dispersed the *flota*, conveying their transatlantic trade in heavily armed register-ships sailing individually or in small squadrons, while the French implemented a convoy system that was under-funded and poorly organized, deficiencies which persuaded shipowners to despatch their vessels to Europe in small, unescorted detachments.[17] Aware that register-ships and 'Martinicomen' were sailing across the Atlantic relying on their own resources for defence, British commerce-raiding venturers responded by setting forth the most powerful units of the eighteenth-century privateering fleet.

A number of outstanding successes were recorded by these large-scale predators. Perhaps the most notable were the capture of two rich register-ships by the *Duke* and the *Prince Frederick*, the destruction of eight 'Martinicomen' by the *Boscawen* and the *Sheerness*, and the various prizes, culminating in the capture of the Spanish '74' *Glorioso*, returned by the *Royal Family*, a fleet of five 'privateers of force' worked by almost 1,000 men.[18] Such heroic actions not only demonstrated the susceptibility of the most valuable elements of Bourbon trade to private men-of-war of a sufficient calibre, but also kindled a 'passion for privateering' of this kind,[19] especially in London and Bristol. This passion persisted until the end of the war, and appears to have revived again at the outset of the Seven Years War with the despatch of a number of 'privateers of force' to cruise in the Western Approaches and the Bay of Biscay. However, conditions proved to be less conducive to this form of predatory activity than venturers had anticipated. French merchants, having sustained heavy losses in the early months of the conflict, and with no semblance of a convoy system in operation, turned increasingly to neutral shippers to convey their colonial goods.[20] While this ploy—which was new only in the extent of its application—intensified the diplomatic dispute over neutral rights, it also rendered redundant the heavy armaments and quasi-naval complements (replete with lieutenants, quarter-gunners, marines and musicians) of the 'privateer of force'. Accordingly, such craft became increasingly rare after the opening twelve months of the Seven Years War, though the prospect of Spanish treasure ships sparked a brief revival of the genre during 1762.

Thereafter, British privateering operations were undertaken in smaller, less powerful vessels. As Table 7.3 indicates, the American Revolutionary War witnessed a marked shift towards the outset of 'Channel' privateers of less than 100 tons—culminating in the privateering mania of 1780–1781—a trend that continued in the 1793–1815 wars. At the same time, smaller crews were deployed aboard the typical 'deep-water' private man-of-war. This reflected the changing character of the target, for the detention and search of a neutral vessel required fewer cannons and men than an engagement with a register-ship or 'Martinicoman'. But it also pointed to the presence of a growing number of 'cruise and voyage' ventures. Traces of this form of activity can be discerned in the Seven Years War as commerce-raiding promoters, frustrated by the dearth of prey in the Western Approaches and the Bay of Biscay, the customary haunts of the 'deep-water' vessel, re-fitted their craft and sent them to the Mediterranean or the Caribbean with orders to take prizes or engage in trade as opportunity offered. Such cruising voyages proliferated in the Caribbean during the American Revolutionary War as conflict with the rebel colonists not only jeopardized Britain's transatlantic trade, but also extinguished the competition of the highly effective colonial privateers in the north American theatre.[21] Faced with a combination of adverse trading conditions and a predatory void, merchants in London, Bristol and, most notably, Liverpool, reacted by setting forth an unprecedented number of truly dual-purpose ships, fitted out *en guerre et marchandise* to seek prizes and cargoes in the Caribbean.[22]

These cruising voyages, generally undertaken in vessels of 250 to 400 tons with complements of between 60 and 140 men, had a significant impact on the internal organization of commerce-raiding enterprises. In the conventional predatory ventures of the 1740s and 1750s, privateersmen normally agreed to serve on a 'no purchase, no pay' basis, relinquishing their right to a wage in return for a predetermined share in a portion of the prize fund generated by their predatory efforts. The element of the profits belonging to the 'ship's people' was generally a half, though it might vary according to local custom.[23] Cruising voyages, however, were essentially 'letter of marque' undertakings, with crews remunerated by monthly wages, as in commercial voyages, as well as a share in a small part, usually a quarter or less, of the net proceeds of any prizes taken.

Thus, the predatory rewards accruing to this dynamic sector of the post-1777 privateering business were neither the sole concern of the financial contract between capital and labour, nor were they distributed as equitably as in the customary form of commerce-raiding agreement. This had important implications for the parties to these contracts. Instead of being related as fellow-venturers united in the quest for prize—however fraught this relationship might prove in actuality—privateer owners and privateersmen now assumed, or resumed, their respective roles as employer and employee, the former having a direct interest in minimizing labour costs, and the latter earning a guaranteed income but diminishing 'the finest opportunity [he] would ever have of making [his] fortune'.[24] As this different form of arrangement appears to have spread from the cruising voyage to other sectors of the commerce-raiding business, either directly as in the case of Liverpool's 'deep-water' ventures in the 1777–83 conflict, or by the sale of shares for wages as occurred in Plymouth's extensive 'Channel' fleet in the

Napoleonic War,[25] it would seem that from the 1770s the restless spirit of privateering was at last conforming to the strictures of the wage labour system prevalent in the shipping industry at large.[26] This was highly germane to the economic significance of the commerce-raiding business.

Diminishing Opportunities

British privateering enterprise was significant in various ways during the 'long' eighteenth century.[27] In a military sense, there were occasions when the operations of private men-of-war severely hampered the enemy's sea-borne trade; thus, in 1744–48, and again in 1756–7, it would seem that privateering venturers truly assisted the navy in distressing French and Spanish shipping, while in the early days of 1781 there were grounds to assert that 'British privateers constituted a naval force sufficient to curb the attempts of the subjects of the neutral powers to convey warlike stores to the enemies of Great Britain'.[28] Equally, there is evidence to support the contention that privateering detracted from the war effort by diverting valuable resources, notably labour, away from the Navy, and by consuming the time of naval personnel charged with policing the activity, as well as wasting the efforts of those obliged to compete with privateersmen for prizes, both on the seas and in the courts.

The question of resource allocation also relates to the economic significance of privateering enterprise. Utilitarians, for instance, might argue that the activity consumed capital and labour which would have been employed more productively in the mercantile marine. Exacerbating these opportunity costs, moreover, were the physical casualties sustained in the pursuit of this high-risk business, the ships and men lost or damaged during commerce-raiding cruises. Advocates of the business, on the other hand, might point to the profits earned by privateering venturers, the prize cargoes diverted to the domestic market, and the service performed by commissioned vessels—the self-protective 'letter of marque' no less than the private man-of-war—in the defence of home trade.

On balance, it would seem that the positive arguments carry the greater weight. While commerce-raiding investments were largely conditioned by demand factors, the spirit of privateering was generally at its height in localities where normal trading options were curtailed.

Thus, wartime depressions in Dartmouth's Newfoundland trade during the 1740s and the late 1770s, and in Liverpool's Atlantic trade between 1777 and 1782, fostered bursts of predatory aggression. Likewise, Bristol's keen interest in the privateering business during the mid-century wars was perhaps a reflection of the port's commercial decline in the face of competition from Liverpool and elsewhere. This clearly suggests that privateering had counter-cyclical attributes, mobilizing idle resources rather than seducing them away from trading activities. Such a contention is supported by the fact that commercially-oriented 'letters of marque' dominated the privateering fleet at times such as 1739–43, 1759–61, and long stretches of the 1793–1815 period, when 'trade flourished and spread her golden wings'.[29] Indeed, it was only on one occasion, during the mania of 1780–1, that domestic commerce-raiding seriously impinged upon Britain's trading capacity. Then, for a short time, bounties were offered to neutral shippers as 'it became impossible to find vessels sufficient to export the corn',[30] while the West India trade suffered because 'the demand for vessels be so great for privateers, and they have sold so high that there's no medling with 'em'.[31]

Generally, therefore, the commerce-raiding business added to Britain's commercial and shipping activity, but only in particular ports during certain phases of a war. Its impact on economic development, even at the local level, was thus impermanent, vacillating and dispersed. Moreover, the long-run trend underlying this role was clearly downwards during the 1739–1815 era. Accordingly, at the start of the period, from 1744 to 1757, the large-scale commerce-raiders set forth from the major ports not only represented an important investment opportunity, but sometimes realized the vast, speculative profits that the business promised. During the 1790s and 1800s, in contrast, relatively few private men-of-war were fitted out, and these were generally limited in scale, based largely in the Channel Islands, and active only in the opening phases of the French Revolutionary and Napoleonic Wars. Drawn from a much larger mercantile marine, these predators were of marginal significance compared to their mid-century forebears, a factor reflected in the contrasting newspaper coverage afforded to privateering activity in the two periods. While the fitting out of commerce-raiders and the return of prizes excited much comment and clearly captured the public imagination in the 1740s and 1750s, such matters were all but invisible in the newspapers of the Napoleonic era.

In the meantime, of course, the privateering business had expanded to an unprecedented degree in the American Revolutionary War. This was not due, however, to any reversal in trend, but to the extraordinarily propitious circumstances which rendered commerce-raiding a favourable option at various stages in the conflict. Not only did the shrinkage in the scale and scope of predatory operations, which had become apparent in the Seven Years War, continue apace during the 1777–83 conflict, but a growing number of ventures were organized along 'letter of marque' lines, with wages rather than prize shares the principal form of remuneration for privateersmen. In itself, this development meant that commerce-raiding enterprise was becoming less significant, for the most distinctive, appealing feature of service in a private man-of-war was that it offered seafarers the opportunity to share directly in the potentially substantial profits generated by their labour. Now, with lesser crews owning a smaller part of less valuable prizes, the privateering business no longer presented seamen with the same chance of breaking through the ceiling imposed on earnings by the wage labour system. Comparison of two court cases encapsulates this long-term change. Whereas in 1749 the able seamen of the *Duke* and the *Prince Frederick* petitioned for their shares in an £800,000 prize fund (worth at least £615 each) accruing from the capture of two Spanish treasure ships, 60 years later the *Snap Dragon's* crew sued for a portion of the profits of less than £6,000 generated by the arrest of 21 neutral vessels.[32] Quite clearly, by the early nineteenth century, after hundreds of years in which it had been sporadically significant, the spirit of British privateering enterprise was ready to rest in peace.

Notes

1. *Morning Chronicle and London Advertiser*, 13 Apr. 1779; *Exeter Flying Post*, 23 Apr. 1779.
2. *Morning Chronicle and London Advertiser*, 27 Dec. 1780.
3. George Shelvocke, *A Voyage Round the World by Way of the Great South Seas Performed in the Years 1719–1722* (1726; reprinted with an introduction by W.G. Perrin, London, 1928); *The Voyages and Cruises of Commodore Walker* (1760; reprinted with an introduction by H.S. Vaughan, London, 1928).
4. *Morning Chronicle and London Advertiser*, 28 Nov. 1778.
5. David J. Starkey, *British Privateering Enterprise in the Eighteenth Century* (Exeter, 1990), 19–34.
6. Anne c.65. 'An Act for the Better Securing the Trade of this Kingdom by Cruisers and Convoys'.

7. David J. Starkey, 'War and the Market for Seafarers in Britain, 1739–1792' in Lewis R. Fischer and Helge W. Nordvik (eds), *Shipping and Trade, 1750–1950: Essays in International Maritime Economic History* (Pontefract, 1990), 25–42.

8. *Morning Chronicle and Daily Advertiser*, 1 July 1779.

9. For instance, see Alan G. Jamieson (ed.), *A People of the Sea: The Maritime History of the Channel Islands* (London, 1986) 109–94; W.R. Meyer, 'Mascall's Privateers' *Archaeologia Cantiana*, XCV (1979), 213–21.

10. Starkey, *British Privateering*, 48–56, 257–8, 269–70.

11. Starkey, *British Privateering*, 38–46.

12. Starkey, *British Privateering*, 293–304.

13. *Morning Chronicle and London Advertiser*, 25 Dec. 1780.

14. Library of the Society of Friends (LSF), Temp Mss 140/1. Daniel Eccleston to Isaac Eccleston, 31 Jan. 1781.

15. David J. Starkey, 'British Privateering against the Dutch in the American Revolutionary War, 1780–1783' in Stephen Fisher (ed.), *Studies in British Privateering, Trading Enterprise and Seamen's Welfare, 1775–1900* (Exeter, 1987), 1–17.

16. Articles of Agreement collected in the Public Record Office (PRO), ADM 43/2–13.

17. Richard Pares, *War and Trade in the West Indies, 1739–1763* (Oxford, 1936), 109–14, 311–25.

18. *Gentleman's Magazine*, XV (1745), 418; Vaughan, *Voyages and Cruises*; PRO, ADM 43/13(2); Starkey, *British Privateering*, 148–50, 316–21.

19. Vaughan, *Voyages and Cruises*, xxxiv.

20. Pares, *War and Trade*, 359–75.

21. Carl E. Swanson, *Predators and Prizes: American Privateering and Imperial Warfare, 1739–1748* (Columbia, 1991).

22. Starkey, *British Privateering*, 49–51, 210–11.

23. Articles of Agreement collected in PRO, ADM 43/2–13.

24. PRO, C 103/130. John Brohier to his brother, 4 Jan. 1747.

25. Articles of Agreement collected in PRO, HCA 25/210.

26. Marcus Rediker, *Between the Devil and the Deep Blue Sea: Merchant Seamen, Pirates and the Anglo-American Maritime World, 1700–1750* (Cambridge, 1987).

27. David J. Starkey, 'The Economic and Military Significance of British Privateering, 1702–1783' *Journal of Transport History*, 9 (1988), 50–9.

28. David MacPherson, *Annals of Commerce* (1805), vol. III, 668.

29. *Williamson's Liverpool Memorandum Book* (1750). This phrase was coined to describe the great expansion which occurred in Liverpool's trade during the 1739–48 conflict due to the port's northerly position and its consequent immunity from French privateering attack.

30. MacPherson, *Annals of Commerce*, vol. III, 657.

31. LSF, Temp Mss 140/1. Daniel Eccleston to Isaac Eccleston, 31 Jan. 1781.

32. *Journals of the House of Commons*, XXVI (1750), 104–5; PRO, C 124/bundle, LH8.

CHAPTER 8

Cruising in Colonial Waters: The Organization of North American Privateering in the War of 1812

Faye Kert

Introduction

The reverberations of the Napoleonic Wars in Europe were echoed in North America in the War of 1812. For Britain, overseas war meant stretching tight resources and lines of communication to breaking point. For America, fighting under the banner of Free Trade and Sailors' Rights, it amounted to a second War of Independence.[1] But for the Canadians in Nova Scotia and New Brunswick, the War of 1812 presented a golden opportunity to capitalize on declining American markets. In the pre-war round of embargoes and non-importation Acts, American merchants, shipowners and seamen found themselves squeezed out of their regular avenues of occupation. The maritime merchants of Halifax and St John were more than happy to fill the vacuum left in the triangular trade between Britain, North America and the West Indies.

Deprived of their peacetime markets, maritime entrepreneurs resorted to the more precarious but exciting business of privateering, or *guerre de course*. The use of private armed merchant ships to supplement naval vessels was a familiar practice in North America. During the American Revolution, as well as in earlier colonial wars, virtually every maritime community had fitted out privateers with some degree of

Map 8.1   The North-Eastern United States and Canada

success. For example, during King George's War (1739–48), a French-Canadian privateer, nicknamed Morpain or Morepang (who may really have been an Irishman named Murphy), reputedly terrorized New

England shipping along the eastern seaboard.[2] The practical combination of patriotism and profit—destroying enemy commerce to enhance one's own—prompted maritime adventurers to view the prospect of war with a more sanguine attitude.

When President Madison declared war in June 1812, neither Britain nor the United States was in a position to undertake a naval war. While Britain had over 1,000 ships in 1811, 70 per cent of them in commission, only 27 could be spared for the North American station.[3] Moreover, all but one ship-of-the-line usually departed for Bermuda from November to July leaving the poorly defended maritime provinces vulnerable to attack.[4] The American navy, on the other hand, had 150 vessels, no ships-of-the-line, and only seven frigates, characterized as 'eggshells armed with hammers'.[5] American naval strategy was based on Thomas Jefferson's gunboat system. These were small vessels, variously rigged, with a crew of 20 and a couple of small cannon. Compared to the $30–40,000 cost of a frigate, a gunboat could be launched for a few thousand dollars.[6] While undeniably cheap, some 200 of these 'miserable vessels . . . lay about in harbours in various conditions of uselessness'.[7] A contemporary analysis reprinted in Niles's *Weekly Register* recommended that the American navy be either enlarged or laid up: 'It is too small as an instrument to chastize England, or to afford our coasts and commerce any valuable protection against her. The arming of merchantmen meets our peculiar approbation.'[8] On both sides of the Canadian–American border, men with ships and money to invest began to organize privateering ventures. Although fast-sailing, manoeuvrable schooners were the preferred vessel, ships, sloops, brigantines and even open rowboats were pressed into service if there were prizes to be made.[9] Adapting a trading vessel for privateering was an expensive but relatively simple task involving the addition of several cannon or swivel guns, and the filling of cargo space with spare masts, sails and rigging to provide for the inevitable wear and tear. A considerably larger crew was also required to allow for the manning of prizes back to the privateers' home port, as well as for the unavoidable crew losses due to sickness, accident and death.

Canadian and American Privateers

The chief difference between Canadian and American privateers was one of scale. While most American vessels hunted larger, more valuable quarry in the West Indies or off the European coasts, Nova Scotian and New Brunswick crews preyed on smaller, less well defended coastal traders closer to home. Garitee estimates the cost of outfitting a Baltimore privateer at $25,000,[10] but the cost of a Nova Scotia privateer would have been somewhat lower. The discrepancy in cost reflects the scope of the two types of operation, and accordingly, the difference in profits. While American privateers such as *America* and *Yankee* are credited with earnings of $1 million and $5 million respectively, they also had to sail farther and risk more to take their prizes.[11] Only one Canadian privateer, the *Liverpool Packet*, approached a million-dollar reputation, but even that is suspected of being an overexaggeration.[12]

The defensive value of privateering has been denigrated by naval historians such as Mahan, as being no more than a secondary nuisance force in any maritime conflict.[13] Nevertheless, it played an important economic role in the communities it touched. Privateering offered investment and employment opportunities, along with a steady stream of prize goods that could be sold, traded or smuggled to markets on either side of the border. According to Vice-Admiralty Court prize documents in the Public Archives of Canada, privateering seems to have been the preserve of a small mercantile community with overlapping family, social, religious, political and commercial relationships. They invested in each other's ventures, served on each other's ships, and ensured that any profits made remained within their fraternity. The small shipbuilding community of Yarmouth, Nova Scotia, provides a good example. Several of the 45 vessels built in Yarmouth between 1812 and 1814 were privateers. In the same period, nine Yarmouth vessels were lost to American cruisers, but local privateers brought in ten prizes. Captures balanced losses within the community, so that overall, more money was made than lost.[14]

By 1812, the practice of privateering had had six centuries to establish a series of internationally recognized legal and administrative regulations governing the capture of property at sea. Every step of the process from obtaining a commission or letter of marque, to taking a prize, to adjudicating the capture was understood (and more or less respected) by the participants. Strict penalties awaited those who transgressed. In Britain and her colonies, the power to determine 'good and lawful prize' fell to the High Court of Admiralty and the colonial Courts of Vice-Admiralty. In 1768 four Vice-Admiralty Courts were created in Halifax, Boston, Philadelphia and Charleston. Judges were appointed at a salary of £600 per year to ensure that privateering ventures in North America followed the accepted rules.[15]

As part of the international law of nations, prize law was based on the assumption that during wartime, an enemy's maritime trade became fair game. In general, enemy goods seized aboard neutral or enemy ships constituted valid prize, while enemy goods aboard a friend's vessel were spared.[16] However, in an era where alliances changed more quickly than news could travel, determining the exact point at which a captured vessel moved from friendly to neutral to enemy status once war was declared, and whether the captor's letter of marque entitled him to seize such a prize, furnished plenty of work for the colonial Vice-Admiralty Courts. According to the late-eighteenth-century jurist, Lord Mansfield:

> The end of a prize court is to suspend the property till condemnation, to punish every sort of misbehaviour in the captors, to restore instantly if upon the most summary examination there don't appear sufficient ground; to condemn finally, if the goods really are prize, giving everybody a fair opportunity to be heard.[17]

Ensuring due process of law could be a fairly time-consuming prospect for the Vice-Admiralty Court and many privateers saw their profits evaporate in legal fees. However, with a well-established court system in place to regulate privateer activities, and England's numerous eighteenth-century wars to serve as a training ground, colonial privateers found plenty of opportunities to familiarize themselves with the process. The frequent condemnation of valuable prizes inspired ongoing commerce-raiding and ensured that privateering would play a prominent role in the War of 1812.

From June 1812 to January 1815, over 500 American privateers and 41 from the Canadian provinces of Nova Scotia and New Brunswick petitioned their governments for commissions to attack each other's merchant shipping. As a legally sanctioned activity, privateering represented a respectable commercial alternative to war-stifled trade. Although of limited strategic use, since they preyed mostly on un-armed merchantmen, the privateers' sea-borne guerrilla warfare aggravated and embarrassed the enemy.[18] While drawn by the lure of windfall profits, privateer investors remained business people first. Expenditures and hazards were carefully calculated, and every effort was made to minimize risk and maximize profits: 'And in its organizational structure, capitalization, method of organization and distribution of profits, privateering as a business was as soberly directed as any conventional commercial, industrial or banking enterprise.'[19] As undertaken by the merchants, shipowners, investors and crews of numerous maritime communities along the eastern seaboard of North America, privateering represented the possibility of lucrative returns for local investment, a means of defence managed at the local level, and employment in a flat economy.[20] From a social and economic standpoint, 'privateering employed the fishermen and all those who depended upon shipping, taught daring seamanship, and strengthened our maritime aptitude and tradition'.[21] More importantly, in addition to these redeeming social, military and economic virtues, privateering was also known to pay better wages and be 'safer and more fun than the army or navy'.[22]

The Organization of Privateering

Central to the practice of privateering was the ship's letter of marque, authorizing private armed vessels to commit acts of war against the enemy. Not only did a valid commission entitle the captor to his prize, it ensured that the act of capture would not be considered piracy. While naval vessels were able to seize enemy prizes immediately upon the outbreak of war, privateers had to wait for official permission to harass the enemy. In Britain after 1708, a General Prize Act usually accompanied every declaration of war.[23] Aside from ordering General Reprisals against the enemy, the Act also generated a set of rules known as Royal Instructions to Privateers. The granting of reprisals empowered the judge of a colonial Vice-Admiralty Court to issue letters of marque in 'the same manner as in England and under the securities and with the regulations prescribed'.[24] In the United States, Congress formally authorized letters of marque and reprisal which were issued to shipowners by the State Department through Collectors of Customs at American ports.[25]

It was a peculiar anomaly of the War of 1812 that, while the United States declared war on 18 June 1812 and immediately began to issue letters of marque, the British were reluctant to formalize hostilities and did not make an official declaration of war until October. This situation left Sir John Coape Sherbrooke in an awkward position. As lieutenant-governor and commander-in-chief of Nova Scotia, as well as head of the Vice-Admiralty Court, he was besieged by requests for letters of marque. His solution was to issue general commissions based on an Order-in-Council given by the Prince Regent on 31 July 1812. It read: 'commanders of His Majesty's ships of war and privateers do detain and bring into port all ships and vessels belonging to the citizens of the United States of America, or bearing the flag of the United States . . . '.[26] The apparent purpose of this order was simply to restrain (but not condemn) American shipping 'being careful to safeguard cargoes so no damage or embezzlement be sustained'.[27] Caught up in the early excitement of the war, merchant adventurers from Nova Scotia and New Brunswick rushed to take advantage of these commissions, only to find themselves embroiled in later legal battles to keep the prizes they had made. In the case of the *Liverpool Packet*, 18 of 20 ships awaiting adjudication in November 1812 were suddenly claimed as Droits of Admiralty for having been seized without a proper commission. A two-year legal wrangle ensued before the ships were finally condemned to the captor and £21,814 in prize money awarded.[28]

A long and inglorious history of commissioned abuse upon the high seas meant that by 1812, applications for letters of marque were closely monitored. Documents from captured American privateers indicate that legal safeguards were similar on both sides. A letter of marque only entitled the bearer to attack ships belonging to the enemy nation specified in the commission. If a new belligerent entered the fray, another letter of marque was necessary before the newcomer's ships could be seized. Each commission had to state the name of the ship, her tonnage, rig, armament, stores, number of crew and days for which she was victualled, as well as the names of the owner and master. Any change in registry, ownership or captain entailed a new letter of marque.[29]

To ensure that having left port, a ship would abide by its commission, at least two investors were required to post a bond of £1,500–3,000 in Canada, or $5,000–10,000 in the United States, depending on the size of the vessel and the number of crew.[30] This guarantee of good behaviour was reinforced by a sworn affadavit or surety, attesting that investors could afford the cost of the bond over and above their debts, if the ship ran foul of the law. Penalties for violation of the ship's commission could range from forfeiture of the bond, to loss of the prize, to prosecution for piracy.[31] While the documents do contain complaints from captives about the theft of ship's stores, small sums of money, and even a pair of pantaloons, if the *Liverpool Packet* is any example, in nine months of cruising with over 100 captures to her credit, there was never any complaint of cruelty or outrage against Captain Barss.[32] Even in a 'captive market', good customer relations seem to have been the order of business for Canadian privateers.

Any shipowner contemplating commerce-raiding had two options. He could fit his ship out as an armed merchant trader, hire a crew for wages, take on a nominal cargo, and carry his commission as no-cost, low-risk insurance should a prize-making opportunity present itself. Or, he could abandon all pretence to trade, invest his money in extra stores and armaments, and sign on four times the usual crew to work for shares. While all privateers had to carry letters of marque, not all letter of marque ships were privateers. The fact that at least twelve Canadian vessels with letters of marque appear not to have taken any prizes would seem to indicate that nearly 30 per cent of Canada's privateers were really armed traders. This coincides with Forester's suggestion that most of the American ships with letters of marque were actually blockade runners.[33] Comparing the reduced annual number of commissions with the gradual decline in number, size and value of American prizes captured in the course of the war, it is clear that for most Canadian privateer investors, there was, eventually, more money to be made in trade.

For those who persisted, however, the profits from a successful privateering venture could be considerable. Eight of the Canadian-based ships obtained two or more letters of marque during the war, accounting for 120 prizes. While their profits are described as 'handsome, though not fabulously large', they were obviously enough to encourage backers to reinvest.[34] The American experience was similar, with roughly 200 or 40 per cent of commissioned ships making one or more cruises and accounting for 1,344 prizes.[35] Considering that the safe return to port of one prize in three was considered good odds, the prize-making potential on both sides was much higher than the actual results.[36] The natural, naval, and legal hazards confronting privateers were often formidable. So why were normally cautious businessmen willing to underwrite the extra expense of a privateer? Liverpool, Nova Scotia, home of one of Canada's most successful privateers, the *Liverpool Packet*, may provide the answer.

The Profits of Privateering: Liverpool, Nova Scotia

Located some 70 miles south of Halifax, the town of Liverpool was a bustling maritime community with 'a reputation of being a rather raunchy and licentious place in the late eighteenth century'. Between

1760 and 1820, Liverpool's population grew from 800 to 4,000.[37] The proximity of Liverpool to Eastport, Maine, and the long-standing trade between the two ports, both legal and illegal, continued throughout the war. Privateering simply added a new dimension to the existing commercial relationships. One author states that smuggling was so prevalent in Liverpool that the preventive officer did not dare interfere without a military back-up.[38] A tightly-knit merchant adventuring elite dominated the economic life of the town. These were men who 'had their teeth sharpened by a long period of incessant sea warfare in which many of them had participated as owners if not operators of privateers'.[39] Liverpool merchants willingly invested not only their experience but their money, accounting for 13 of the 27 privateers registered in Nova Scotia.[40]

One of Liverpool's most famous sons was Simeon Perkins, a Connecticut-born entrepreneur who emigrated to Liverpool in 1762. His diaries, written over 45 years, offer a fascinating glimpse of the diversity of the late-eighteenth-century colonial economy. A well-respected member of his community, Perkins was involved in trade, fishing, lumbering, shipbuilding, politics and law, as well as being a pillar of the Methodist Church. It was Perkins who built Liverpool's first privateer, *Lucy*, in 1780 and owned shares in virtually every Liverpool privateer until his death in 1812.[41] The long-term participation of such a prominent citizen in privateering is proof that these ventures were both socially acceptable and commercially sound.

Needless to say, Perkins did not invest alone. In fact, documentary evidence suggests that most merchants in Liverpool were involved in privateering. The capture of the schooner *Falun* in 1814 illustrates the extent of the business. Taken jointly by the privateers *Liverpool Packet* and *Retaliation*, the prize was carried into Liverpool harbour. While awaiting adjudication, she was broken into and her cargo damaged. Acting on the owners' behalf, William K. Reynolds of Halifax petitioned the Vice-Admiralty Court to have the ship removed to Halifax so that the loss could be evaluated by disinterested parties. He argued:

> your petitioner has been informed and verily believes that most of the respectable people in Liverpool are interested in the privateers *Liverpool Packet* and *Retaliation*, and tho they are in the opinion of your petitioner honest men, yet he most humbly conceives that they may be prejudiced by their interest.[42]

That Reynolds himself, as a one-time bondsman for the *Retaliation*, and part-owner of the Halifax privateer *Retrieve*, might not have been completely disinterested is not raised in the court case. A survey of 33 owners and investors from Liverpool reveals that nine of them invested in two or more privateering cruises, with five men investing in four or more.[43] According to Garitee's Baltimore-based study of the same period, the frequency of investment indicates the degree of commitment. Marginal investors backed one voyage, while active investors sponsored four or more.[44] No other location in the maritime provinces supported as many privateering ventures with as many different investors as Liverpool. The only other multiple investor, Halifax merchant Enos Collins, was a native of Liverpool. Reputed at his death to have been the wealthiest man in Canada, Collins's $6–9 million estate may have originated in his partial ownership of the 67-ton schooner, *Liverpool Packet*.[45]

Bought for £440 at a prize auction in 1811, the *Liverpool Packet*, formerly the *Black Joke*, began her career as a tender to an American slave ship.[46] She was purchased by Enos Collins, his brother-in-law Benjamin Knaut, and the brothers John and James Barss, all of whom were ex-privateers and ship-mates.[47] Recognizing the suitability of her deep draught and narrow, Baltimore clipper lines, the owners quickly converted her to privateering the moment America declared war. The commission for the *Liverpool Packet* confirms that she carried a crew of 40, five guns, 25 muskets, 40 cutlasses, and enough food for 60 days.[48] Her first captain was John Freeman, whose father Joseph was a three-time bondsman for the vessel. On her first cruise, from August to December 1812, she brought in 19 prizes. The value of just six vessels and their cargoes captured in November 1812 is estimated at $50,000.[49] An article from a New England newspaper recounts the American side of the story:

> The *Liverpool Packet* has just captured and sent in [to Liverpool] the *Dolphin* of Beverley with flour and tobacco; the *Columbia* of Dennis with 600 barrels of flour and 203 kegs of tobacco; *Two Friends* of Boston with a cargo of flour; and the *Susan* of Sandwich with a cargo of flour. She could have captured many more but had only seven men left to navigate her to Liverpool.[50]

Thomas Freeman, the captain's brother and prize master for the *Columbia*, made £530 as his share of the prize money.[51]

Cruises under subsequent letters of marque in February 1813 (Joseph Barss, master), November 1813 (Caleb Seely), and October 1814 (Lewis Knaut) were equally successful. In all, Vice-Admiralty Court prize records list 50 ships for which the *Liverpool Packet* was sole or joint captor.[52] Since several sources credit her with up to 100 captures, it would appear that at least half of these were either destroyed, released or restored in court. Even with half her prizes and only a quarter of the prize money conservatively ascribed to her, the *Liverpool Packet* earned her reputation as 'the evil genius of the American coasting trade'.[53] The seriousness of the threat presented by the schooner can be measured in the $25 bounty on each crewman, more than twice the standard American bounty on British captives.[54] Even capture in 1813 by the American privateer *Thomas* of Portsmouth, New Hampshire did not halt the *Liverpool Packet's* career. No sooner was she put up for sale, than she was bought back by Collins and resumed her depredations. In a nice irony, the *Thomas* was brought into Halifax soon after by the Royal Navy, bought by John Barss, and turned loose to torment her former countrymen as the Canadian privateer *Wolverine*.[55]

Prize ships and cargoes filling the harbour at Liverpool served as incentive for the privateering business. Owners, with bonds posted and commissions in hand, sought experienced captains and prize masters. A successful cruise really relied on the captain's flair 'supplemented by an intimate knowledge born of experience, of the trade routes and the seasonal variations of commerce and the ways of the merchant captains both in convoy and proceeding independently'.[56] Men who had sailed the New England coast knew the shoals and harbours where a ship could lie in wait for likely prizes. The area around Cape Cod and Block Island was one of the *Liverpool Packet's* favourite hunting grounds.[57] With such a reputation for success, the *Liverpool Packet* never seemed to have any trouble obtaining a crew. Compared to the standard seaman's wage of $15–30 per month,[58] Snider estimates that each sailor aboard the *Packet* in 1812 made at least £156 apiece, roughly $700 for six months' work.[59] Profits from each cruise were shared by owners, investors and crews in agreed-upon proportions (usually 64ths) according to a sliding scale.[60] There were also bonus shares for being the first to sight a prize, board her, or perform some other valuable service.[61]

To ensure that everyone knew what he had signed on for, a set of Articles of Agreement was read to the assembled crew before sailing. Each man signed or made his mark guaranteeing that everyone from the captain to the cabin boy had a vested interest in the cruise. Prize crews who left the ship to sail prizes back to port remained eligible for shares in subsequent captures.[62] The Articles even provided for shares of prize money for sick or wounded seamen, or their widows, orphans or elderly parents.[63] It is indicative of the non-violent character of Canadian privateering that less than half a dozen privateersmen were actually killed in action during the course of the war.[64]

As a business, however, privateering was only viable as long as there was money to be made. Once the British naval blockade closed in along the American seaboard at the end of 1813, the opportunity for prize-making decreased substantially. For Nova Scotian investors, the extra cost of a privateer cruise by then did not justify the risk of falling victim to storms or American privateers. The presence of an expanded garrison in Halifax furnished an ample market for goods obtained through conventional trade. Thanks to the war, by 1814 the booming economy of the Canadian maritime provinces eliminated the need for commerce-raiding entirely.[65] In the United States, privateering declined because any ships that managed to sneak through the blockade could not bring their prizes back home for condemnation. The gradual tightening of the blockade squeezed American trade to a trickle and plunged entire communities into real hardship. When the war finally drew to its inconclusive close, privateers and public on both sides were ready to return to their peacetime pursuits.

Conclusion

Sharing a legal and historical tradition that reached back two hundred years, American and Canadian privateers encountered many similar experiences during the War of 1812. Both sides enjoyed close personal and professional relationships within their own mercantile communities. Privateering cruises were subject to the same international regulations, and their judicial procedures followed the British model. Their ships were similar, sometimes the same vessels, and their crews, for lack of official uniforms, very often appeared interchangeable. Early in the war, the organization of a privateering venture presented similar opportunities and risks for investors on either side. Without the decisive weight of the British naval blockade by 1814, it is likely that the more numerous American privateers would have decimated Canada's maritime trade. Instead, investors persisted as long as there were profits to be made, and began to agitate for peace when prospects diminished. Fortunately for Nova Scotia, New Brunswick and their American neighbours, by January 1815 both privateering and the war were history.

Notes

1. Kate Caffery, *The Lion and the Union: The Anglo-American War 1812–1815* (London, 1978).
2. Howard M. Chapin, *Privateering During King George's War 1739–1748* (Providence, 1928).
3. H. Niles (ed.), *The Weekly Register*, vol. 1. Baltimore, 7 Sept. 1811 to Mar. 1812, vol. 1, no. 2, 3. Also vol 1, no. 9, 145.
4. Walter Ronald Copp, 'Military Activities in Nova Scotia During the War of 1812', in *Collections of the Nova Scotia Historical Society*, vol. 24 (Halifax, 1938), 59.
5. Niles, *Register*, vol. 1, no. 5, 79 quotes the number of American ships from Blodgetts Economica. The types of ships are listed in Howard Chapelle, *The History of American Sailing Ships* (New York, 1982), 51. See also John K. Mahon, *The War of 1812* (Gainesville, 1972), 8.
6. J.P. Cranwell, and W.P. Crane, *Men of Marque* (New York, 1940), 26.
7. James Barnes, *Naval Actions in the War of 1812* (New York, 1896), 10.
8. Niles, *Register*, vol. 1, no. 14, 251.
9. Cranwell and Crane, *Men of Marque*, 19. S.E. Morison, *The Maritime History of Massachusetts, 1783–1860* (Boston, 1961), 199. Morison refers to five Salem privateers that were open boats filled with men with muskets.
10. Jerome Garitee, *The Republic's Private Navy* (Middletown, 1977), 111.
11. Major James Ripley Jacobs and Glenn Tucker, *The War of 1812: A Compact History* (New York, 1969), 170. Also William McFee, *The Law of the Sea* (New York, 1950), 121.
12. C.H.J. Snider, *Under the Red Jack: Privateers of the Maritime Provinces of Canada in the War of 1812* (Toronto, 1927), 51.
13. A.T. Mahan, *The Influence of Sea Power upon History, 1660–1783* (London, 1965), 132–3.
14. Clement Crowell, *Nova Scotiaman* (Halifax, 1979), 4.
15. Carl Ubbelohde, *The Vice-Admiralty Courts and the American Revolution* (Chapel Hill, 1960), 130.
16. James Stewart, *Reports of Cases argued and determined in the Court of Vice-Admiralty at Halifax, Nova Scotia from the commencement of the War in 1803, to the end of the year 1813 in the time of Alexander Croke LLD., Judge of that Court* (London, 1814), vii.
17. Stewart, *Reports*, 319.
18. Donald Macintyre, *The Privateers* (London, 1975), 189.
19. Garitee, *Private Navy*, xv.
20. Morison, *Maritime History*, 29.
21. Morison, *Maritime History*, 199.
22. Mahon, *War*, 24.
23. E.S. Roscoe (ed.), *Reports of Prize Cases determined in the High Court of Admiralty before the Lords Commissioners of Appeals in Prize Cases and before the Judicial Committee of the Privy Council from 1745 to 1859* (London, 1905), vol. 1, vii.
24. Stewart, *Reports*, 401.
25. Cranwell and Crane, *Men of Marque*, 18.
26. Stewart, *Reports*, Appendix, vii. The Public Archives of Nova Scotia contains the notice from the Lords of High Admiralty, 5 Aug. 1812.

27. Public Archives of Canada (PAC), RG 8, IV, vol. 73. Letter of Marque for the *Liverpool Packet*, 24 Nov. 1812.

28. Snider, *Red Jack*, 29.

29. Timothy Runyan (ed.), *Ships, Seafaring and Society* (Detroit, 1987), 253.

30. Cranwell and Crane, *Men of Marque*, 18.

31. Macintyre, *The Privateers*, 4.

32. Janet E. Mullins, *Liverpool Privateering 1756–1815* (Nova Scotia, 1936), 53.

33. C.S. Forester, *The Naval War of 1812* (London, 1957), 76.

34. W.S. MacNutt, *The Atlantic Provinces: The Emergence of Colonial Society 1712–1857* (Toronto, 1965), 151.

35. E.B. Potter (ed.), *Sea Power: A Naval History* (New Jersey, 1960), 213.

36. Garitee, *Private Navy*, 170.

37. James H. Morrison and James Moreira (eds), *Tempered by Rum* (Nova Scotia, 1988), 64.

38. Dave MacIntosh, *A History of Canadian Customs and Excise* (Toronto, 1984), 235.

39. Morison, *Maritime History*, 64.

40. Faye Kert, unpublished MA thesis, Ottawa: Carleton University, 1986, Appendix 2, 144.

41. John Leefe, *The Atlantic Privateers* (Halifax, 1978), 18.

42. PAC, RG 8, IV, vol. 105, *Falun*. Affidavit from William K. Reynolds.

43. Kert, Appendix 2, 144–51.

44. Garitee, *Private Navy*, 33.

45. Peggy Anderson, 'Enos Collins 1774–1871', in *Canadian Arts and Antiques Review* (Toronto, 1982), 29.

46. Leefe, *Atlantic Privateers*, 6.

47. Mullins, *Liverpool Privateering*, 43.

48. PAC, RG 8, IV, vol. 73. Letter of Marque for the *Liverpool Packet*.

49. Mullins, *Liverpool Privateering*, 43.

50. Leefe, *Atlantic Privateers*, 10.

51. Mullins, *Liverpool Privateering*, 26.

52. Kert, Appendix 3, 152–69.

53. Mullins, *Liverpool Privateering*, 145.

54. Mullins, *Liverpool Privateering*, 25.

55. Snider, *Red Jack*, 48. The *Wolverine* eventually took 13 prizes, eight of them destined for Boston. Kert, Appendix 3.

56. Forester, *Naval War*, 77.

57. PAC, RG 8, IV, assorted files.

58. Mullins, *Liverpool Privateering*, 68.

59. Snider, *Red Jack*, 137.

60. Crowell, *Nova Scotiaman*, 12. Also, Chapelle, *American Sailing Ships*, 131.

61. Chapin, *Privateeering*, 7.

62. Roscoe, *Reports*, 549. Decision by Sir William Scott, Lord Stowell, Judge of the High Court of Admiralty re *Ceres*, 26 Nov. 1805.

63. Richard Pares, *Colonial Blockade and Neutral Rights* (Oxford, 1938), 9.

64. Mullins, *Liverpool Privateering*, 68.

65. MacNutt, *Atlantic Provinces*, 137.

CHAPTER 9

Experience, Skill and Luck: French Privateering Expeditions, 1792–1815

Patrick Crowhurst

A Privateer and its Crew

In September 1813 Benoist Joseph Foube fitted out the 87-ton lugger *Génie* 'pour faire la Course sur les Ennemies de l'Etat pendant soixante jours de Mer effectifs'.[1] Foube chose as captain a Dunkirk man, Louis Joseph Amand Piquendaire, a 'captaine au long cours', whose experience had been in the Dunkirk colonial trade. This is an interesting choice of captain, for the year 1813 was almost at the end of two long wars, in which opportunities for sailing 'au long cours' were limited. Some trade in sugar, coffee and other colonial goods had continued with Tobago, Martinique and Guadeloupe for a time but by 1811 these had all fallen into British hands, leaving Piquendaire without an occupation. As a captain in the colonial trade he was one of the few men who had continued to brave the British naval patrols as a captain of a privateer, for he knew the English Channel from the landfalls off the Soundings to the Straits of Dover and had carried colonial goods to ports in the North Sea. He was also a man whose whole adult life, apart from the brief Peace of Amiens, had been spent at sea during war and he had been given the command of at least one ship already. In September 1813 when the *Génie* was ready to sail from Boulogne he was aged 32; at the outbreak of war in 1793 he had been too young even to sail as cabin boy.

The choice of captain was of crucial importance to the success of a privateering voyage. The *armateur* provided general instructions for the voyage but the decision where and how to attack trade had to be left to the captain. Only he could decide which areas might offer good prospects for prizes or which should be avoided because of British naval patrols. Privateer captains were usually in their early thirties, in the prime of their life and with 15–20 years experience at sea. Piquendaire was 1.64 m tall, slightly shorter than his officers and many of his men, though no doubt force of character and physical strength more than compensated for this. His duty as captain was to mould the crew of young men as quickly as possible into an effective force. Privateer crews were traditionally unruly and could only be controlled by strength of personality and the prospect of prize money.

The second captain, officers, ensigns and master and assistant boatswain also played an important part in the effective control of the crew. Most of those employed on the *Génie* were from Calais or Dunkirk, with one man, Roskamp, from Papenbourg, a small north German port close to the Dutch border. Most had a common background of experience and language. As a further check on the management of the ship at sea, Foube appointed as writer Charles Benoît Constant Foube, aged 37, either a brother or close relative. When these appointments had been made the *armateur* was able to consider the men who were required for the administration of the ship: the purser, the master and assistant carpenter, and the master sailmaker. The other petty officers, the master and assistant gunner and surgeon completed this list. The petty officers were from diverse backgrounds and most were comparatively young. The youngest was the surgeon, who at 17 can have had little experience of his profession. The oldest was the master sailmaker, Gonzalve da Silva, a Portuguese aged 51. The petty officers formed the main element of the crew and were responsible for discipline, leadership, the control and proper use of stores and maintaining the effectiveness of the ship's armament.

Recruitment for a Privateering Voyage

The seamen's main job was to bring the privateer within gunshot of any potential prize, provide a prize crew and then to take the captured vessel safely into the home port so that it could be sold. They were seldom expected to capture a prize by hand to hand fighting. Normally a shot across the bows of a merchant ship was enough to make the captain surrender. The sight of a large number of armed men was usually sufficient to overawe the small crew of a merchant ship. The privateer's crew would then board the prize and seize whatever they could. The only restriction was that by tradition certain items were reserved for the privateer's captain.[2]

The main criteria in choosing men for the crew were experience, age (they were ideally in their twenties) and a reasonable willingness to understand and obey the captain's and petty officers' commands. In theory this would logically mean that the crew were all French and possibly from the same region, on the grounds that they would share a common dialect and cultural background. In practice this was seldom the case. This was partly because of difficulty in recruiting young men—when privateering was popular there were never enough for all the crews—and partly because it was sometimes useful to have foreigners who could control the crew of a prize vessel. The choice of men for the crew depended on which sailors were available in the port when the vessel was being fitted out. All French able seamen were registered with the Commissaire des Classes, so that they could be called into naval service if necessary. In consequence privateer crews tended to be made up of men who were not registered as seamen, either because they were listed as cabin boys and apprentice seamen, or because they were foreigners.

The outbreak of war left a number of seamen stranded far from home, either because the master decided not to risk the voyage back and sold the ship or because all vessels remained in harbour. During the wars few ships sailed from French ports and seamen became desperate to find work. One example is of a Swede, Carl Frederick Ribe, who in 1797 sailed on an American ship from Hamburg to Morlaix, where the ship was sold. He went to Brest to seek work, but fell ill and used up his savings in doctor's fees. When he had recovered he signed on the privateer *Vautour* because that was the only work he could find.[3] The example of Ribe helps to explain why foreigners signed on for French privateering ventures even though they might be called upon to seize a ship from their own country. Though Sweden was neutral, a Swedish ship might be taken carrying British goods.[4] The concept of nationality at the end of the eighteenth century was different from that of today. Nationality was conferred by residence rather than birth; seamen who moved from Belgium to Dunkirk spoke the same language and were regarded before long as 'French' for all reasonable purposes. The modern concept of nationality is a product of the Napoleonic period and of the nationalist movements of the nineteenth century. Although British seamen were regarded as traitors if they fought for France against England, other foreigners from countries not at war with Britain who were captured on board French vessels were listed in Admiralty records as French.[5] The presence of many different nationalities on board the *Génie* thus causes no surprise. The crew consisted of French (from Brest, Dunkirk, Gravelines, Cherbourg, Caen, Marseilles, Calais and St Cosme (?) in the *département* of Gard), Flemish (Brussels, Bruges, Ostend), Danish (Bellingsberg), Dutch (De Ryp near Amsterdam, Dorb (?), Amsterdam), Prussians (Königsberg), Americans (New York), and Portuguese (Brazil)—seven nationalities in a crew of only 52.

According to an order of 2 prairial Year XI (2 May 1803), the number of foreign sailors on French privateers should have been limited to two-fifths of the total crew.[6] However, a lack of experienced seamen forced managing owners to hire large numbers of foreigners. This appears to be a feature of privateering throughout the Napoleonic War, for as early as 1804 the Bayonne privateer *Général Augereau* had a crew which was predominently Spanish—43 of the total of 67 seamen, novices and cabin boys.[7] The shortage of seamen during the Napoleonic War shows that a large number of French ships were captured by British naval forces and their crews were kept prisoner in Britain.[8] This demonstrates the effectiveness of British naval patrols. The decision to keep prisoners of war for a long time represents a change in the attitude towards them. In earlier wars the custom had been to return prisoners within a year of so of capture. Even if they had not been formally exchanged they were allowed to return on parole but were not free to fight again until their exchange had been formally agreed. Towards the end of the Revolutionary War the Consulate announced that it was abandoning the care of French prisoners to the British government and would only maintain the (smaller) number of British prisoners that it held.[9] It was much harder to justify the exchange of prisoners under these circumstances and men remained in prison hulks and camps in Britain much longer.[10]

Foube decided that 52 men were not enough for a vessel of 87 tons and on 20 September recruited a further 36 men for 30 *jours de mer effectifs* for the *Génie*. On 20 September the group showed a similar variety to the first group: there were French (from St Vaast, Dunkirk, Estinay (?), Honfleur, Boulogne, Saussay la Vache in the *département* of Eure, Calais, Trouville, Havre, St Pierre d'Arène), Portuguese (from

Biema, the Island of Fayol, Lisbon), Gibraltarese, Spanish (Majorca, Carthagena, St Felin (?) in Catalonia, Cadiz), Venetians, Swedish (Stockholm), Sardinians, Flemish (Nieuport, Bruges), and Italians (Rome). Thereafter the crew remained fairly static, apart from the transfer of some men to the *Lynx* privateer and others to captured vessels as prize crews. To replace the latter several were added when the *Génie* called at La Hougue and Fécamp from time to time between the end of September and mid-November. In the final stages of the voyage—the *Génie* was captured on 19 December 1813—it seems to have become more difficult to recruit experienced seamen of any nationality. On 22 October Piquendaire hired Thomas Védic, a labourer in the wine trade, as volunteer; on the 24th Ferdinand Porquib, spice merchant, was added as ensign; Pierre Gulle of Calais, *ouvrier civil*, as *capitaine d'armes*; Jean Degrave of Dunkirk, a ropemaker, as volunteer, and Charles le Prêtre, also of Dunkirk, a carpentry workman, as pilot.

When hiring seamen, Piquendaire bargained with each within a customary wage range. Rates for officers were more strictly defined: Piquendaire as captain received an advance of 400 francs, his second officer received 350 francs, lieutenants 300 francs and ensigns 250 francs. Towards the end of the voyage another *capitaine au long cours*, the 38-year-old François Racine of Brest, was hired as a coastal pilot for an advance of 500 francs. This made him the highest paid of all the officers on board and reflected the importance given to an experienced pilot. In the case of the volunteers the advances varied from 80 to 180 francs, though most were paid 120 francs. Why some were paid more than others is hard to say; the *rôle d'équipage* gives no indication of any special qualities or experience. It is likely that a man who was able to demonstrate considerable experience at sea was able to drive a harder bargain and command a higher wage. The best paid were a 26-year-old Portuguese, Joseph Belborde, and a 30-year-old Swede, Nicolas England; the lowest paid volunteers were men with no previous seafaring experience: 19-year-old Auguste Marbier and a 16-year-old novice Philippe Germe, both of Calais. These wages paid to seamen on the *Génie* were very similar to those paid to seamen on the Bayonne privateer *Général Augereau* in 1803 noted above.[11] Although it is dangerous to generalize, it is clear that both crews were recruited when there was a shortage of trained seamen and wages were high. The wages seem to have remained high during the war because so many were captured and remained in British prisons during this war.[12] This would help to explain why so many foreign seamen were prepared to serve on board privateers. They were not necessarily more successful in taking prizes but the wages were good. By comparison, wages noted by Simon Ville for the English shipping industry in the same period fluctuated very considerably, reflecting greater availability of seamen, seasonal fluctuations in demand, and higher wages in war than peace.[13]

One of the main features of these privateer crews was that most of the seamen were under 30 years old. Since comparative youth and vigour were considered important, one must ask whether the ages shown in the *rôle d'équipage* were accurate, or whether men claimed to be older or younger than they really were. There is no means of knowing the exact date of birth of some of the men who signed on the crew of the *Génie*, since many of them were born abroad. As to the others, the ones in their teens probably exaggerated their age in order to get a place on the lugger, though, as will be seen, most were probably approximately accurate. Some recent research on a sample of 1,800 seamen at Port Louis and Riantec for 1750–62 compared the ages shown in *rôles d'équipage* and legal documents such as marriage registers, which provided accurate details of age.[14] This research has shown that teenage boys at those two small ports overstated their ages by up to three and a half years, though men gave ages which were usually accurate to within a year or two. The same was probably true of the crew of the *Génie*. In the case of skilled craftsmen such as the carpenters and sailmakers, many of whom were older, experience was more important than age and there was no reason to give a false age. In any case, it was less difficult to get alternative work ashore and the men were less dependent on privateering.

The skill of the officers and seamen formed the main resource of commerce-raiding rather than the vessel or type of armament. The strategy for each cruise was decided in the first place by the *armateur* and subsequently agreed between him and the captain. The type of vessel chosen reflected this strategy. Opportunities for taking prizes varied from port to port but in each case the captain employed a blend of guile and courage. A voyage from a northern port such as Dunkirk was fundamentally different from one at an Atlantic port such as Nantes. Part of the difference was geographical, but the experience of the merchant-turned-managing-owner and his captain differed from place to place. The nature of Dunkirk privateering is well known: attacks on trade in the North Sea and English Channel, often in the dark winter months when visibility was limited, formed the normal pattern. But beyond that there was a range of choices: should the privateer attack the colonial and American trade as it returned to London in the autumn? Should it attack the coasting trade which continued throughout most of the year, except for the winter months when gales made navigation more dangerous? Should it attack the commerce between London and the Dutch ports, or Bergen or the Baltic trade? Each had its particular cycle of departure and arrival and the potentially richest prizes had the best convoy protection. A cruise might be launched to allow the captain a judicious choice between all of these, but it should be remembered that a voyage was normally for 60 days at sea, allowing for short visits to port to take on board more stores or carry out repairs. Two-month cruises could be and often were repeated, but each one had to be profitable or offer reasonable prospects.

It is these considerations that required careful judgement by the managing-owner at the outset and governed his choice of captain and type of vessel. One of the most interesting choices was to use an English or other foreign built vessel of a distinctive design to make it appear as if this was a merchant ship rather than a privateer. Many ports and harbours along the English coast had developed a type of vessel to suit the local conditions and these were sometimes captured and sold in France. With a vessel built at, say, Deal, a captain could cruise unnoticed in the area to wait for isolated coasting vessels. An observer on the shore would eventually notice that the vessel was staying at sea too long and the sound of gunfire would announce the capture of a prize. Or the privateer might cruise further along the coast, appearing to be one of the small coasters that were commonly seen or an American ship engaged in trade.[15]

For this policy to be successful the crew had to contain one or more fluent English speakers, which helps to explain the presence of some Americans on board privateers. This would provide adequate disguise for casual meetings with neutrals that could not be seized and which would otherwise report the presence of the corsair to other shipping. It would not fool naval captains, who would be more careful in their questioning of captains of vessels they met at sea. A disadvantage of this strategy from the point of the *armateur* was that many of the potential prizes were, like the privateer, small and of little value.[16] A larger vessel such as the *Génie*, which was registered at $87^{76}/_{97}$ tons, could cruise for longer and carry a larger crew. As noted already, part of the complement was intended to be used for prize crews. Ships from other ports along the north coast of France followed a similar pattern; many were relatively small (under 100 tons) and the captains cruised in the areas they knew best, along the south coast of England. St Malo stands at the margin of this English Channel war. Most seamen were experienced deep-water mariners, who sailed to the cod fisheries of the Grand Banks in peacetime. Traditionally, many had sailed to southern Ireland and had taken part in the more general French coasting trade. Using this experience, St Malo privateers cruised principally off Ireland, the Scilly Isles and south-west England.[17]

Local Conditions of Privateering

Privateering strategy was different in the Atlantic ports. The experience of merchants and captains from Nantes, La Rochelle and Bordeaux was in deep-sea commerce. Nantes was engaged in the triangular trade, to the west coast of Africa for slaves, thence to the Caribbean and home with cargoes of sugar, coffee, and a variety of other commodities. La Rochelle was engaged in commerce with North America and the West Indies, and in the distribution of colonial goods. Bordeaux had been the principal port for the Caribbean trade in the 1780s. The ships fitted out to cruise from these ports were normally merchant ships and were sent to the Soundings and the approaches to Cape Clear for the English trade returning from the Caribbean and North America in the autumn. This was the trade that the Nantes captains knew from personal experience and the ships and crews were ideal for this task. Some merchants had experience of the commerce with Portugal and fitted out smaller vessels to attack the British trade that sailed directly from England and also the returning cod fishing fleet that made its landfall from Newfoundland at 'the high land at Viana'. Since all these potential prizes usually sailed in convoy, the aim of the captain (and managing-owner) was to seize isolated ships that had become separated by bad weather or whose captains had pressed ahead of the convoy to reach the market early. The same strategy would have been followed at Bordeaux if the resources had been available. Before 1789 its merchants had suffered heavy losses in their management of the plantations and many of their assets were seized during the Revolution. There were two other factors which made privateering a less attractive proposition at Bordeaux. The first was the family structure of shipowning in the colonial trade, which was different from that of other ports. Ships were owned by three or four

Map 9.1   North-Western Europe

families, and privateering demanded a wider sharing of the risks than
this.[18] The other was the availability of trade goods in 1797–8 when
privateering was popular elsewhere. Although there were many bankruptcies at the end of the summer of 1797, there were also profits to be
made from trading in Portuguese cotton and other goods, which

continued to be attracted to Bordeaux because of the reputation of the
port as a commercial centre. From Bordeaux merchants sent these
goods to destinations in northern Europe, especially Belgium, and at
times their profits were very large. Charles Fieffé, for example, made
profits of over 50 per cent on shipments of cotton to Lille during the
cotton famine.[19] Privateering was unlikely to make such large gains.

The activity of British naval patrols seems to have had comparatively
little effect on privateering at the Atlantic ports. Bordeaux was never
completely blockaded and large numbers of corsairs were able to enter
and leave Nantes. Commerce-raiding was more important at Nantes
than Bordeaux partly because there were fewer bankruptcies at Nantes,
so there was enough speculative capital, and the commercial population did not suffer such heavy losses from the Revolution. Furthermore
there remained, at least for a time, a steady demand for trade goods
that could not be obtained in any other way. Increasingly from 1797
neutral merchants preferred to ship their goods elsewhere, especially to
northern European ports such as Hamburg, and offered the goods at a
lower price. It was this continued demand for goods in France and
Switzerland, and the resources to support privateering, that made
Nantes the main privateering port during this period in terms of the
size of her ships, the level of investment, and the number of men
employed. Close behind Nantes in terms of the number of voyages—
though by smaller ships—came Bayonne and its outport St Jean-de-
Luz. Traditionally engaged in trade with Spain and Portugal, these
ports offered many prospects for raiding Portuguese and Spanish
commerce when France was at war with these countries. Another
advantage of Bayonne was that its ships were designed to be rowed as
well as sailed. When leaving the River Garonne it was often necessary
for the crew to row into the prevailing westerly wind. This provided
the ideal vessel and crew for attacking the Portuguese trade, because
these relatively small vessels were highly manoeuvrable and their crews
could capture merchant shipping at will in light winds, often in sight
of their escorts.[20] On the other hand, it was difficult for the British
navy to patrol the mouth of the Garonne because of the westerly wind
and a dangerous lee shore.

In the case of the Mediterranean, Revolution and the Terror
damaged the prospects for privateering at Marseilles as at Bordeaux.
Only at the beginning of the Revolutionary War was there any
significant interest. For the rest of the time the port imported grain
carried by small Genoese vessels which avoided the British blockade off

Toulon. The combination of British naval patrols, shortage of finance and the prospect of alternative trade with neutral shipping made privateering a less attractive proposition at Marseilles than elsewhere. A small number of vessels were fitted out elsewhere in the Mediterranean, principally in Corsica, after being supplied with letters of marque by French consuls, but these did not play a significant part in the privateering war. Their main target was the variety of trade from Italian as well as neutral states that might be found carrying British, Austrian or other enemy goods. Venetian ships were often enemies of France, so too from time to time were boats from ports in northern Italy, depending on the state of diplomacy, especially in the Napoleonic War.

The Economy of Privateering

So far this chapter has concentrated on the way in which privateering voyages at ports in different areas tended to be organized according to local conditions. There remain four factors which have to be considered: the need for privateers to carry some form of armament; the cost of a privateering voyage; profitability; and the question whether sailing *en guerre et marchandise* constituted a true privateering voyage.

The armament of a privateer was as much a matter of psychology as of reality. Few if any privateers, including the comparatively large ships which cruised in the Indian Ocean (which do not form a part of this study), were able to fight off a naval warship. They carried guns which appeared to represent a substantial armament. In fact the carriage guns were comparatively small and a number of what appeared from a distance to be guns were in reality wooden dummies, which were run out with the others to overawe a potential prize. More valuable were the bow and stern chasers that were used to fire warning shots towards a potential prize or give some cover against attack by a naval vessel while the crew threw almost everything overboard to lighten the ship to try and escape. Stocks of these small guns must have formed part of the normal stores in any shipbuilder's yard, to be used from time to time. They were also comparatively easy to make in one of the local iron foundries that supplied the basic needs of each port. The other weapons were sabres and a variety of firearms that were also generally available and could be easily made in any locality. The cost of these was comparatively modest and formed a small proportion of the total cost of fitting out. A typical example is that of the *Julie*, fitted out at

Nantes by Felix Cossin in 1797. The vessel carried 12 6-pounder cannon, two 12-pounders, 40 rifles and sabres and 30 pistols. These cost a total of 18,724 francs, around 10 per cent of the total cost of 196,500 francs.[21]

The *Napoléon*, of St Malo, fitted out by Blaize *et fils* and Robert Surcouf in Year XI (1803) was a different type of venture.[22] Although the tonnage is not known, she cost 346,858 francs to build and fit out and carried 25 32-pounder carronades and a brass 40-pounder. These were heavy guns that could severely damage a ship and the *Napoléon* had to have a strengthened deck to be able to carry and fire them. Because these were so much larger than the usual privateer guns, the 32-pounders had to be bought at Brest and the 40-pounder at Nantes. Four small cannon were also carried, together with 42 sabres for the crew. The total cost of the carronades, cannon and sabres was 60,672 francs, representing 18 per cent of the total. It could be argued that the expense was unnecessary, since the *Napoléon* was not intended to fight a naval warship and 20 32-pounder carronades and a 40-pounder were the wrong weapons. The *armateur* wanted a prize undamaged so that it could be sold for a high price. The four small carriage guns were adequate for this task. Whether the other main items of expenditure were equally unrealistic is hard to say: 57,766 francs for timber, 47,289 for labour, 38,283 for cordage and 15,792 for advance payments to the crew and sundry expenses. On top of this the *armateur* received 5 per cent commission on the final total: 16,517 francs. More realistic is the example of the St Malo privateer *Bougainville*, which cost 23,640 francs to build in Year VI, and carried ten 6-pounder cannon, two 4-pounders, ten swivel guns and sundry firearms and sabres. However, the total cost of all armaments and personal weapons was approximately the same as the cost of the timber, which is the same proportion as for the much larger *Napoléon*.

Without knowing the full details of each ship it is impossible to compare the costs of building them. No one can say whether the larger compass timbers required for a relatively big privateer such as the *Napoléon* were more or less expensive for a given weight and size than those required for the *Bougainville*. The price of timber was bound to fluctuate, although it is possible that some of the smaller vessels were built with cheaper, relatively green timber. A ship built primarily for speed rather than carrying capacity was less useful in peacetime than war and by sharing the cost of the venture among many it was possible to write off the ship fairly quickly if sufficient prizes were captured. In the same way prices for iron, hemp, pitch and possibly even labour rates in the dockyards could vary according to the quality of the material and supply available. It is unlikely, for example, that the best Swedish tar and iron were used if there was a cheaper alternative, and when privateering was popular and many ships were being built the prices were bound to increase. This highlights the importance of sound management of the whole venture. The *armateur* had to get the ship to sea as cheaply as possible if he was to have any chance of profit. On the other hand, he benefited from a high cost, since he was paid a commission on this that varied from 1 to 5 per cent according to the law in force. The example of the St Malo corsair *Magicienne* demonstrates the problems.

Final account of the *Magicienne* [23]

To the sale of the Swedish prize *La Sophie*, sold at Nantes 11 July 1807		11,541 fr.
To the sale of the English prize *l'Ocean*		3,650 fr.
	Total	15,191 fr.

Crew's account

One third	4,645 fr.
Less advance payments, on which the *Droits des Invalides* have been paid	10,486 fr.

Therefore nothing to be paid to the crew, and the crew's share is to be paid to shareholders and managing owners

Shareholders' account

Two thirds		9,290 fr.
+ crew's one third		4,645 fr.
	Total	13,935 fr.

Less

The cost of fitting out, including the *armateur*'s 2 per cent commission		37,965 fr.
and the cost of repairs and decommissioning at Cherbourg, Audierne, Aberwrach and Bréhat		5,115 fr.
	Total	43,080 fr.

Loss on the venture	29,145 fr.

This demonstrates some of the problems facing managing-owners: the absolute need to capture prizes and to continue to do so all the time the ship was at sea. Merely staying at sea cost money in food for the crew and wear and tear on the vessel, rigging and sails. The payment of advances to the crew was only the beginning. A man who made an unwise choice in his captain, petty officers or seamen would guarantee a costly failure. Even Surcouf, returning to St Malo as the hero of the Indian Ocean, could not continue indefinitely as managing-owner when his ventures proved to be a mixture of success and failure.

Finally, was the combination of trading voyage and privateering venture—a voyage *en guerre et marchandise*—any better? Was it a true privateering voyage? As a voyage designed for two purposes—trade and prize money—it was not a true privateering venture. There were theoretical advantages to it, since it appeared to offer profits from both, and prices of many goods increased during the war. In reality it was impossible to do both properly and the cost of these voyages were very high in terms of insurance and wages. Either the captain concentrated on arriving safely at his destination and returning to his home port or the trade would be no more than a by-product of a potentially risky venture. The main danger was from British naval patrols off the home port and the Caribbean and many ships which sailed on this type of voyage were captured. In addition, as time went by more and more of the French islands fell into British hands and even neutral islands were closed to trade.

Conclusion

The main conclusion to be drawn from this is that there was no typical privateering voyage during these two wars. Each geographical area was different and even within a particular area there were major differences between ports. The old pattern of the *guerre de course*, domination by Dunkirk and St Malo, gave way to a surge of interest at Nantes and Bayonne and a relative decline at the English Channel ports which were separated from the areas of growing economic importance. The reason is the close relationship between commercial opportunities that came from privateering and the cycle of trade. Privateering flourished when there was a need for the goods that could not be supplied in the usual way. The interest in privateering at Nantes reflects the commercial prospects that privateering seemed to offer at a particular period. At Bordeaux, by comparison, there was comparatively little privateering, in spite of the earlier importance of the port in colonial trade. This lack of interest was partly because of the effect of the Revolution and subsequent bankruptcies and partly because Portuguese ships supplied the merchants' needs. There was no need to wage war to try and capture the goods. Equally significant, the focus of economic development was shifting to the north and east, and Dunkirk and St Malo were not part of this industrial network. During the Napoleonic period Hamburg replaced the Atlantic ports as the entrepôt for coffee, cotton and other goods and American ships supplied these at lower prices than Nantes and Bordeaux. The economic decline of France during the Napoleonic period offered a limited market for captured goods and nowhere did the scale of privateering match that of the Revolutionary War. Privateering lost most of its incentive: it was always at best a marginal economic activity for most merchants, though not to the men who were employed in the different aspects of it. Success was always elusive and surrounded by myth and legend. What mattered most was the quality of the management of each venture and of the leadership at sea. Successful voyages were a blend of experience, skill and luck and were for this reason comparatively rare.

Notes

1. The following is based on Archives départementales du Pas-de-Calais, 6U, Tribunal de Commerce, Boulogne, the *Génie*.
2. Principally the captain's personal possessions.
3. Public Record Office, Adm 98/107, 26 Dec. 1797.
4. If Edouard Plucket is to be believed, he recruited about 15 Dutch sailors for his venture in February 1793 and subsequently captured eight prizes, two of which were Dutch ships: *Mémoires de Plucket (Pierre Edouard) de Dunkerque; ancien lieutenant de vaisseau et Chevalier de la Légion d'Honneur* (Paris, 1843; new edn, Dunkirk, 1979), 162–3.
5. An unusual case concerned 15 Prussians captured on board a Dutch East Indiaman late in 1795 or early in the following year. They wrote to the Admiralty asking to be released because they were neutrals. The Admiralty, however, decided that because they had been taken on board an enemy merchant ship—the Dutch Republic was at war with Britain—they should remain prisoners. Finally it was decided that because they could not have known about the war when they left India they should be released; Public Record Office, Adm 99/92, Minutes of the Transport Office, ff 68, 92, 6 and 16 Feb. 1796.
6. J.E. Even, 'Les corsaires de l'Adour sur les Côtes nord de l'Espagne, sous la Révolution et l'Empire', XXXVIIe Congrès d'Etudes Régionales, Pau, 1985.
7. *Ibid.*

8. For an estimate of the numbers captured during the Revolutionary and Napoleonic Wars, see P. Crowhurst, *The French War on Trade: Privateering 1793–1815* (Aldershot, 1989), 207–9.

9. Crowhurst, *The French War*, 173. This meant that Britain had a heavier financial burden, which was Napoleon's intention.

10. For example, over 900 men were captured on board Boulogne privateers during the course of the Napoleonic War, of which approximately one-third were taken in 1810; Crowhurst, *The French War*, 209.

11. Some 168 men were captured on Bayonne privateers during 1804; Crowhurst, *The French War*, 209.

12. In the Revolutionary War a total of 28,456 seamen were captured on board French privateers; many were returned comparatively quickly, though there were delays in 1796. During the Napoleonic War 11,841 were captured and most remained in prison in Britain. Crowhurst, *The French War*, 208–9.

13. S. Ville, 'Wages, Prices and Profitability in the Shipping Industry during the Napoleonic Wars; a Case Study' *Journal of Transport History,* 2 (1981), 48–51.

14. P. Zerathe, 'Les origines géographiques et sociales des matelots et officiers mariniers du Port Louis et de Riantec (1750–1762)' *Annales de Bretagne et de Pays de l'Ouest,* 97 (1990), 39–57.

15. A similar case is the 60-ton brigantine *Jeune Emilie*, built in New England in 1783, which sailed from St Malo in 1793; Crowhurst, *The French War*, 88.

16. The example of the *Julie*, fitted out by Felix Cossin at Nantes in 1797, shows the problem clearly. The total cost of construction and fitting out was 196,500 francs. The first cruise produced only 55,457 francs from six prizes ranging from 4,628 to 27,326 francs and the second 56,468 francs from three prizes, of which a Danish prize, the *Anna*, produced over 83,000 francs; Schweizerisches Wirtschaftsarchiv, Basel, Segerhof Archiv, Schiffahrtdokumente, the *Julie*.

17. Eight ships were captured off Cape Clear, another off the Skelligs a little to the west, a third off Cable Island and another in Latitude 46° off the coast of Ireland; the ships that cruised there were from St Malo, Bordeaux, Nantes, Granville, Brest and Morlaix. Public Record Office, H.C.A. 32/609, 867, 844, 513, 579, 672, *Eclair, Triton, Surveillant, Amis de Bordeaux, Adour, Duguay Trouin, Achéron, Grand Indien, Hardi, Invincible Napoléon,* Archives départementales du Morbihan, Lz 1598, *Sans Culottes*, ibid., Lz 939, *Hardi*.

18. P. Butel, 'Les difficultés de commerce maritime bordelais sous le Directoire; example de l'adaptation à la conjoncture de guerre maritime', Quatre Vingt Quatorzième Congrès Nationale des Sociétés Savantes, (Pau, 1969), II, 340.

19. Butel, 'Les difficultés', 344.

20. Crowhurst, *The French War*, 64.

21. Schweizerische Wirtschaftsarchiv, Basel, Segerhof Archiv, Shiffahrtsdokumente, the *Julie*.

22. Archives départementales d'Ille-et-Vilaine, 2 Um/87.

23. Archives départementales d'Ille-et-Vilaine, 2 Um/7, the *Magicienne*.

CHAPTER 10

The Organization of a Privateering Expedition by the Middelburgse Commercie Compagnie, 1747–1748[1]

Corrie Reinders Folmer

Preparing a Privateering Voyage

In 1747, when after 34 years of neutrality the Dutch Republic got involved in the War of the Austrian Succession, the thoughts of merchants engaged in overseas shipping and trading inevitably turned to the possibilities this situation offered for the business of privateering. Especially so if those merchants worked with capital gained in previous privateering enterprises as was the case with the directors of the Middelburgse Commercie Compagnie. This overseas shipping and trading company in the town of Middelburg in Zeeland was founded in 1720, partly with money made from privateering during the War of the Spanish Succession.[2]

By May 1747 and particularly after the occupation of Bergen op Zoom by the French army in September, the directors must already have been toying with the idea of privateering.[3] It was an opportunity to combine patriotic zeal with financial gain. The idea of providing a ship with a letter of commission was first explicitly mentioned in the minutes of the directors' meeting on 29 November 1747.[4] At that time they were fitting out the frigate *Vryheyd* for a trading voyage to St Eustatius. A few days later they decided to apply for a letter of commission as soon as these letters should become available so that the ship would be in a stronger position to defend itself when unexpectedly attacked.[5] At the same meeting they resolved to consult with the members of the company's board of supervision on organizing an active privateering enterprise against the French with one or more ships. In December 1747, at a combined meeting of the directors, the members of the board and the principal shareholders, it was decided unanimously to leave the matter entirely in the directors' hands.[6] Letters were sent to Pieter Buteux, member of the States General for Zeeland, asking for interpretation and clarification of the *Placcaet* issued by the States General on 11 December 1747.[7] This *Placcaet*, or edict, laid down the legal basis for privateering expeditions. On some points the *Placcaet* was somewhat vague or in contradiction with other *Placcaeten* concerning the definition of contraband, ownership of goods, to which ports prize seized ships could be brought, and so forth. The directors wanted to be sure on these matters before they sent their ships out to sea. They also corresponded with their agent in Amsterdam, Jacobus Sappius.[8] By the end of February, after having finally received the official clarification from Their High Worships,[9] they decided to get the ships underway as soon as possible.[10]

In the meantime, on 29 December 1747 they had started preparations by resolving to announce the enterprise open for underwriting by the general public, not only in Zeeland but in Amsterdam as well.[11] This was to be another topic of interest in the correspondence with Sappius.[12] He recommended advertising in the Amsterdam papers like other entrepreneurs were wont to do. The directors decided otherwise and told him that they did not want their planned expedition publicized in this way. It was to be completely clear that they had only embarked on this enterprise out of patriotism and they were certainly not begging for money as if the company was not able to finance a privateering expedition on its own. The company itself was going to keep a large share in the financing, and aspiring participants would only get a share of 25 or 30 thousand guilders per ship at most. It seems they succeeded in getting their message across or the enthusiasm for investing in privateering fell far short of their estimation. Only 13 people ever bought a share in the venture for a grand total of 25,200 guilders for all three ships together.[13]

Problems with Recruitment

On 2 January 1748, the ships to be fitted out as privateers were

Map 10.1   The Netherlands

designated, *viz.* the frigates *Jonge Wilhem*, *Princes van Oranje* and *Prins van Oranje*.[14] The appointment of officers commenced on 9 January, beginning with those for the *Jonge Wilhem*; contracts were put out for great quantities of victuals and ammunition and regulations set up such as those pertaining to the ships' surgeons.[15] On 24 January the signing on of seamen for the *Jonge Wilhem* began in Middelburg and

Vlissingen. Monthly pay was to be 15 guilders, two months down. Not enough men signed on. This was a common occurrence and the directors were not unduly worried. Whenever this had happened in earlier years, they wrote to one of their business relations in Amsterdam or to a middleman asking him to provide the officers and men they needed.[16] Consequently they wrote to Hendrik Edelhoff, a middleman in Amsterdam, asking for men. As the captain of the *Princes van Oranje*, Laurens Kraeg, lived in Amsterdam they wrote to him too.[17] They should have realized things were going to be difficult. As early as November 1747 Sappius and Edelhoff had written about problems in engaging men for the *Vryheyd*.[18] The main reason for these problems lay in the fact that the burgomasters of Amsterdam had ceased issuing permits for the recruiting of seamen in their city.[19] This had been done at the request of the Admiralty of Amsterdam because it had had trouble manning its own ships, a situation which, in the eyes of the company's correspondents, was not going to get any better if the Admiralty kept its pay pegged at 11 guilders per month.[20] The lack of a permit meant that signing on could not be done legally in front of the water-bailiff and with bailsmen who guaranteed the company would get the down payment back in case the seaman failed to enter on board ship in Middelburg.[21] It was a disappointment and a nuisance. But sailors had to be found if the expedition was to go through. Buteux was asked if he could get the *stadthouder*, Prince William IV, or any other authority to intercede for them with the burgomasters.[22] The company's attorney in The Hague, R.A. Hoyman, was also asked to help and Captain Kraeg was sent from Amsterdam to The Hague to impress upon these gentlemen the absolute necessity of getting permission for recruiting. He was even to try to see the Prince personally.[23]

In the meantime the directors worked on a method to evade the prohibition by getting the men to travel to Middelburg themselves where they could then sign on. The recruiting officer in Amsterdam was to promise them reimbursement of their travel expenses.[24] But this ran up against the problem that the crimps in Amsterdam did not want to let the seamen in their control get out of their sight without contracts.[25] On 16 February Sappius wrote that the authorities in Gouda allowed recruiting in their town. The directors were delighted and immediately sent Captain Jacob Dirksen of the *Jonge Wilhem* there, as Gouda was much nearer to Amsterdam than Middelburg. As it turned out, recruiting in Gouda was not permitted![26] Although in practice the prohibition was not adhered to as strictly as in Amsterdam, the results were very discouraging.[27] The efforts to get the Prince interested in the company's plight did not amount to anything either.[28] By mid-April the directors were in such a state of desperation that they were prepared to go to any lengths to get men. Edelhoff was asked if he could find a solution, any solution, but he had nothing to suggest.[29] Especially aggravating was the fact that there was an ample supply of men. At least that was what the directors in Middelburg were told.[30] Finally, on 30 April, they gave up. There was no chance of finding the necessary seamen in sufficient numbers, although the burgomasters of Amsterdam had finally—and unofficially—relented insofar that recruiting was allowed in the surrounding countryside at a distance of at least 100 *roeden*[31] from the city limits.[32] The directors called off the enterprise and told Captains Dirksen and Kraeg to come home.[33] Captain Hendrik de Beer of the *Vryheyd* was to keep on trying as his ship was meant for a regular trading voyage. He was even allowed to offer up to 20 guilders per month, starting immediately, when signing on.[34] All to no avail, for on 14 May the privateers were paid off and on 17 May the decision was taken to withdraw the *Vryheyd*.[35]

The Organization of a Privateering Expedition

During the same months that the directors' representatives were active in Holland, they themselves were very busy in Middelburg. As mentioned above the *Jonge Wilhem*, the *Princes van Oranje* and the *Prins van Oranje* were designated as privateers. At that time the *Jonge Wilhem* and the *Princes van Oranje* had already been commissioned, but the *Prins van Oranje* was still at the building stage. All three frigates, together with the *Vryheyd*, were the largest ships the company possessed. The records of the *Jonge Wilhem* and *Princes van Oranje* are fairly extensive and are easy to differentiate from those of their regular trading voyages. They are also both of the same nature for each ship and provide us with a good insight into the organization of a privateering expedition. The records of the *Prins van Oranje* are few, while those of the *Vryheyd* do not permit us to separate normal fitting-out activities and expenditure from those for potential privateering purposes as the ship was destined for a regular trading voyage to St Eustatius.

The *Jonge Wilhem* was bought in 1745 from the West India Company and had made two round trips to St Eustatius before being fitted out as a privateer in 1747 and 1748.[36] Her overall length was 96 ft and she could carry 94 last. On the trading voyages to St Eustatius the ship mounted 16 4-pounder guns and carried a crew of 37.[37] For privateering use she was to be armed with 36 guns.[38] The planned crew was to number between 250 and 275.[39] The *Princes van Oranje* was built in Zaandam in 1745 and bought on 8 August 1747.[40] Her overall length was 105¾ ft and she measured 105 last.[41] The company had not yet used the ship for a regular trading voyage before fitting her out as a privateer. For the voyage to the West Indies after the war, however, she was mounted with 26 guns and 81 men.[42] For privateering use she was to carry 30 guns and 220 men.[43]

Although the hundreds of extra seamen, necessary to go privateering, were never found, the Zeeland labour supply in January was not too bad. Jacob Dirksen was appointed captain of the *Jonge Wilhem* on 9 January 1748. Probably because he was the first one of the company's captains to enlist crew, he managed to find a nearly full complement of officers, petty officers and other 'specialists' totalling 43 men including himself. Their pay ranged from 72 guilders for the captain (12 guilders more than the normal 60) to 40 for the mates to 19 for the quartermasters and 14 for the cook's second mate. The able seamen received 15 guilders a month, which was 2 to 3 guilders more than in the years shortly before the war. Apprentice seamen and boys got between 12 and 6 guilders (see Appendix 10.1). The muster-roll shows 59 names in these categories, which means the ship still lacked approximately 150 seamen when the expedition was called off. Of this total of 102 men, 60 gave a town in Zeeland as their place of origin. Twenty men came from other parts of the Dutch Republic. The remaining 22 were foreigners. The captain himself was from Fredrikstad (Schleswig-Holstein?) but he had been in the company's service since 1734 and wrote Dutch very well.[44] As was usual, the men's wages started on the day the ship actually put to sea, although they were expected to assist in making the vessel shipshape and bringing her out into the roads. It is no wonder they became restless as time passed by. On 27 March they petitioned the directors to start their wages as they had fulfilled their obligations to make the ship ready for sailing.[45] Although obviously very unhappy with setting a precedent, the directors resolved to begin wages on 1 April.[46]

On the *Princes van Oranje*, Laurens Kraeg was appointed captain on 16 January 1748.[47] Hiring in Zeeland for his ship began on 4 March. Thirty-eight men signed on in Middelburg, eight of whom were reimbursed for their travel expenses. Captain Dirksen's recruiting activities in Gouda and Amsterdam between 27 March and 3 May enlisted another 25 men. Thirty-three of the total fell within the category of officers, petty officers and 'specialists', and 27 signed on as able seamen. Three boys completed the list. The captain himself (not included in these lists) came from Amsterdam. He had served the company once before, as captain of the *Jonge Wilhem* on her second voyage to St Eustatius. Eight men came from Zeeland, 15 from other parts of the Republic, and the remaining 40 were foreigners.[48] Their wages were the same as those for the crew of the *Jonge Wilhem*. However, it was clear by March that the local labour supply had run dry and men of foreign origin—normally found in Amsterdam—were not available.

We find no instances of an able seaman being paid more than 15 guilders. Of course in privateering monthly wages were not all a man expected when signing on. The chances of prize money probably figured greatly in the men's minds. In signing on they accepted and signed the *Articulen ende Ordre* that spelled out the kind of voyage the ship was going to make, the conditions of employment, their rights and duties, and last but not least the apportioning of their due parts in the spoils should their ship take a prize.[49] Besides the *ordinaire plunderinge* the whole crew was entitled to 10 per cent of the net income in various proportions according to their rank (see Appendix 1). For example, the captain received 40 portions, the boatswain 12 and an able seaman three.[50]

Ships and Equipment

Apart from the important and, as it turned out, decisive business of finding enough crew, the ships themselves had to be fitted out, repaired and altered if necessary, and more guns mounted. As the possibility of damage due to fighting had to be taken into account a good supply of spare material for repairs at sea had to be on board. The sources give no data on exactly what kind of work was done on the ships themselves. Only the cost of raw materials and labour in port is given.[51] Quite a number of items on the list of expenses for the *Jonge Wilhem* have to do with the mounting of and trials with the guns and with the purchase of small arms and powder.[52] The expense account of the *Princes van Oranje* is almost totally lacking in these items. Either the ship must have been in perfect fighting condition or—more probably—the directors never got as far as making arrangements. The accounts of both ships show the wages paid to personnel, including the recruiting costs.[53]

Very prominent in the accounts are the expenses for food and drink.[54] Victualling lists show what kind of food the directors planned for each of the ships and the amount per man per day. Provisions had to be adequate for a period of six months. In some instances there were different qualities for use in the cabin and for the men. Some delicacies were obviously for cabin use only, such as ox tongues and French brandy.[55] The lists are too extensive to give many details but the following may serve as an example: groats 1½ sacks a day for the whole crew; bread at 4 lb per man per week; butter 5¼ lb per 7 men per week; bacon 2 lb per man per week. The other main articles of food and drink were stockfish, salt beef, peas, cheese, beer and wine. Added to this were smaller quantities of smoked ham and beef, speciality cheeses, sugar, spices, dried fruits and coffee beans. Candles, tallow and lamp oil were also required.

Not all of these goods were in fact bought and paid for in full. The directors probably slowed down their purchases when recruiting turned out to be difficult. Nevertheless, the shipbooks show a total expenditure of 36,637 guilders on the fitting out of the *Jonge Wilhem*[56] and 23,796 guilders on the *Princes van Oranje*.[57] In these amounts the value of the ship itself is not included. The *Jonge Wilhem* was estimated at 6,600 guilders on return from St Eustatius on 14 September 1747, and the same estimate was also used when starting the accounts of the trading voyage after the war.[58] The *Princes van Oranje* was bought for 30,000 guilders and this was also the starting value for the voyage of 1749–52.[59] Not all the expenditure on the ships was lost when the privateering venture was called off. Quite a lot of the stores were used for the voyages after the war and for the fitting out of other company ships generating proceeds of 19,223 guilders for the *Jonge Wilhem* and 12,484 guilders for her consort. Net losses therefore amounted to 28,726 guilders, 17,414 arising from the *Jonge Wilhem* and 11,312 from the *Princes van Oranje*.

To complete the accounts of the privateering venture of the Middelburgse Commercie Compagnie, we have to add the loss incurred in building the *Prins van Oranje*. Although never explicitly mentioned as such, it is highly probable that the directors had privateering in mind when they started building the ship in May 1747 in the neighbouring dock in Middelburg specially rented for this occasion from the West India Company.[60] Although she was not finished in time to go to sea, the records contain her letter of commission dated 26 February 1748. It mentions the captain, Jan Jansen de Jonge, who was appointed on 16 January 1748.[61] No other crew was ever hired, although some victuals were contracted.[62] By the end of 1748 the ship appeared on the company's balance-sheet at a total value of 33,208 guilders.[63] In August 1749 the directors decided the *Prins van Oranje* would be of no further use to them and tried to sell her.[64] They could not find commercial buyers for their *extraordinaris* ship.[65] To prevent further expenses she was finally sold in 1750 to the Admiralty of Zeeland for 39,500 guilders at a loss of 4,079 guilders.[66]

The case of the *Vryheyd*, the fourth ship involved in the privateering plans of the company, is different. This frigate was the largest ship the company owned and measured an overall length of 113.5 ft with a carrying capacity of 130 last.[67] During her four round trips to the Caribbean in the years 1738–47, she had mounted between 24 and 28 guns and carried from 76 to 105 men.[68] On 1 August 1747 the directors had decided on another voyage to St Eustatius and ordered Captain Hendrik de Beer to start preparations.[69] In Middelburg and Vlissingen recruiting began on 31 October, offering an able seaman 16 guilders a month, two months down. Not enough crew could be found in Zeeland and a letter went out to Edelhoff in Amsterdam asking him to hire a total of 46 officers and men as cheaply as possible.[70] As we know, this proved an impossible task and on 17 May the voyage was called off. The ship still lacked men, the cargo had been stowed for such a long time that it had deteriorated appreciably and, last but not least, now that the war was over profits of a trip to St Eustatius were doubtful.[71] In August 1749—at the same time as they were deliberating on the *Prins van Oranje*—the directors decided that this ship too could not be of further use to the company.[72] No buyers came forward. Finally in 1753 the *Vryheyd* was broken up.[73]

Luckily the finances of the company had been in pretty good shape at the beginning of the whole venture, thanks to some very good returns from their shipping and trade to Africa and the Caribbean in 1746 and 1747.[74] As the fitting out of the three ships was never completed we do not know the extent of capital necessary for the whole of the projected enterprise. Neither do the sources provide us with enough data to make a reasonably reliable estimate. But the company could easily afford the sums spent between January and May 1748. Nevertheless the loss of 28,726 guilders on privateering weighed heavily on the annual result for 1748 as the books show a deficit of

18,993 guilders for that year.[75] Naturally this was very different from what the directors had hoped for but in no way disastrous. There is no evidence of any final settlement with the 13 outside participants. They received their money back and that was it.

Conclusions

With hindsight we cannot help but wonder whether the directors had not been somewhat overly optimistic when they decided on fitting out ships for privateering. There is no reason to doubt their initial patriotic enthusiasm and expectations of handsome profits, but they severely underestimated the problems of hiring the large crews necessary. We can only speculate on their reasons for keeping at it through the months of March and April. Fear of loss of face in their local community may have had something to do with it, as did possibly a lack of knowledge about the progress of the peace talks at Aix-la-Chapelle. They may have been lucky to escape with a relatively light loss. On 5 May 1748, Hoyman wrote to the directors that the peace preliminaries ending the War of the Austrian Succession had been signed in Aix-la-Chapelle on 30 April.[76] In the end, they themselves laid the blame for the failure squarely on those Amsterdammers who begrudged the Zeelanders success in their enterprises.[77]

Although the enterprise itself was a failure and we will never know what the financial results might have been if the ships had ever sailed, the surviving records provide us with a good insight into the way such a privateering expedition was set up in the middle of the eighteenth century. In a kind of microcosm we find several elements already mentioned by Verhees-van Meer for the beginning of the century.[78] In the *Vryheyd* we have a regular (albeit fair-sized and fairly heavily armed) merchant ship on a normal trading trip furnished with a letter of commission to be used in defending herself in a possible confrontation with ships of the French enemy. The *Jonge Wilhem* and *Princes van Oranje* were the same kind of ship but manned and armed intentionally for seeking out enemy ships to inflict losses on French trade and make a profit in doing so. On the other hand, it seems that the directors unwittingly crossed the vague borderline between merchant and navy ships in building the *Prins van Oranje*. When finished, the ship turned out to be unsuitable for mercantile use and ended up with the Admiralty. Another aspect is the strict legality with which the directors wanted to conduct their business. There is absolutely no hint of the slightly unsavoury piratical flavour that sometimes seems to accompany privateering. This privateering expedition was organized and was going to be executed as an honourable combination of war and business within the laws of the land.

Notes

1. The main sources for this chapter can be found in the Rijksarchief Zeeland, Middelburg, The Netherlands, where the extensive records of the Middelburgse Commercie Compagnie (MCC) are kept. If not otherwise stated all numbers in the notation are from the inventory of those records.
2. W.S. Unger, *Het archief der Middelburgsche Commercie Compagnie* ('s-Gravenhage, 1952), 3–4. J.Th.H. Verhees-van Meer, *De Zeeuwse Kaapvaart tijdens de Spaanse Successieoorlog 1702–1713* (Middelburg, 1986), 136–57.
3. At this time the management of the company was in the hands of the following six directors, the year of their appointment in brackets: Casparus Ribaut (1720); Abraham van de Bussche (1733); Hendrik Boursse (1724); Bartholomeus van de Coppello (1734); Abraham Claudore (1733); Daniël Jansz. Schorer (1734)
4. MCC 19 *Notulen* (=Minutes of the directors' meetings), 24 Nov. 1747.
5. MCC 19, 29 Nov. 1747.
6. MCC 19, 28 Dec. 1747.
7. MCC 94, letters to Pieter Buteux, The Hague, 29 and 30 Dec. 1747. MCC 95, letters to Buteux, 3 and 6 Jan. 1748.
8. MCC 95, letter to Jacobus Sappius, Amsterdam, 2 Jan. 1748. MCC 65, letter from Sappius, 8 Jan. 1748.
9. MCC 1562, Certified extract from the Resolutions of the States General, 14 Feb. 1748.
10. MCC 19, 23 and 27 Feb. 1748.
11. MCC 19, 29 Dec. 1747. MCC 660, unfinished draft of certificate of participation.
12. MCC 65, letter from Sappius, 8 Jan. 1748. MCC 95, letter to Sappius, 12 Jan. 1748.
13. MCC 1562, 'Lijst van intekenaers . . .' from 5 Jan. through 20 Feb. 1748. MCC 1562, 'Conditie na welke de Directeuren . . . de vryheyt geven . . . Intrest te nemen . . .'. Certificates of participation in the fitting out of the *Jonge Wilhem*, the *Princes van Oranje* and the *Prins van Oranje*.
14. MCC 19, 2 Jan. 1748 ff.
15. MCC 19, 9 Jan. 1748. Unlike the usual practice of the company, the ships surgeons were to be examined upon their qualifications by a doctor of medicine before they were engaged.
16. MCC 19, 15 Sept. and 7 Nov. 1747.
17. MCC 95, letters to Hendrik Edelhoff and Laurens Kraeg, Amsterdam, 26 Jan. 1748.
18. MCC 65, letters from Sappius and Edelhoff, 10, 11, 17 and 21 Nov. 1747.
19. MCC 19, 6 Feb. 1748. MCC 95, letter to Buteux, 13 Feb. 1748. Gemeente Archief Amsterdam, Archief Burgemeesteren nr. 5023, 11e Groot Memoriaal, 40–41.

20. MCC 65, letters from Sappius, 28 Nov. and 9 Dec. 1747; from Edelhoff, 1 Dec. 1747; from Hendrik de Beer, 28 Dec. 1747; from Kraeg, 31 Jan. 1748. MCC 78, letters from Rudolf Abraham Hoyman, The Hague, 17 Feb. 1748; from Kraag, 8 Mar. 1748. J.R. Bruijn, *De Admiraliteit van Amsterdam in rustige jaren, 1713–1751: Regenten en financiën, schepen en zeevarenden* (Amsterdam, 1970), 157–61.

21. MCC 95, letter to Edelhoff, 6 Feb. 1748.

22. MCC 95, letter to Buteux, 6 Feb. 1748.

23. MCC 19, 13 Feb. 1748; MCC 95, letters to Buteux, Hoyman and Kraeg, 13 and 14 Feb. 1748. MCC 78, letter from The Hague from Kraeg, 8 Mar. 1748: he was received by the Stadtholder and had spoken with him for over 15 minutes. His Serene Highness had listened very carefully and told him to petition the States General.

24. MCC 19, 6 Feb. 1748.

25. MCC 65, letters from Sappius, 30 Jan. 1748; from Kraeg, 8 Feb. 1748. Kraeg wrote on 19 Apr. 1748 that the men could not come even if they wanted to because they were not their own masters on account of their debts to the crimps. In 1780 the same situation existed according to G.J.A. Raven, 'Aanhoudend sukkelen om bootsvolk' *Tijdschrift voor Zeegeschiedenis*, 2 (1982), 134.

26. MCC 65, letter from Sappius, 16 Feb. 1748. MCC 95, letters to Sappius, 19 and 27 Feb. 1748; letter to Dirksen, 23 Feb. 1748. MCC 19, 5 and 19 Mar. 1748.

27. While Captain Kraeg of the *Princes* was travelling between Amsterdam and The Hague, Captain Dirksen of the *Wilhem* travelled between Gouda and Amsterdam in search of men. On 27 March he managed in Gouda to get six men to sign on for the *Princes*. In Amsterdam he found five men between 14 and 18 April and a further 14 men in the beginning of May.

28. MCC 19, 19 Mar. 1748.

29. MCC 95, letters to Sappius and Edelhoff, 19 Apr. 1748.

30. MCC 65, letters from Edelhoff, 5 Jan. 1748; from Kraeg, 31 Jan. and 8 Feb. 1748. MCC 95, letters to Buteux, 13 Feb. 1748; to Dirksen, 19 Apr. 1748.

31. 1 *Roede*=appr. 3.68 metres.

32. MCC 19, 22 Apr. 1748. MCC 65, letters from Kraeg, 25 and 30 Apr. 1748. MCC 78, letter from Hoyman, 29 Apr. 1748.

33. MCC 95, letters to Edelhoff, Sappius, Dirksen and Kraeg, 30 Apr. 1748.

34. MCC 19, 30 Apr. 1748. MCC 95, letter to De Beer, 30 Apr. 1748.

35. MCC 19, 14 and 17 May 1748.

36. MCC 646 *Scheepsboek* = shipbook. Purchase price 8500. MCC 655 Printed notice for sale.

37. MCC 646, and a separate enclosed Certificate of registry (dated 15 November 1747) from the Admiralty of Zeeland. The company, however, used a different method of measuring from the Admiralty, which in most cases resulted in higher figures. If available I use the dimensions the company itself used. 1 last=2 ton.

38. 10 eight-pounders, 18 six-pounders and 8 lighter ones.

39. MCC 660.

40. MCC 948 *Scheepsboek*, 6. The ship was then named *Marseliaanse Galey*, owner Lambert Fokkes in Amsterdam, purchase price 30,000 guilders.

41. MCC 956. In this case all sources agree on the tonnage but differ concerning the

length. The Admiralty of Amsterdam measured the ship's length *binnen steven* (from bowsprits to stern post) as 99 ft while the builder, Pieter Lynse Roggemeester at Zaandam, and the harbour authorities in Amsterdam, give 105¾ ft *lang over steve* (forward of bowsprit to after stern post) which is also the length used by the company.

42. MCC 948, 6. MCC 949 *Monsterrol* 10 Jan. 1749.
43. MCC 948, 1 (28 six-pounders, 2 four-pounders and 2 three-pounders).
44. MCC 659 'Monsterrol ter Kaap, Jonge Wilhem, 1747'. MCC 660 'Lijst van de maentgelden . . . Jonge Wilhem . . .'. The only 'specialists' not found were one mate, two sailmakers and one gunner's mate.
45. MCC 648.
46. MCC 19, 29 Mar. 1748.
47. MCC 19, 16 Jan. 1748.
48. MCC 951 'Monsterrolle ter kaap . . . Princes van Orange . . . begonnen . . . 4 maart 1748.' MCC 952 'Lijst van de maentgelden . . . Princes van orange . . .'. MCC 952 'Rolle van het gehuurde manschap . . . Princes van Oranje . . .'.
49. MCC 660 'Articulen . . . Jonge Wilhem . . .'. MCC 952 'Articulen . . . Princes van Orange . . .'.
50. MCC 19, 6 Feb. 1748. The directors gave as their reasoning that everything was to be done as was usual in the previous war. By *ordinaire plunderinge* or normal plunder was meant the right of the crew to the personal possessions of the prize's crew (Verhees, *Zeeuwse Kaapvaart*, 54–55).
51. MCC 646, 110, *Jonge Wilhem* 2,655. MCC 948, 1, *Princes van Oranje* 2,090. The local currency in Zeeland was the pound Flemish. For convenience sake I use the Dutch (Holland) guilder. The rate of exchange was: 1 Flemish = 6 Holland. Amounts of less than one guilder are disregarded.
52. MCC 646, 107–10. Powder to the amount of 2,661 guilders.
53. MCC 646 *Jonge Wilhem* 5,196 guilders. MCC 948 *Princes van Oranje* 2,664 guilders.
54. MCC 646 *Jonge Wilhem*: bread 1,663 guilders, other foodstuffs 10,742 guilders. MCC 948 *Princes van Oranje*: bread 1452 guilders, other foodstuffs 5,511 guilders.
55. MCC 949 'Lyst wegens de victualie . . . Princesse van Orange voor 6 maanden voor 220 coppen'. MCC 1562 Victualling list for the *Jonge Wilhem* for six months for 250 hands, put out for contract 6 January 1748. This list stated also the amount of ammunition needed for the guns at 70 shots per gun, as well as the small arms with their shot and powder. The same kind of list for the *Princes van Oranje* for 220 hands.
56. MCC 646, 110.
57. MCC 948, 3.
58. MCC 646, 105 and 113 resp.
59. MCC 948, 6.
60. MCC 19, 5 May 1747. MCC 957.
61. MCC 1562. MCC 19, 16 Jan. 1748.
62. MCC 19, 26 Jan. 1748.
63. MCC 1694, 170.
64. MCC 19, 5 and 12 Aug. 1749.

65. MCC 19, 16 Aug. 1749. The ship's overall length was 110 ft and it could mount 42 guns. Tonnage was not given.
66. MCC 19, 23 Feb. 1750. MCC 957. MCC 1695, 43. The Admiralty renamed the ship *Jonge Prins van Oranje.*
67. MCC 1263, 1.
68. MCC 1263, 1, 33, 66 and 94
69. MCC 19, 1 Aug. 1747.
70. MCC 94, letters to Edelhoff, 20 Oct., 7 and 14 Nov. 1747.
71. MCC 19, 17 May 1748.
72. MCC 19, 5 and 12 Aug. 1749.
73. MCC 20, 7 Nov. 1752. MCC 1263, 193–6. MCC 1695, 44.
74. MCC 1694, 133: 1746 a profit of 30,008 guilders; 166: 1747 a profit of 130,710 guilders.
75. MCC 1694, 184.
76. MCC 78, letter from Hoyman, 5 May 1748.
77. MCC 95, letter to Dirksen, 26 Apr. 1748.
78. Verhees-van Meer, *Zeeuwse Kaapvaart*, 39–46.

Appendix 10.1

Crew as planned for the projected privateering venture of the *Jonge Wilhem* January 1748

Rank	number	monthly pay in guilders	portions of the 10%
Kapitein (Captain)	1	72	40
Opperluitenant (1st lieutenant)	1	60	32
Onderluitenant (2nd lieutenant)	1	54	28
Derde luitenant (3rd lieutenant)	1	50	25
Schipper (master)	2	40	20
Stuurman (mate)	6	40	17
Secretaris (clerk)	1	30	13
Bootsman (boatswain)	1	30	12
Bootsmansmaat (boatswain's mate)	2	19	8
Schieman (boatswain's mate)	1	25	12
Schiemansmaat (boatswain's mate)	1	19	8
Constabel (master gunner)	1	25	12
Constabelsmaat (gunner's mate)	2	19	8
Oppermeester (master surgeon)	1	42	13
Seconde meester (2nd surgeon)	1	30	10
Ondermeester (surgeon's mate)	2	21	8
Kok (cook)	1	25	12
Koksmaat (cook's mate)	2	14–19	8
Bottelier (steward)	1	25	12
Botteliersmaat (steward's mate)	2	19	8
Opperzeilmaker (sailmaker)	1	?	10

Appendix 1—*continued*

Rank	number	monthly pay in guilders	portions of the 10%
Onderzeilmaker (sailmaker's mate)	1	?	6
Oppertimmerman (ship's carpenter)	1	40	12
Ondertimmerman (carpenter's mate)	2	28	8
Kwartiermeester (quartermaster)	8	19	8
Kuiper (cooper)	1	19	8
Scheepscorporaal (ship's corporal)	1	22	10
Scheepscorporaalsmaat (corporal's mate)	1	18	5
Trompetter (trumpeter, bugler)	?	?	10
Tamboer (drummer)	?	?	8
Matroos (able seaman)	c. 200	15	3
Oploper (apprentice seaman)	6	10–12	?
Jongen (ship's boy)	11	6–10	1

Buglers and drummers usually signed on as able seamen but could receive a somewhat higher wage. In the lists they are not separately named, however, and it is not clear if any were engaged.

As the ship never had a full complement of able seamen we do not know how many would have been signed on if there had been a sufficient labour supply. Assuming that the total crew size was between 250 and 275, approximately 200 able seamen would have been required. The number of apprentice seamen and boys is that of the (young) men actually engaged.

Sources: MCC 659 and 660.

CHAPTER 11

The Risky Alternative: Dutch Privateering During the Fourth Anglo-Dutch War, 1780–1783

Jan van Zijverden

The Fourth Anglo-Dutch War, 1780–1783

On 20 December 1780 Great Britain declared war on the Dutch Republic, by means of the publication of the 'Manifesto'. This was the culmination of a series of disputes between the two sea-powers. The origin of their discord can be found in the struggle between the 13 rebellious colonies in North America and Britain, which started in 1775.

As early as 1775 an extensive smuggling trade grew up between Dutch traders on St Eustatius and the American rebels. This smuggling enabled the rebels to replenish their stock of arms, munitions and other equipment needed for the war. In March 1778 Britain declared war on France because of the treaty on trade and friendship that the French had concluded with the American rebels. Merchants from the Dutch Republic exploited an excellent opportunity to start a neutral trade with the belligerents, especially France, taking full advantage of the old rule of 'free ship, free goods'. This rule entailed that when a vessel sailed under neutral colours, the cargo should be considered neutral too. This had been laid down in 1674 in the Treaty on Commerce and Navigation between the Dutch Republic and Britain.

Dutch merchants supplying France and the American rebels with armaments were, however, not acceptable to the British government.

Sir Joseph Yorke, the British ambassador in the Dutch Republic, regularly protested to the States General about the course of action adopted by Dutch merchants. In September 1780 a draft contract between merchants of Amsterdam and the rebellious colonies was found on board the *Mercury*. According to H.M. Scott this contract was in reality: 'a piece of commercial opportunism by Holland's leading town and aimed only to secure for its merchants a privileged position, should the Americans gain independence'. For the British government it was the legal grounds for declaring war on the Dutch Republic.[1]

So the Dutch policy of neutrality and the possibility it afforded for making profits from it came to nought. Willem V, the stadtholder of Holland, allowed the armaments trade with France only under the pressure from merchants, pro-French patriots and the French government. This trade was indispensable to France, and was one of the most important areas of trade for the Dutch Republic. On the other hand, Willem V tried to keep in with the British government by doing his best to impose restraints on this trade. Eventually this policy of neutrality resulted in the British declaration of war on 20 December 1780.

In January 1783 an armistice was concluded, followed in 1784 by a peace treaty. During the war only one minor sea battle took place, the battle of the Dogger Bank on 5 August 1781. Both parties claimed a victory.

Maritime Forces

The Dutch navy was almost halved in size between 1714 and 1750. Because of the enormous expenses incurred during the War of the Spanish Succession (1702–13), the Dutch Boards of the Admiralty had run into debt. They were unable to keep their ships in repair and they could not even begin to think about replacing old ships. This state of affairs was reinforced by the policy of neutrality which had been pursued by the Dutch government since 1714. Despite the Treaty on Defence of 1678, between Britain and the Dutch Republic, the latter stayed out of the wars that were waged by the British.[2] This treaty made the necessity of a Dutch fleet which was able to compete with the British fleet more or less superfluous. In the middle of the eighteenth century the size and quality of the Dutch fleet reached its lowest ebb. In the second half of the century the fleet was slowly improved, as is shown in Table 11.1.

Table 11.1
The Size of the Dutch Fleet 1741–1782[3]

Guns	1741	1751	1761	1771	1779	Dec. 1780	Oct. (on the 1782 stocks)	
SHIPS OF THE LINE								
96–80	1	0	0	0	0	0	0	
87–70	6	5	5	4	4	3	7	(6)
68–60	9	9	7	8	9	9	20	(8)
56–50	18	16	17	13	15	15	12	(0)
TOTAL	34	30	29	25	28	27	39	(14)
FRIGATES								
48–40	16	9	8	6	7	7	15	(2)
38–34	3	2	9	15	16	14	12	(0)
28–20	6	5	11	18	18	13	15	(0)
18–12	3	4	2	2	3	0	0	(0)
TOTAL	28	20	30	41	44	34	42	(2)
TOTAL FLEET	62	50	59	66	72	61	81	(16)
Average age in (years)	12	14	12	13	17	?	?	?

In 1771 the total Dutch fleet consisted of 66 ships, 25 of which were considered ships of the line. Of these only 20 could be used on active service, the other five being in a deplorable condition. For the next six years, 'country-provinces' and 'sea-provinces' were engaged in a battle with each other, the former wanting to enlarge the army, the latter to refit the fleet.[4] The final outcome was the construction of a limited number of new ships of the line. In the autumn of 1780, 36 men-of-war were ready for active service. This number was much fewer than the Boards of the Admiralty thought necessary for the defence of Dutch trade. In this condition the Dutch navy was unable to provide an adequate convoy service for the merchant marine.[5] During the war itself the Boards of the Admiralty built a wide range of new ships.

The British navy, meanwhile, was confronted in the Channel by the superior force of a combined Franco-Spanish fleet. Therefore from 1778 onwards the British stationed their 'European' fleet in the Channel. In spite of the fact that the British 'Channel' fleet was smaller in number and of inferior quality, it succeeded in beating off several enemy attacks. In view of its lack of quality, the Channel fleet was only capable of taking defensive action.[6] There was not only a shortage of ship's tackle, but the navy also had to cope with a manpower problem.[7] Seamen were not only scarce but also mostly unskilled. It was in this condition that Britain went to war with the Dutch Republic, which added an extra burden to the tasks of the Channel fleet.

In contrast to the Dutch fleet, the British were capable of organizing convoys for the merchant marine. However, the quality and number of the ships that were used for escorting merchantmen left much to be desired: 'The forces available for the North Sea were therefore very much the left-overs and there could be no hope of offensive operations.'[8] At the time Britain went to war with the Dutch Republic, a part of the Channel fleet was brought into action for this convoy service. The British Admiralty tried to provide regular convoys, especially to the Baltic. Trade with the Baltic was of great importance to the British because of the supply of naval stores from this area. Coastal trade and fishing was protected as well as possible. Because of the enormous variety of routes and voyages undertaken, protection was very difficult. Pearsall concludes that the British convoy service 'were successful in the main object of maintaining British trade. The convoys were effective in preventing losses and only a few losses along the coast were reported of ships sailing independently.'[9]

The Dutch Merchant Marine During the War

Overseas trade played a very important role during the Fourth Anglo-Dutch War. The British tried to blockade Dutch trade while maintaining their own. The Dutch, on the other hand, tried to advance their own commerce. The British seemed to be fairly successful in the disruption of Dutch trade. On this subject Marcus writes: 'Before their [the Dutch] fleet could be fitted out their trade had been driven off the seas.'[10] Scott even calls this a 'devastating onslaught on Dutch shipping and commerce'.[11] During the war 129 Dutch vessels were captured by British privateers and another 195 by the British navy.[12] By far the majority of these vessels were taken during the first three months of the war.[13] I believe that this was due to the position of the British fleet in the Channel, and the enormous number of privateers that was stationed there.[14] Most of the Dutch homeward-bound ships were unaware of the war with Britain, and thus it was very easy for the British navy and privateers to catch these unwary victims. This is confirmed by the research on British privateering by Starkey. From his results one may conclude that Dutch merchantmen were especially threatened by privateers sailing out of southern English ports.[15]

At first the States General could do no more than forbid ships to leave Dutch ports until all necessary measures had been taken. Indeed, in January 1781, the States General forbade all ships in Dutch ports to put to sea. With the intention of fitting out as many men-of-war as possible, they also forbade the export of naval stores and the charter or selling of ships to foreign countries. The poor condition of the Dutch navy made regular convoys an impossibility and the recovery of the navy was considerably speeded up. Meanwhile the merchant marine had to languish unemployed in the Dutch ports. Gradually all resolutions concerning the putting out and selling of ships were abandoned. On 15 November 1781 all ships were allowed to sail, with the exception of large fishing boats and whaling ships. On 15 November the prohibition on the sale of ships was abrogated.

Research has shown that only during the first few months of the war was Dutch shipping really at a standstill. At the beginning of 1781 Dutch shipping seems to have fallen into decay but half-way through the same year shipping had made a strong recovery. In 1782 it had almost reached pre-war levels. In 1783 shipping was once more at a normal level.[16]

Did neutral traders take over Dutch trade or were Dutch merchants, in spite of the British threat, not afraid to put to sea under Dutch colours? Previous research has shown that Dutch shipowners neutralized their vessels on a large scale. Dutch shipowners organized sham-auctions to neutral foreign trading-companies. From March 1781 requests were made to the States General to sell merchantmen to foreign countries.[17] These requests were almost all without fail immediately conceded, although this remained officially forbidden by the same States General until November 1781. In Amsterdam and Rotterdam about 715 merchantmen were neutralized. For the country as a whole the number may have been closer to 900 merchantmen.[18] The number of ships which made up the Dutch merchant marine is not precisely known but it is thought to have been 1,871 ships in 1786.[19]

Between them British privateers and the navy seized 324 Dutch merchantmen. Almost all of these 324 ships were taken during the first three months of the war during which Dutch vessels were still sailing under Dutch colours, because there were as yet no neutralized vessels! So one might say with some truth that neutralizing ships was a fairly successful way of defending the merchant marine.

Dutch Privateering During the Fourth Anglo-Dutch War, December 1780–January 1783

Twenty-nine Dutch privateers were fitted out during the Fourth Anglo-Dutch War. Compared to previous wars, this number of privateers is particularly small.[20] The first Dutch privateers only put to sea from June 1781; most of the privateers from Zeeland were only fitted out in 1782.

On 12 January 1781 Willem V was permitted by the States General to write out letters of commission. It is remarkable that it was three weeks before these letters of commission were actually issued. Usually privateers were fitted out as soon as war broke out so as to capture merchantmen which were not yet aware of the state of war or could not reach a safe port in time. However, since British merchantmen were already protected against American, French and Spanish enemies, the chance of finding any non-protected English merchantmen on the high seas was fairly small. Therefore there was little incentive for Dutch shipowners to fit out privateers as soon as the war had broken out. The Dutch government supported privateering in many ways. The States General offered premiums for seizing hostile ships-of-war, they reduced the warrants for privateers who were putting to sea and they established an indemnification for privateer-owners in the event of a peace treaty being concluded within one year. In spite of this positive attitude taken towards privateering by the Dutch government, the number of privateers remained small.[21]

Before a letter of commission could be acquired, a privateering company had to be established. These privateering companies were usually 'share-holder companies' so that the high risks of the business

Table 11.2
Dutch Privateers by Home Port 1781–1783[22]

Zeeland		Holland		Other	
Vlissingen	9	Rotterdam	5	Palermo (Italy)	1
Vlissingen		Amsterdam	5	Unknown	1
Middelburg	1	Maassluis	1		
Veere	1	Dordrecht	1		
Middelburg	1	Den Haag	1		
Zierikzee	2				
Total	14	Total	13	Total	2

were spread out. To fit out a privateer was an expensive business and success could not be guaranteed. The manager-owner of a privateering company was the person who was responsible for the financial part of the voyage and the fitting-out of the privateer. A manager-owner usually came from the 'shipping world', and could use his contacts to get the best result. Closer examination shows that most of the manager-owners also held high positions in the local community. Frequently they took charge of more than one vessel. The other share-holders were often members of the manager-owner's family, the captain of the privateer or people connected with the shipping business. In this war, too, most of the privateers originated from Zeeland, with Vlissingen once again the most important port for privateering activities, as is shown in Table 11.2.

The North Sea and the Channel, sometimes very close to the English coast, became the theatre of operations for most of these privateers. Hostilities were forbidden in the Sound and the Baltic.[23] Most Dutch privateers steered clear of this area, with the exception of Henri Koelberg. This Swedish captain of the Dutch privateer *Veerenaar* attacked British vessels close to the Swedish coast. The British government protested to the Swedish Crown about his activities.[24] Although difficult, it was definitely worthwhile to cross the Channel. The most successful Dutch privateers were *de Goede Verwachting* and the *Vlissinger*. These privateers operated most frequently close to the French coast.[25] The privateers which did cross the Channel probably attacked the British coastal trade. This is shown by the cargoes of the captured vessels: of 22 seized vessels six were loaded with coal and seven were fishermen.[26]

During the Fourth Anglo-Dutch War the fast-sailing cutter was the most favoured type of vessel for Dutch privateering activities. These cutters, which were relatively heavily armed, were small, fast and manoeuvrable vessels. They could easily be used in the choppy waters of the Channel. For this reason they were especially used by smugglers and the excise.[27] Since Dutch privateers operated in the North Sea and the Channel it is likely that they preferred the cutter for the same reasons. In his article on privateering during the Second and Third Anglo-Dutch Wars, Bruijn also indicated that there is a relation between the size of a privateer and its theatre of operations.[28]

The average crew on board a privateer consisted of 86 seamen.[29] This is considerably less than in the War of the Spanish Succession. It was certainly due to the use of the cutter as privateer vessel, a factor

Table 11.3
Size and origin of Dutch Privateering Crews[30]

Name vessel	Number	Du	Fr	Br	Swe	Dan	Other	Cap	Dep.	Dep.
Amazone	78	x	x	–	x		Var.	Du	Du	Du
Doggersbank	85	x		5			Var.	USA	Du	USA
Gooten Turc	13		x	–			Var.	Fr	Fr	Fr
Hercules	162	x		–			Var.	Du	Du	—
Mars	140	x		–	x			Du	Swe	Swe
Middelburger	34	x	x	–			Var.	Fr	Fr	Fr
Valk	37	x	x	–	x	x		Fr	Swe	–
Vliegende Visch	35	x		–	x	x	Ge	Du	Du	Du
Vlijt	14			2			Var.	No	Mal	Swi
Zeeuwsche Waterleeuw	50	30	x	–			Var.	USA	Du	Fr

Abbreviations:
Dep.=Deponent, usually the 2nd Captain and the 1st lieutenant
Var.=Various

Du=Dutch	USA=American
Fr=French	No=Norwegian
Br=British	Mal=Maltesian
Swe=Swedish	Swi=Swiss
Dan=Danish	Ge=German

confirmed by the increasing number of ships with a crew consisting of less than 60 seamen. Information about the crew is only available for those vessels that were taken by the British as a prize, as shown in Table 11.3.

From this information the conclusion can be drawn that Dutch privateers were often manned by a considerable number of foreigners with French seamen in particular found on board these vessels. The presence of British members of the crew on the *Doggersbank* and the *Vlijt* is noteworthy.[31] During its first voyage the *Vlijt* was even under the command of a British captain, John Bannister. Strangely enough when the privateer was seized on her second voyage John Bannister appeared to be second captain. Bannister was subsequently accused of piracy. He was also accused of seizing a British vessel, called the *Sally*, in conspiracy with the Dutch privateer *Vervackton*.[32] Because of the spelling, it is not clear whether Bannister was sailing on the *Goede Verwachting* or on the *Niet Verwagt*. Eventually Bannister was sentenced to death 'at Justice Hall in the Old Baily convicted of piracy' for serving as second captain on the *Vlijt*.[33] On 23 December 1782 he received the pleasant news that he would be released at the next general pardon 'for the poor convicts in Newgate'. He was released only on the condition 'of his entering and continuing to serve us in our Royal Navy'.[34] The further adventures of John Bannister are unknown. During the Fourth Anglo-Dutch War several British seamen, who had served on hostile privateers, were released on the same condition![35]

It is remarkable that 15 out of the 29 privateers were commanded by foreign captains, mostly French or American. It is not difficult to find an explanation for the presence of French captains, especially on privateers from Zeeland. When the war broke out French privateering had already been going on for almost two years. Experienced Dutch privateering captains were not available with the exceptions of Lavens Hendrikse and Jan Hoogenboom, who became famous on a French privateer as *Jan Aardappel* (John Potato).[36] I presume that young French privateersmen of the lower ranks went to the nearby Dutch ports in search of a higher-ranking position. This was an attractive proposition because of the higher wages and the higher share of the prize money for the more important members of the crew of a privateer.[37] Most of these French seamen were very young.

The presence of American captains on Dutch privateers is also explicable. In Dunkirk, for example, 47 American captains were in command of 78 of the 150 privateers that were fitted out there.[38] The lower-ranking American seamen on privateers might have had the same motives as their French colleagues. The remarkable presence of American privateering captains in France and the Dutch Republic might be explained as follows: American privateers were instructed to capture only British ships-of-war and naval support ships, which was far more dangerous and maybe less lucrative than the capture of possibly richly laden merchantmen.[39] It would seem obvious that American seamen especially the lower-ranking, would try to get signed on a European privateer.

The 29 Dutch privateers captured 61 British merchantmen and ransomed 40 British merchantmen between December 1780 and January 1783. They also recaptured one French vessel. Sixteen of the 29 privateers were lost, all having failed to achieve any result. Yet, in spite of this, I suggest that nine shipping companies still made profits from the privateering business. Nine other companies must surely have lost money on their privateering ventures. The returns of one company are not known.

Dutch Privateering in Relation to Trade

The number of Dutch privateers during the seventeenth- and eighteenth-century wars fluctuated widely. Privateering flourished in the seventeenth century and reached its climax at the beginning of the eighteenth century, during the War of the Spanish Succession. In Dutch publications little attention has been paid to the difference in scale between privateering activities during their height and privateering during the second half of the eighteenth century. A connection has been made between the number and success of privateers and the naval force of the belligerents, but this link has hardly been developed. It is based mainly on the nineteenth-century publication of De Jonge, *Geschiedenis van het Nederlandsche Zeewezen*.[40] The central theme of his argument is the idea of the 'weak' Dutch navy confronted by a 'strong' British opponent, which made privateering an uninteresting, risky business.

The Dutch fleet was indeed very weak when the war broke out, but a recovery programme was started immediately. The British navy, on the other hand, was patrolling the North Sea with only a few remnants of its 'strong' fleet. While the Dutch fleet only put to sea a few times, the British navy was very effective in protecting 'their' merchant marine. Dutch privateers and merchantmen could not bank on the support of the national navy. The only promising areas for Dutch privateers to operate were the not-too-well-protected British coast and the southern entrance to the Channel. The blows that were dealt to Dutch privateers by the British must surely have had a negative influence on the amount of investment in Dutch privateering. During the summer of 1781, two recently built privateers, the *Hercules* and the *Mars*, were seized by the British within a week of their putting to sea. During the summer of 1782 five Zeeland privateers, all originating from different shipping companies, were seized by the British. None of these vessels had seized a British vessel!

Recently, Bruijn has provided a new starting-point for studying the scale of privateering; he says that during the Second and Third Anglo-Dutch Wars not all shipowners had to remain unemployed or to try to continue trading activities under neutral colours. The fitting out of privateers offered alternative employment.[41] Research on British privateering also shows the connection between trade and privateering. The main function of a privateer was, according to Starkey, economic: namely, to make profits for the owners of the privateer. Starkey's conclusion regarding the motivation of British shipowners who invested in privateering is: 'They were respectable merchants who engaged in privateering activity when the prospects of gain were brighter in this occupation than in other trades.'[42]

The research of Crowhurst on French privateering also shows this economic function of privateering. His explanation of the limited scale of privateering in Nantes during the War of American Independence is: 'The lack of privateering activity does not indicate that the port was in decline . . . in fact, privateering was badly supported at the port because many merchants were able to continue trading.'[43] In his view this situation symbolizes the state of French privateering in this war and explains why privateering was much less in vogue than during the War of the Spanish Succession: 'Many French merchants were reluctant to invest in privateers, because they could make more profits from trade.'[44] Crowhurst concluded that 'Merchants invested in privateering as a substitute for the trade.'[45]

The main reason why shipowners in Britain, France and, probably, the Dutch Republic invested in privateering was to make profits. When trade was in decline, privateering flourished; when trade picked up, the scale of privateering shrank. Great success or heavy loss naturally brought changes in any situation.

It is hard to say what 'supposed' Dutch privateer-owners might have thought about the potential of privateering, the risky alternative, during the Fourth Anglo-Dutch War. It is clear that in December 1780 and January 1781 Britain was hit by a privateering mania, while in the Dutch Republic only a few plans for privateering existed at the beginning of 1781. Because of the lack of capital, these plans were slow to become a reality.

Dutch Newspapers and the Small Number of Dutch Privateers

Through reading the shipping reports and political news in Dutch newspapers, I have tried to get an idea of the reactions in the maritime world to the outbreak of war. In Britain an enormous run on letters of marque started as soon as war broke out, while most people in the Dutch Republic were not even aware that a war had broken out. Only by the beginning of January 1781 did people know about the declaration of war on the Republic.[46]

Because of the delay in spreading the news about the war, many vessels putting to sea even after the declaration of war might have been

Fig. 11.1   Captain Nicolaas Jarry seizing a British collier, 24 October 1782. J. Kobell after J. Perkois, around 1782 (Netherlands Maritime Museum, Amsterdam)

NICOLAAS JARRY
CAPITEIN OP HET VLISSINGSCHE KAPER SCHIP
DE VLISSINGER.

Fig. 11.2 Nicolaas Jarry, Captain of the Dutch privateer *Vlissinger*, 1782.
P.W. van Megen en M. de Sallieth after J. Perkois, around 1782
(Netherlands Maritime Museum, Amsterdam)

in danger of being taken by the British. On 5 January there was a ban
on the departure of ships and on 12 January privateering was permitted. It took almost a week for the news about privateering to be

published. The *Amsterdamsche Courant* and the *Middelburgsche Courant* published this report respectively on 18 and 20 January.[47]

The war was just one month old when, at the end of January, the first rumours about an imminent peace were published.[48] These rumours were probably the reason for a request to the States General by a few Dutch privateer-owners for an indemnification in the event of peace.[49] Meanwhile, fear of the British was growing. In almost any edition of the newspapers from the beginning of January lists of Dutch merchantmen seized by the British navy and private men-of-war were published. The number of captures had declined by the end of March. As well as this, there was news about the enormous number of English privateers in the newspapers. The number 545 was mentioned several times.[50] The newspapers also started to publish reports on confrontations between British privateers and their Dutch victims.

In spite of the slow start to the Dutch campaign, the hope for peace and the heavy losses in the merchant marine, some plans for privateering companies were published. On 6 January 1781, for example, when privateering was still not allowed in the Dutch Republic, a privateering company was projected in the *Rotterdamsche Courant*.[51] It is not clear who was behind this plan, which could be subscribed to at the office of the Rotterdam broker Jan Ys van der Vliet. The authors made an appeal to patriotic and wealthy citizens. Privateering companies were officially permitted from April 1781 onwards, but no plans from the province of Holland were subsequently published. This is probably because money was being invested in a safer alternative, the neutralization of vessels.

In Zeeland most privateers were fitted out at the very end of 1781 and the beginning of 1782. I presume that this was due to the attitude of the States of Zeeland towards the war. Even before the war, Zeeland turned its back on measures taken by the States General which could lead to war. Several times it was suggested that Zeeland should negotiate with Britain because war would destroy overseas trade, especially that of the Zeeland merchants who were heavily involved in trade with Britain. During the war, the Zeelanders also insisted on peace negotiations.[52]

When privateering got under way, the Zeelanders became fairly enthusiastic, due to the great successes of Pierre le Turq and Nicolaas Jarry, which certainly encouraged the fitting out of a large number of privateers in Zeeland in May 1782. Whether there is a connection with a decline in Zeeland's trade is difficult to prove, though there is one

Fig. 11.3 The explosion of the Dutch privateer, *Dappere Patriot* in which all members of the crew died, 14 August 1781 (Netherlands Maritime Museum, Amsterdam)

indication that makes it a plausible explanation. The *Amsterdamsche Courant* published this report from Zeeland on 18 May 1782:

> On the cutter, called the *Zeeuw*, Captain Le Turq will be in command. At the moment a heavy privateer cutter has been fitted out, called the *Doggersbank*, and two other privateer ships, called the *Zeeuwsche Waterleeuw* and the *Hoop*, while within a few days a fourth one will be launched. Through all these activities and the tempting sight of men-of-war and frigates in the roads, the sorrows of the war and the decline of overseas trade seem to have been put aside and appeased.[53]

This enthusiasm for privateering was soon dampened by the heavy losses in June 1782.

Conclusion

The financial gains of Dutch privateering enterprises during the Fourth Anglo-Dutch War were varied. Almost half of the companies lost money; the other half may have proved lucrative. This confirms the idea that the Dutch privateers did have the opportunity to make profits. But, in spite of this, during the two years of the war, privateering involved only a small number of vessels. This was not only due to a 'weak' Dutch navy and its 'strong' British adversary, as has been suggested by De Jonge; several other reasons contributed to the decision not to invest in privateering activities.

The newspaper material suggests that the Dutch were afraid of the British navy and privateers. However, research by Pearsall shows that the British navy was not really 'strong', but in fact merely used its 'left-overs' in an effective way. It was very easy for British privateers and men-of-war to seize the homeward-bound Dutch merchantmen, which were as yet not aware that war had broken out. The newspaper material also shows that the Dutch were hoping for a prompt peace. The promise of an indemnification by the States General in the event of a peace treaty concluded within a year could not change the ideas of potential privateer-owners.

Another major factor that influenced the number of privateers was the possibility, from March 1781 onwards, of neutralizing merchantmen. Interest in privateering was limited, if trade could be continued. The great majority of Dutch merchantmen were indeed able to continue their trading activities during the war by setting out under neutral colours.

Although privateering did offer an opportunity for making profits, catching prey was not as easy for a Dutch privateer as it was for his British counterpart. There was almost no chance of capturing a British vessel that was unprepared for war, which was yet another reason for the limited scale of Dutch privateering activities during this war.

To this list I would like to add the original cause for the war. The British tried to blockade Dutch trade, and the Dutch tried to maintain that very same trade. For the British especially, privateering was an important means of destroying the trade of the enemy. The Dutch tried, where possible, to avoid hostilities with the British to protect their vulnerable overseas trade.

The slow reaction in Zeeland probably reflected the wish of the Zeeland authorities to start peace negotiations. The upsurge in Zeeland privateering confirms that the phenomenon of 'privateering' was still alive, but due to the heavy losses in June 1782, privateering came to a standstill in Zeeland. At the same time this flourishing period of privateering underlines the connection between privateering and trade. At this point further research is necessary.

One may conclude that there was no real question of a decline in Dutch privateering at the end of the eighteenth century. However, besides patriotic ideals and a small chance of making profits, there was no reason to invest money in privateering.

Notes

Abbreviations:
PRO=Public Record Office, London.
HCA=High Court of Admiralty.
ARA=Algemeen Rijks Archief, The Hague.

1. H.M. Scott, 'Sir Joseph Yorke, Dutch Politics and the Origin of the Fourth Anglo-Dutch War' *Historical Journal*, XXXI (1988), 574.
2. Treaty on Defence: A treaty concluded between the Dutch Republic and Great Britain, which implied that whenever one of the two countries was being attacked by another European country (i.e. France), the other country would support the victim with troops and ships-of-war.
3. Sources: J.R. Bruijn, *De admiraliteit van Amsterdam in rustige jaren 1713–1751* (Amsterdam/Haarlem, 1970); J.C. de Jonge, *Geschiedenis van het Nederlandsche zeewezen*, vol. IV (2nd edn, Haarlem, 1861); J. Reedijk, *Nederlandse marineschepen in de tweede helft van de achttiende eeuw* (Strijen, 1990). Unpublished paper, University of Leiden.
4. J.S. Bartstra, *Vlootherstel en legeraugmentatie 1770–1780* (Assen, 1952).
5. De Jonge, *Nederlandsche zeewezen*, vol. IV, 405.
6. G.J. Marcus, *A Naval History of England, Vol. I 'The Formative Centuries'* (London, 1961), 423.

7. Marcus, *Naval History*, vol. I, 416.
8. A Pearsall, 'British Convoys in the North Sea, 1781–1782' in W. Minchinton (ed.), *Britain and the Northern Seas* (Pontefract, 1988), 106.
9. Pearsall, 'British Convoys', 108.
10. Marcus, *Naval History*, vol. I, 431.
11. Scott, 'Joseph Yorke', 572.
12. D.J. Starkey, 'British Privateering against the Dutch in the American Revolutionary War, 1780–1783' in S. Fisher (ed.), *Studies in British Privateering, Trading Enterprise and Seamen's Welfare, 1775–1900* (Exeter, 1987), 15.
13. Starkey, 'British Privateering against the Dutch', 15.
14. About 500 British privateers were directly involved in privateering activities against the Dutch merchant marine. This number is based on D.J. Starkey, *British Privateering Enterprise in the Eighteenth Century* (Exeter, 1990).
15. Letters of Marque against the Dutch and Dutch prizes classified by port group, 1780–3:

Port Group	Letters of Marque against the Republic	Number of Dutch prizes
London	295	12
Bristol	91	8
Liverpool	189	11
Channel Islands	94	6
East England	53	15
South-east England	154	19
South-west England	184	38
West England and Wales	24	—
West Scotland	59	—
East Scotland	14	—
Ireland	39	3
Overseas	16	1
Unknown	21	16
Total	1,233	129

Source: Starkey, 'British Privateering against the Dutch', 12–14.

16. E.S. van Eyck van Heslinga, 'De vlag dekt de lading. De Nederlandse koopvaardij in de Vierde Engelse oorlog' *Tijdschrift voor Zeegeschiedenis,* 1 (1982) 2, 102–13.
17. Van Eyck, 'De vlag dekt de lading', 106.
18. Van Eyck, 'De vlag dekt de lading', 110.
19. I owe this information to J.R. Bruijn.
20. J.Th.H. Verhees-van Meer, *De Zeeuwse Kaapvaart tijdens de Spaanse Successieoorlog 1702–1713* (Middelburg, 1986); J.R. Bruijn, 'Dutch Privateering during the Second and Third Anglo-Dutch Wars' *The Low Countries Yearbook, Acta Historiae Neerlandicae,* XI (1979), 79–93.
21. PRO, HCA 32 inv. nr. 332/1/1–41 *Vlissinger,* Nicolaas Jarry, nr. 41. 'Placaat van de Staten-Generaal betreffende de primie voor commissievaarders'. *Nieuwe*

Nederlandsche Jaarboeken, of vervolg der merkwaerdigste geschiedenissen die voorgevallen zijn in de Vereenigde Provincien, de Generaliteitslanden en de Volksplantingen van den staat, 1781 deel A (Leiden-Amsterdam, 1766–1798) 78, 400, 647 and 762.

22. Source: J.C. de Jonge, *Het Nederlandsche zeewezen* IV, passim; H. Jordaan, *Nademaal, het den koning van Groot-Brittannien goedgedagt heeft . . . De activiteitenen organisatie van de Nederlandse kaapvaart tijdens de Vierde Engelse oorlog 1780–1784* (Leiden, 1981), 11; ARA, admiraliteitsarchieven, Inventarisnummers: 96 Copie commissiebrieven en copie-instructiën, uitgegeven door de admiraliteit op de Maze, 1758–1791; 96 A Instructiën voor de gezagvoerders der kaperschepen de *Valk*, de *Havick* en de *Gier*, door de reeders van die bodems blijkbaar overlegd aan de admiraliteit op de Maze, 5 February 1782–9 November 1782; 1330 Copie commissiën en copie-instructiën van zeeofficieren en commissievaarders, 19 November 1748–4 February 1794; 1201 Journaal, gehouden door den schrijver C. de Haas op het kaperschip de *Gier*, onder bevel van den kapitein I. Jansz. Former gedurende zijn reis in de Noordzee, 26 April 1782–6 July 1782; XXXI Collectie Bisdom: 202 Stukken door de admiraliteit op de Maze medegegeven aan den kapitein J. Visser, voerande het kaperschip het *Algemeen Belang*; PRO, HCA. 32 inv. nr. 266/16/1–39, 309/1/1–15, 332/1/1–41, 345/17/1–28, 352/10/1, 352/12/1, 393/19/1, 399/15/1–3, 401/41/1–26, 470/7/1–34, 475/18/1–27, 475/20/1–28 and 491/5/1–19.

23. PRO, HCA 32 inv. nr. 266/16/1–39 *Amazone*, Cornelius Loeff, nr. 37. 'Ordonnantie van de Staten-Generaal betreffende het plegen van vijandelijkheden in de Baltische zee', 18 June 1781.

24. *Nieuwe Nederlandsche Jaarboek*, 1782 deel B. 1249–53.

25. This can be concluded from a list compiled by H. Jordaan on the ports where Dutch prizes were seized. Jordaan, *Nademaal*, 19–21. Unpublished paper, University of Leiden.

26. Of British vessels seized by Dutch privateers 1781–1783, six carried cargoes of coal, seven carried fish, five carried other specified cargoes, and seven carried unknown cargoes. Jordaan, *Nademaal*, 19–21.

27. J. van Beijlen (ed.), *Maritieme encyclopedie*, vol. IV (Bussum, 1971), 175–6.

28. Bruijn, 'Kaapvaart', 417.

29. Jordaan, *Nademaal*, 17; De Jonge, *Nederlandsche zeewezen*, deel IV, 759–60; PRO, HCA 32 inv. nr. 266/16/1–39, 309/1/1–15, 332/1/1–41, 345/17/1–28, 352/10/1, 352/12/1, 393/19/1, 399/15/1–3, 401/41/1–26, 470/7/1–34, 475/18/1–27, 475/20/1–28 and 491/5/1–19.

30. Source: PRO, HCA 32 inv. nr. 266/16/1–39, 309/1/1–15, 332/1/1–41, 345/17/1–28, 352/10/1, 352/12/1, 393/19/1, 399/15/1–3, 401/41/1–26, 470/7/1–34, 475/18/1–27, 475/20/1–28 and 491/5/1–19.

31. PRO, HCA 32 inv. nr. 309/1/1–15 *Doggersbank*, James Pile, nr. 1 t/m 3 Verslag van de ondervraging van de bemanningsleden van de *Doggersbank* z.d.; PRO, HCA 32 inv. nr. 475/20/1–28 *Vlijt*, Jens Willemsen, nr. 2 t/m 4 Verslag van de ondervraging van de bemanningsleden van de *Vlijt* z.d.

32. PRO, HCA 1 inv. nr. 25 nr. 38 Indictment of John Bannister, serving in Dutch privateer. PRO, HCA 1 inv. nr. 25 nr. 39 Indictment of John Bannister, piracy against *Sally*.

33. PRO, HCA 1 inv. nr. 25 nr. 52 23 December 1782, Warrant for pardon of John Bannister.
34. *Ibid.*
35. PRO, HCA 1, Oyer and Terminer Records 1535–1834.
36. De Jonge, *Nederlandsche zeewezen*, vol. IV, 665; *Leydsche Courant*, 19 Dec. 1781; *Nederlandsche Jaarboek*, 1781 deel A, 241.
37. PRO, HCA 32 inv. nr. 266/16/1–39 *Amazone,* Cornelius Loeff, nr. 34 Nota van de reders voor Cornelius Loeff betreffende de verdeling van de te behalen buit, z.d.
38. H. Malo, *Les derniers corsaires. Dunkerque 1715–1815* (Paris, 1925), 116.
39. J.M. Morgan, 'American privateering in America's War for Independence, 1775–1783' in M. Mollat (ed.), *Course et Piraterie: Etudes presentées a la commission internationale d'histoire maritime a l'occasion de son XVe colloque international* (San Francisco, 1975) vol. II, 560.
40. De Jonge, *Nederlandsche zeewezen*, vol. IV 662 and 675.
41. Bruijn, 'Kaapvaart', 411.
42. Starkey, 'British Privateering against the Dutch', 9.
43. P. Crowhurst, *The Defence of British Trade 1689–1815* (Folkestone, 1977), 29.
44. *Ibid.,* 64.
45. P. Crowhurst, *The French War on Trade, 1793–1815* (Aldershot, 1989), 199.
46. *Amsterdamsche Courant*, Dec. 1780–Dec. 1782; *Rotterdamsche Courant*, Dec. 1780–Dec. 1782; *Middelburgsche Courant*, Dec. 1780–Dec. 1782; *Leydsche Courant*, Dec. 1780–Dec. 1782.
47. *Amsterdamsche Courant*, 18 Jan. 1781; *Middelburgsche Courant*, 20 Jan. 1781.
48. *Amsterdamsche Courant*, 30 Jan. 1781; *Leydsche Courant*, 31 Jan. 1781.
49. *Nieuwe Nederlandsche Jaarboek* 1781 deel A, 647 en 762.
50. *Rotterdamsche Courant*, 27 Jan. 1781.
51. *Rotterdamsche Courant*, 6 Jan. 1781.
52. *Middelburgsche Courant*, 9 and 30 Jan. 1781; *Rotterdamsche Courant*, 13 Jan. 1781.
53. *Amsterdamsche Courant*, 18 May 1782.

CHAPTER 12

Profit and Neutrality: The Case of Ostend, 1781–1783

Jan Parmentier

An 'Economic Boom in Ostend'

This chapter deals with the neutral status of the port of Ostend during the Fourth Anglo-Dutch War (1780–3) and more specifically with the use and abuse of the neutral imperial flag in international trade and shipping. Then it discusses the economic benefits this situation brought to Flanders and Brabant. There will also be an attempt to assess whether this 'economic boom' was essentially artificial, due solely to the participation of foreign merchant houses.

During the Fourth Anglo-Dutch War the Austrian Netherlands remained neutral in a conflict that involved the three major maritime nations. Privateering and naval activity seriously disrupted the overseas trade of the belligerents and obliged them to use neutral shipping for the continuation of their commercial activities. The Austrian Netherlands had a geographical advantage in being situated right in the midst of these maritime nations. Moreover, on 11 June 1781, Emperor Joseph II proclaimed Ostend a free port. From that date on, Ostend, and to a lesser extent Bruges and Ghent, became attractive places for Dutch, French and English firms to continue their commercial traffic.

We have been able to discern two main methods used by foreign firms to operate under a neutral flag. Firstly, they might set up a branch in a Flemish town. This branch took care of the necessary neutralization of ships and cargoes. It was even more to the advantage of the foreign merchants to contract a Flemish or foreign commissioner in Ostend, Bruges or Ghent to charter neutral ships. Secondly, a lot of English, French and Dutch firms sold their ships to an imperial commissioner, but only for the duration of the war. A variation on this phenomenon was the inception of several new trading companies under the stipulation that at the end of the Fourth Anglo-Dutch War they would be liquidated.

Another aspect to be taken into consideration is the harbour conditions of Ostend. The entrance to the port was obstructed by shallows and the channel only allowed passage for ships of less than 250 tons.[1] Compared to the neighbouring ports of Dunkirk, Middelburg and Flushing, Ostend could be described as a small seaport with an antiquated harbour infrastructure which was unsuited to long-distance merchant shipping and not really fit to play a prominent role in European commerce. On the other hand, due to the closure of the Scheldt—the main seaway to Antwerp—since the seventeenth century, Ostend had been the only trading port in the Austrian Netherlands.

During the pre-war period around 480 arrivals per year were noted in Ostend, all from European destinations. Approximately 60 per cent of the vessels came from Holland and England. During the first years of the American Revolution, a modest increase in traffic was noticeable. Until the English blockade of the Channel near Calais in 1778, this conflict offered several Ostend merchants the opportunity to smuggle large quantities of weapons and ammunition from Liège to France.[2]

The economic boom of the port of Ostend started in the second half of 1781. At that moment Ostend accommodated only 11 merchant houses which had developed some overseas trade.[3] By 1782 over 50 foreign firms were settled there and 1,173 new 'burghers' had been officially registered.[4] The population of Ostend increased spectacularly by 65 per cent from 6,000 to 10,000 inhabitants in the space of two years.[5] This town became the transit-market for belligerents for all kinds of goods. During this period every week the *Gazette van Gent*, the most important newspaper in the Austrian Netherlands, announced several public sales of European and Caribbean products in Ostend.[6] It developed into a port at which all kinds of neutral ships (Danish, Swedish, Prussian and others) sought cargoes. On this matter the Ostend merchant W.J. van Iseghem, in his capacity as consul for Denmark and Norway, wrote to his superiors that the English sent their export products for the Mediterranean to Ostend, where these cargoes were neutralized and shipped in Danish and Swedish vessels, provided with Turkish or Algerian passports, to Portugal, Spain and Italy.[7] The facilities for arranging profitable ventures via Ostend even attracted the major Copenhagen firm de Coninck & Reiersen. In this way this merchant house organized voyages to St Thomas and the Atlantic slave trade under the imperial flag.[8]

Foreign Merchants in Ostend

When the newly established branches of foreign firms are examined we note that a large colony of French and English merchants, mariners and shipowners was present in Ostend. The French mainly originated from Dunkirk.[9] This phenomenon was fairly normal for, ever since the seventeenth century, there had been a constant stream of migration between Dunkirk and Ostend or *vice versa*, depending on the economic situation of both towns. For example, the large-scale privateering business organized from Dunkirk during the War of the Spanish Succession attracted a lot of Ostend seamen.[10] Between 1720 and 1735 we can trace a reverse movement via the Ostend Company, the lion's share of the foreign sailors on board the Ostend Eastindiamen coming from Dunkirk.[11]

The Dunkirk *armateurs* most active in soliciting imperial passports were François De Vinck & Co., with a fleet of 157 ships, and the firm of Pierre de Gravier & Anthoine Willems, with 135 Ostend sea passes.[12] François De Vinck acted as sole commissioner for companies all over Europe. The main sources which shed light on his trade are the Ostend notary archives.[13] Almost every day during the war De Vinck shipped cargoes under the imperial flag. Most of these goods never even entered Ostend; he often drew up contracts with 'neutral' captains to transport cargoes directly from France and Spain to Holland. Notwithstanding his large 'masked' fleet, he often chartered Prussian and Danish ships for this purpose. We assume he was also one of the major commissioners for the English coastal traders, because after the war he gave back 41 of his sloops to the firm of Fennings & Haern in Harwich.[14] François De Vinck returned to Dunkirk in 1783, but he never entered the ranks of the leading merchants there.[15] Willems and De Gravier, on the other hand, had already established careers in Dunkirk. Anthoine Willems was a well known shipowner, specializing in the colonial and slave trades.[16] Pierre de Gravier had a reputation as a smuggler and was also involved in the West India trade. Tobacco imports yielded the most important revenues for his company.[17] This trade, and the preparation of the tobacco, expanded rapidly in the north of France during the second half of the eighteenth century, and Dunkirk became famous for its high quality tobacco.[18] De Gravier's contacts with England and Holland were excellent; his father-in-law was a Dutch merchant. Willems & De Gravier only remained in Ostend for the duration of the war. One remarkable detail in their 'neutral' activities was their purchase of 12 English prizes in Cherbourg, Le Havre and Caen. We presume these were commissioned by their former English owners.[19]

Joseph Stival and the house of Forcade & Son were the other main Dunkirk firms which settled in Ostend. Both merchant houses had 39 neutral ships. We have found very little information on the Forcade firm, except that its fleet sailed chiefly from France across the Atlantic to Martinique.[20] Before moving to Ostend, the Dunkirk merchant Stival set up a gin distillery in 1777.[21] His geneva was in demand as contraband in England.[22] The sources reveal that his trade was highly diversified. At the start of the war (1778), with several Irish and English smugglers, he moved first from Dunkirk to Flushing, at that point the centre of the illicit trade with south-east England.[23] But the involvement of the Dutch Republic in the Fourth Anglo-Dutch War forced him to migrate temporarily to Ostend.[24] When we analyse his fleet, we note that it contained five small cutters, ideal for smuggling, which still carried on traffic with Zeeland. Possibly the lack of good contraband in Ostend obliged him to find his outward-bound cargoes in Middelburg and Flushing. The destinations of his larger brigantines and frigates showed that he acted in commission for Dutch companies trading to Curaçao, Suriname and the United States of America.[25] In October 1782 he fitted out four French herring-busses at Nieuwpoort, a small fishing port on the Flemish coast, and strangely enough he got permission from the local Admirality to sell his catch in France.[26] We have to emphasize that the Dunkirk fishing industry prospered greatly during this war, because their complete fleet, around 70 ships, sailed under the imperial flag. Moreover, the French government agreed with the British authorities not to hail each other's fishing craft. English and French privateers taking fishing boats were reprimanded by the authorities and had to return their prizes.[27]

The ports of Le Havre, Honfleur and Dieppe respectively were represented in Ostend by the firm Famin & Rigoult and the house of Le Baron & Son.[28] For the overseas trade of Le Havre in this period, a study of Pierre Dardel informs us that the entire slave trade and the direct West India traffic was organized under the imperial flag. Before the outbreak of the war only four or five Ostend ships per year visited Le Havre. This number suddenly increased to 28, 39 and 34 imperial arrivals in the years 1780–2, and decreased in the following decade to the pre-war average of four ships yearly.[29] With 131 imperial sea passes, the firm of Famin & Rigoult played a key role in neutralization, but other foreign and Flemish merchant houses active in the Austrian Netherlands also looked after the fleet of Le Havre.[30]

Other French ports with extensive Atlantic interests, like Rouen, Nantes and Bordeaux, did not have a branch in Ostend or Bruges, but thanks to the international network of commercial relations these merchants easily obtained valuable imperial passports.[31] Compared to the rest of the maritime companies in France, the traders in the Mediterranean ports of Marseilles and Sète preferred to entrust their consignments to Scandinavian and Prussian vessels, which were protected by Algerian sea passes.[32]

Finally, in our survey of the French colony in Ostend we found two traders who created an association with Flemish merchants. One of them was the Dunkirker Jean-Baptiste Vercoustere who started a continuous trading route between Ostend and Margate with the Ostender Flaneghan. But the real owner of the ships and the cargoes was an Englishman named Minet, and even the captains and crew were English.[33] This association kept 12 ships under sail. Besides smuggling, they traded with Martinique and San Domingo.[34] The second collaborative venture was that of Louis Tribou from Saint-Valéry and the Ostend merchant, Derdeyn. Tribou married Derdeyn's sister and became *poorter* of Ostend. He owned several fishing boats with Calais as home port. Through his marriage he received neutral passports for all his ships, which continued to operate from Calais.[35]

English traders resident in Ostend formed the largest group of foreigners. Their activities were mainly confined to the coastal trade and smuggling. Only Alexander Hubbert, representative of the firm Hubbert of London, was involved in the West India trade. He controlled a fleet of 15 brigantines, frigates, flutes and snows with an average size of 350 tons.[36] The majority of his outward-bound cargoes consisted of food, beverages and domestic articles for planter families on Grenada, St Thomas, and St Christopher, and his West Indiamen returned with the usual colonial products.[37]

Profits from contraband provided the major revenue for more than 80 per cent of the English colony at the Flemish coast. The most important firms were the eight merchant houses that migrated from Flushing, namely John Holman, Hayman & Fox, Thomas Holman Junior & Co., Story & Hunt, Buchanan & Co., Joseph Hodges, Thomas Cullen, and John Fottrell. Smuggling or trading contraband from Ostend to south-east England was one of the most profitable activities the Fourth Anglo-Dutch War brought to the Austrian Netherlands. The local authorities were well aware of this and offered these newcomers all kinds of facilities to keep them in Ostend. For instance, the tax on the distillation of gin was lowered by one-third.[38] A new distillery especially for the smugglers, which could produce the high quality geneva of Holland, was opened in Nieuwpoort.[39] Eight warehouses for the smugglers were built on the quay in Ostend and foreign coopers were engaged to cope with the increased demand for small casks.[40]

Most of the contraband cargoes were composed of gin, tea and tobacco. England was an excellent market for continental gin or geneva as prices for alcohol rose in the second half of the eighteenth century by 122 per cent. Tea prices on the London market were also much higher than in Amsterdam or Nantes.[41] Furthermore, there was always a great demand for luxury products like Virginia tobacco and other colonial products from the West Indies. A government report of 1781 mentions that, at the beginning of their trading on one day, 68,970 lb of tea (value 85,250 guilders) and 30,400 lb of geneva was already shipped to England, a considerable amount of trade.[42]

In the wake of the English colony, three Irish merchant houses arrived in Ostend, namely Edward & Philippe Connelly, Murdoch & Co., and David Michael Gallwey.[43] The first two firms had been based in Dunkirk since the middle of the eighteenth century.[44] The house of Murdoch combined the function of commissioner for several Dutch merchants with an intensive trade of its own to Norway, Ireland and the West Indies. This firm had 47 ships registered in Ostend.[45] David Michael Gallwey was descended from the merchant family Gallwey of Cork which had departed to France around 1750.[46] During the Anglo-Dutch War members of the Gallwey clan ran respectable firms in Nantes and Bordeaux. David Michael Gallwey had a fleet of 17 imperial ships and specialized in the traffic from Bordeaux and Rotterdam to the West Indies.[47] The connection with Ireland was important for this trade because Cork functioned as one of the main ports of call for West Indiamen before crossing the Atlantic.[48]

It is surprising that only a handful of merchants from the Dutch Republic moved to Ostend, because most of the 'masked' ships were

Dutch. Shipowners from Middelburg, Zierikzee and Rotterdam in particular bought imperial passports with the assistance of Flemish commissioners.[49] This is reflected in the reports of the Dutch Navy; in 1782 about 80 per cent of all ships passing Hellevoetsluis—the entrance to the port of Rotterdam—sailed under imperial colours, while in Zeeland waters as many as 90 per cent of all vessels had imperial sea passes.[50] According to the Ostend Admiralty, Pierre Gavanon was the major Dutch solicitor, neutralizing 82 ships for the Amsterdam firms. We may view this merchant as a special case. He was already a citizen of Ostend prior to 1777, the year he married in Amsterdam. He lived in the Dutch capital, on the Prinsengracht, and received Amsterdam citizenship in 1778.[51] According to our sources he was not of Flemish origin. We think his full family name, Gavanon de Valleraugue, reveals his origins. Valleraugue is a town in the Cévennes (France). So we believe our Franco-Dutchman with imperial nationality set up a 'paper firm' in Ostend for it was not necessary for him to be resident in Flanders to acquire the imperial passes. Several Flemish notaries were very willing to send blank documents abroad to the port of departure of the ship. Also there is no reference to the firm Gavanon in the well-preserved notary archives of Ostend.

Another interesting Dutchman was Guillaume Candé. He became *poorter* of Ostend in April 1781[52] and was associated with, or a figure-head for, a few Dutch merchant houses trading to Curaçao and Suriname.[53] In this capacity he neutralized 27 ships and even more cargoes.[54] On several occasions he also shipped sugar and coffee from Martinique and San Domingo under orders from the Dutch firm F.L. Delcourt, which had its headquarters in Bordeaux.[55] Candé was one of the few new Ostenders who traded with the Baltic. At the end of the war he sold all his ships in Amsterdam and Zaandam.[56]

At the first sight Christiaan Dutilh from Rotterdam did not seem to be an active merchant. He only needed four imperial passes, but he is the only foreigner who became an 'Ostender' purely to continue his personal trade.[57] Two other Dutch merchants were associated with Ostend traders for the duration of the war. In 1782 one of them, F.J. van den Broek from Amsterdam, started a firm in association with the Ostend family, Verbeke. In this joint-venture Michael Verbeke acted as manager in Ostend and Van den Broek became the correspondent in Amsterdam.[58] So this Dutch trader also stayed in Holland. The second Dutch-Ostend company was called Van Iseghem, De Vries & Co. Besides the fact that 13 ships sailed for this firm to Cayenne, the

Antilles and back to several Dutch ports and Copenhagen, we have found no data on how this merchant house functioned.[59] Before the war the firm Van Iseghem was already involved in an active trade with Scandinavia and the Baltic.[40]

Apart from the presence of merchants from the belligerent nations in Ostend, a small number of Swiss and German firms tried to make their fortune by neutralizing ships and cargoes. François Henri Christyn was born in Yverdon (Vaud) and specialized in the trade to the West Indies.[61] In 1782 six of his ships sailed to Curaçao and two other vessels were bound for Suriname.[62] Probably his brother Louis, who lived in Amsterdam, arranged the outfitting for the Dutch West Indies. During this war the Christyns were associated with Mathias Evertz in Curaçao. This merchant was given a procuracy by Christyn to charter neutral ships bound for Ostend.[63]

In 1781 the Hamburg merchants Schultz and Tamm contacted Jean Baptiste Serruys, a young lawyer with no commercial experience, from Torhout (West Flanders). Nevertheless, this firm worked very professionally by sending circular letters to the main merchant houses in Paris and Bordeaux, offering their services to neutralize ships, crew and cargoes lying in French ports in exchange for a lower than usual commission fee.[64] Their way of obtaining the necessary imperial documents proved to be a notorious fraud, which is discussed later in this chapter. Schultz, Serruys, Tamm & Co managed to neutralize 29 ships in 1782. In the following two years we note that all these vessels were returned to their original owners.[65]

Finally, to round off our survey of foreign participation in the Ostend trade during the war, we will provide an example of the foundation of a new foreign firm in Ostend, especially created for war-profiteering. The London merchant Crinsoz was associated with George Cottens, a commissioner in Ostend. In December 1781 the firm of Crinsoz & Cottens started a new merchant house in conjunction with Charles Le Goux, a Swiss trader from Neuchâtel. Le Goux was to travel to the Danish island of St Thomas and establish there a new firm under the name Charles Le Goux & Co. Le Goux was not allowed to spend more than 6,000 guilders on the firm's foundation. Crinsoz promised to ship merchandize worth 100,000 guilders to St Thomas every year. Le Goux received two-thirds of the profits (losses) on the sale of these cargoes. His task was to purchase colonial products for the Ostend market. He would receive 2 per cent commission on the sale of these cargoes. The duration of this contract was to be only three years and the contract would be automatically broken if the war ended.[66]

The Austrian Netherlands and International Trade

The contribution of Flemish firms to this international web of commerce was by no means negligible. In 1782 the five major Ostend merchants had a fleet of 327 ships registered in their names. The data of the Ostend Admiralty indicate that the House of Romberg with 153 vessels under its flag could be considered the most important shipowner in the Austrian Netherlands.[67] The founder of this company was Frédéric Romberg, a self-made man from Westphalia who had settled in Brussels around 1755. In ten years he had built up a successful career as a banker and trader, mainly concentrating on the transit-traffic from Ostend to Germany, Switzerland and Italy. It could be said that he created an international courier-service ahead of its time. For this purpose he set up three branches situated in Louvain, Nancy and Lindau. The government supported his initiatives and regularly asked his advice on commercial affairs.[68] For Romberg the Fourth Anglo-Dutch War was an undreamed of opportunity to expand his company. Right from the beginning of the war, he tried to profit from contraband transport. His excellent contacts with several firms in the belligerent nations gave him the facilities to make a fortune by neutralizing ships and cargoes. In 1781 his fleet already numbered 94 vessels. In order to manage his increasing activities more efficiently, he created new branches in Ostend, Ghent and Bruges. In conjunction with the major merchants of Bruges, he founded a maritime insurance company in 1782, the *Société d'Assurances maritimes établies à Bruges*. This company enjoyed great success as long as the war lasted.[69] Frédéric Romberg also became a very active slave-trader in collaboration with the Brussels banker and industrialist Jacques Joseph Chapel. This consortium was largely financed by banks in Paris, London and Amsterdam.[70] In 1782 ten of his ships left Ostend for West Africa and Angola, and possibly more of his vessels sailed via France to Africa. After the war the Romberg family moved its commercial centre to Bordeaux.

In contrast to Frédéric Romberg's enterprise the other Flemish firms remained fairly small, many being established in the stimulating environment of the 'economic boom'. On the other hand the few merchant houses which were already trading out of Ostend before the war expanded rapidly and could cope with the new competition. The major Ostend firms, besides Romberg, always combined their own trade with the function of commissioner. For instance the Ostend association Liebaert, Baes & Derdeyn launched an intensive trade to the West Indies with a part of their own fleet and at the same time they neutralized more than 50 Dutch and French vessels.[71]

When we look at the trade organized in Bruges during the Fourth Anglo-Dutch War we note that only 268 sea passes were issued by the authorities in the years 1781–3, while the Admirality in Ostend signed 1,944 similar passports during the same period.[72] In consequence, the foreign merchant colony of Bruges was restricted to a group of British and Irish firms, one Amsterdam merchant, and a colleague from Basel. The English associations, like Mason, Blundell & Masterson and Henry Oshea, invested exclusively in the triangular trade.[73] The enterprise of the Irish merchant David Lynch, who had already settled in Bruges before the war, expanded rapidly thanks to the neutrality of the Austrian Netherlands. He shipped large quantities of linseed from the north of France to England and Ireland.[74]

The most active foreigner in Bruges was the Dutchman Daniël Cornelis Wesselman. In Amsterdam he ran a shipyard and was also known as a timber broker. When he arrived in Bruges, he was running an iron foundry in Brabant.[75] As well as the office in Bruges he also opened one in Ostend. His ships were practically all destined for Guinea and the West Indies, often under commission from Dutch merchants.[76] It is interesting to note that he became the supervisor of the affairs of the Copenhagen firm Frederik de Coninck & Niels Reiersen in the Austrian Netherlands. In this way part of the Danish slave trade was organized under the imperial colours.[77] In contrast to Ostend, the local merchants of Bruges concentrated on their own expeditions and the neutralization of foreign ships was limited. Only three Bruges merchant houses were in possession of 'masked' ships, namely Cipriaen De Beir, Valentin Jacobi, and Willaert de Bare & Co.[78]

The contribution of the Antwerp merchants to this sudden commercial windfall can be discerned in a few preserved merchant archives. From 1781 onwards, several new companies sprang up, in Antwerp, the major new associations being De Wael, Veydt, Van Ravestijn & Co., De Gruyter & Solvijns, and Solvijns, De Wolf & Co. Many of these merchants lacked experience in international trade. Before the war Van Ravestijn was a lace merchant and the brothers Laurent and Maximiliaan Solvijns specialized in furs and cheese respectively.[79] The firm De Wael, Veydt, Van Ravestijn & Co. was actually a joint-venture by five Antwerp merchants and one or two traders from Amsterdam. From the Dutch capital this firm equipped a few ships to Suriname under the imperial flag. Besides his partnership in this firm Frans Veydt, a former teabroker, managed to neutralize 18 Dutch vessels, which were bound for St Thomas and Curaçao.[80] According to their book-keeping the second new Antwerp company, De Gruyter & Solvijns, had eight ships under sail. Laurent Solvijns and his associate were only responsible for a quarter of the capital in this enterprise. Possibly the other financers lived in France, for all their ships sailed via Bordeaux or Nantes to the French Antilles.[81] According to the Admiralty, De Gruyter & Solvijns possessed a fleet of 38 vessels, so we may assume that the greater part of these crafts were 'masked' ships.[82] The company Solvijns, De Wolf & Co., also called De Oostendse Handelsmaatschappij, was founded in February 1782 and was directed by Max Solvijns and C.J.M. De Wolf. The capital of this firm amounted to 240,000 guilders divided into 40 shares of 6,000 guilders each. The major shareholders were not merchants but rich investors from Antwerp. This firm was joint owner of several ships trading to the West Indies and Suriname.[83]

According to the Admiralty register the participation of merchants from Ghent and Brussels in Ostend shipping was limited to a small group which only required imperial passports for neutralizing foreign ships.[84] On the other hand, the mercantile archives of the wealthy cloth traders Jean and Joseph de Potter reveal that more than one firm in Ghent participated in shipping and in this way expanded their trade to new markets, but they made use of several commissioners in Ostend to obtain the necessary passports. Thanks to the Fourth Anglo-Dutch War Joseph de Potter purchased four ships in conjunction with the Rotterdam company Jan Osy & Sons. The Amsterdam merchant houses of Daniël Crommelin and J. Brentano also had some financial interest in this association. This Flemish-Dutch group shipped a lot of Flemish cloth to Curaçao, St Croix, and Philadelphia in 'neutral' vessels, conducted under the name of the 'paper' owner Liebaert, Baes & Derdeyn or Philippe Connelly.[85]

Procedures for Neutralization

According to the Admiralty the neutralization of Dutch ships was more important than that of ships of French or English origin. Of the

1,944 imperial passports that were officially issued in Ostend, 37.2 per cent were used for ships of Dutch origin, while the French and the English vessels represented 22.3 per cent and 20.6 per cent respectively. About 15 per cent of the ships cannot be identified and the other craft were built in the Austrian Netherlands, Ireland and America.[86]

The need for neutral passports and the minimal governmental control led to a lot of abuses, like the simulated sale of ships. Using the example of the neutralization of a Dutch expedition to the Antilles by a Flemish merchant we will illustrate how the system worked.[87] In October 1781 François Hugues, resident in Amsterdam, contacted Laurent Janssens of Ghent with a view to starting a joint-venture. François Hugues descended from a Protestant family originating in the Cévennes.[88] His relatives controlled an international network with branches in Marseilles, Bordeaux and San Domingo, while Laurent Janssens ran a tiny local merchant house.

According to the deed of sale, dated 19 October 1781 and passed before the Amsterdam notary Martinus Dorper, Hugues sold his frigate *Petrus en Alexander* to Janssens for 17,000 guilders. This was the official version, but a private arrangement, dated 1 November 1781, shows that Janssens 'purchased' this frigate for the price of 30,000 guilders under the following conditions:

a. Hugues procured the necessary credit to finance the sale, under the explicit condition that Hugues could always reclaim his ship as long as Janssens had not paid the proceeds.

b. Hugues promised to take back his ship for the same price either at the end of the war or if the economic situation changed.

c. Hugues could sell his ship to a third party, at an even higher price, on condition that he absolved Janssens of the debt of 30,000 guilders. If Hugues received more than this amount for his frigate, Janssens should get 1 per cent of the surplus value.

d. In exchange for the credit Janssens agreed to equip the frigate under the imperial flag and she would sail under the new name of *les Trois Soeurs*. Furthermore, Janssens had to send all the accounts of the expeditions to Hugues.

e. All profits (or losses) devolved on Hugues, except the 1 per cent commission for Janssens.

f. Laurent Janssens undertook to claim the ship and cargo if it was taken by privateers or confiscated by men-of-war.

This was not a standard contract, there are several obvious variations, but the main items like credit for the purchase, the ownership of the vessel, a commission fee, the fact that the ship would sail under imperial colours and the condition that the commissioner would act as the owner when confronting the belligerents were quite similar to those in other extant contracts.[89]

The destination of this voyage from Amsterdam was Bordeaux with a cargo of iron, nails, vinegar and oil for a merchant called Ferrière. This trader would seek a new cargo, provided by several Bordeaux firms, bound for Martinique. In the Caribbean *les Trois Soeurs* had to call at a few islands to complete her cargo before returning to Bordeaux with colonial products. So this ship, like so many others, never entered an imperial port.

The path taken by Hugues and Janssens to get hold of the requisite imperial documents is interesting. First the Dutch captain, Thijs Ketel, and the supercargo of les *Trois Soeurs* travelled to Ghent and stayed at the inn *The Swan* for about seven days. During this short period the captain and the supercargo were made burghers of Ghent by a deed of *poorterije*, sworn before the local notary, Drieghe. These documents were validated by the city council for the price of 25 *Vlaams*. Furthermore, the British consul in the Austrian Netherlands confirmed the authenticity of the documents. A similar procedure was followed to legalize the imperial ownership of the frigate. On this latter document we also find the signature of the French consul.

When the frigate *les Trois Soeurs* was ready to sail from Amsterdam, François Hugues asked Janssens to send him a blank muster-roll, certified by a notary of Ghent. This muster-roll was filled in on board when the crew was completed. Janssens also had to falsify the ship's destination on the muster-roll, namely 'om te zeilen van Gent naar Amsterdam en vandaar naar Bordeaux' (to sail from Ghent to Amsterdam and from there to Bordeaux). Finally we find another falsification of documents on this expedition in the bills of lading drawn up in Bordeaux. Jean-Jacques Bethmann, the consul of the Austrian Netherlands in Bordeaux, neutralized the complete cargo even though he knew that the real owners of these goods were French. Laurent Janssens earned a 1 per cent commission fee on this neutralization in Bordeaux.

The instructions of François Hugues to the captain and the supercargo give an idea of how they exercised caution to deceive the billigerents. When the crew arrived in Amsterdam, they had to stay on board the ship. If anybody did have shore leave, the captain had to check that he did not bring on board letters or papers directed to persons in Holland, France or Spain. If such papers were discovered after the ship had sailed they had to be burnt immediately. The only papers allowed on board were the imperial documents. The captain also had to see that no contraband (weapons, ammunition) was loaded.

The expedition of the frigate *les Trois Soeurs* highlights several abuses in the neutralization system. To receive neutral passports one had to be registered in the Austrian Netherlands, but on different occasions an Ostend firm purchased false citizenship in Veurne and Lo, two little towns near the French border, for foreign captains, who were resident abroad. It became common knowledge that the town councils of Veurne and Lo did not check the identities of the applicants, so in this way 883 French, English and Dutch captains and sailors were accepted as new *poorters* of Veurne.[90] These papers were used to neutralize ships which never entered Ostend. The firm Schultz, Serruys, Tamm & Co. specialized in these transactions. To acquire three new burgherships for French captains, this company sent one of its servants with the original French birth certificates to Veurne, Lo and Nieuwpoort and he received the desired documents without any difficulty under pretence that these captains' ships were ready to sail from Ostend.[91]

In Ghent in this period there was also a traffic in burgherships, organized by the lawyer Bruno d'Hert with the knowledge of the notary Buyck and the city council.[92] During the winter of 1781–2 in the Ghent register of burghership a crowd of Dutch fishermen from Vlaardingen, Maassluis and Middelharnis were noted.[93] More than 280 fishermen stayed a few days in Ghent to acquire an imperial passport for themselves and for their vessels. When we consider the fact that, around 1780, the fishing fleets of Maassluis, Vlaardingen and Zierikzee were comprised of 150 hookers, and 44 gaff ships from Middelharnis and Zwartewaal sailed for the cod-fishing, we may assume that almost the whole fishery of the area around Maassluis was protected by the imperial flag.[94] Bruno d'Hert likewise acted as commissioner for neutralizing 40 Frisian koffs and tjalks.[95] The captains of 26 *bomschuiten* (Dutch fishing craft) received their neutral passports in Blankenberge—in the eighteenth century still a small fishing village—through the intermediary of the Dunkirk merchant Pierre Pollet.[96]

At the outbreak of the Anglo-Dutch conflict, several Dutch firms had ships and cargoes in the Antilles. They chose to contact imperial commissioners in order to bring these vessels safely to Europe. For this purpose the company Liebaert, Baes & Derdeyn were given three contracts by the Zierikzee firm Gillis van Ijsselsteyn & Co. to collect one of its frigates and her cargo in Curaçao. The Ostend merchant house engaged *pro forma* the Dutch captain Pieter Balmer and provided him with imperial burghership. Furthermore, Liebaert, Baes & Derdeyn purchased 'on paper' the Zierikzee frigate, which was anchored in the roads of Willemstad, and sent Balmer to Curaçao in one of its own brigantines.[97]

Another rather common abuse regarded the use of double bills of lading. Sometimes, when a ship anchored in the Ostend roads, the captain went ashore for a few hours to meet a commissioner who changed the destination of his bill of lading. This Ostend merchant then went directly to a notary, who confirmed that the Ostend commissioner was the real owner of the cargo and that these goods were being shipped from Ostend to another port in Europe or in the Antilles. This false statement was thereupon certified by the consuls of the belligerent nations. In this way, the captain did not have to pay harbour-dues in Ostend.[98]

In Dunkirk Louis Delattre, the consul of the Austrian Netherlands, discovered some excellent falsifications of the neutral Ostend passport. The false certificates, made by Dunkirk merchants, were used by French privateers to bring their prizes safely to Dunkirk.[99] On one occasion we know that the English authorities were also swindled by two Ostend merchant houses; Vercoustere & Flaneghan and Pierre de Gravier purchased several French and Spanish ships in London for the former French owners via their agent in London, the Widow Doudeuil & Co., and provided these vessels with imperial ship's papers.[100]

One last question to be answered is whether the imperial flag guaranteed complete protection during the Fourth Anglo-Dutch War. On the whole English privateers respected the neutrality of the imperial merchant fleet, but the frequent abuses of the Ostend passports provided the opportunity for the seizure of several imperial vessels. We estimate that about 2–4 per cent of the imperial ships were captured.

Conclusions

At first sight we might conclude that the benefits for Ostend and for the Flemish merchants were limited to being no more than inter-

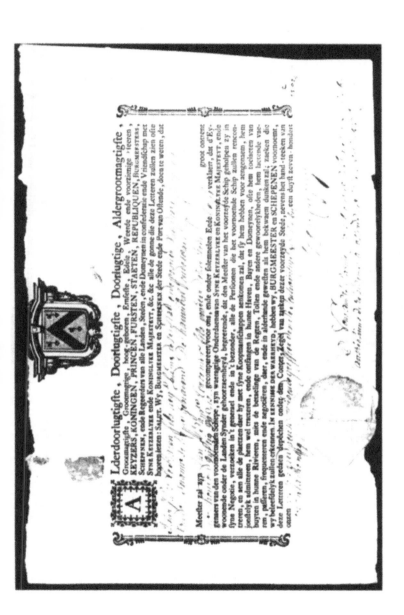

Fig. 12.1 An authentic Imperial passport, signed by the Ostend town-council, for the snow *Hannibal*, which sailed under Imperial colours on behalf of the company Le Baron & fils. This firm from Dieppe acted as commissioner for merchants of Dieppe, Granville and Le Havre. On paper the fleet of Le Baron fils extended to 28 vessels during the war.

(Nationaal Scheepvaartmuseum Antwerpen)

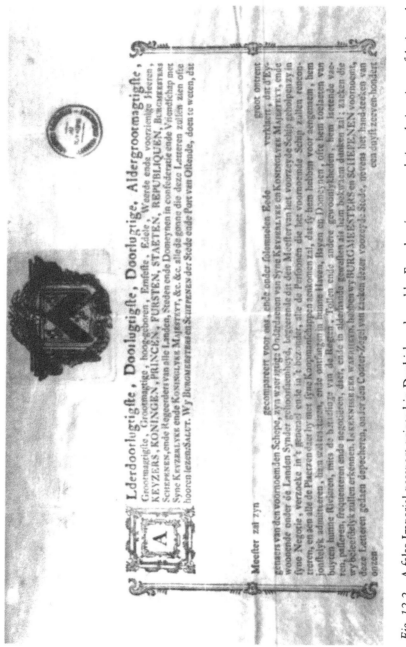

Fig. 12.2 A false Imperial passport printed in Dunkirk and used by French privateers to bring their prizes safely into the harbour. These excellent falsifications were discovered by Louis Delattre who worked as consul for the Austrian Netherlands in Dunkirk. (Algemeen Rijksarchief Brussel)

mediaries for the three belligerent powers, but after the war the Ostend trade did not die away completely. Thanks to the 'economic boom', the port infrastructure had been improved and it could now compete with its neighbours Dunkirk and Flushing. According to the traffic lists of Ostend, the arrivals in the period 1784–8 dropped drastically by 46 per cent but still stayed 221 per cent higher than during the pre-war period. Only the long distance trade to the West Indies and Africa disappeared. In 1786–7 the imperial fleet was comprised of 130 ships, which was still 60 per cent higher than in 1779.

During the Fourth Anglo-Dutch War, the number of Flemish merchants and bankers who invested in Ostend shipping was impressive. Due to high freight rates, shipowning became a very profitable business. On this matter Delplancq, an advisor to the Finance Council, wrote: 'de riches capitalistes de ce pays achetèrent des navires par la certitude que deux ou trois voiages, même à simple fret, doubleroient leur mise'.[101] Estimates in government reports show that about one-third of all neutral ships in Ostend were effectively owned by Flemish firms. We think that many of these opportunist shipowners combined these investments with the neutralizing of foreign ships for a commission fee. But, at the end of the war, the freight rates decreased rapidly, so that it became difficult to compete with the maritime nations. Therefore a great number of ships in the imperial fleet were sold to the Dutch and the French.

Notes

1. R. Baetens, 'Het uitzicht en de infrastructuur van een kleine Noordzeehaven tijdens het Ancien Régime: het voorbeeld van Oostende' *Mededelingen van de Academie van Marine van België (MAMB)*, XXIII (1973–1974–1975), 47–62.

2. A. de Dorlodot, 'Les ports d'Ostende et de Nieuport et les fournitures d'armes aux insurgents américains, 1774–1782' *MAMB*, VII (1953), 141–56.

3. Algemeen Rijksarchief Brussel (ARB), Kanselarij van de Nederlanden te Wenen (KNW), nr. 651.

4. Vereniging voor Familiekunde Oostende (VVFO), Archief Commissie Openbare Onderstand (COO), nr. 4, f° 515–25.

5. This information was kindly supplied by Daniël Farasijn. He is one of the few historians still active, who did research before 1940 in the local Ostend archives, which were destroyed during World War II.

6. Universiteitsbibliotheek Gent, *Gazette van Gent*, 1781–3.

7. Rigsarkivet Copenhagen, Kommercekollegiet nr. 1128, Konsulatssekretariatets Journalsager 1781.

8. K. Klem, 'Om Fr. de Conincks og andre rederes udnyttelse af den Danske

neutralitet isaer i perioden 1781–82' *Handels- og Søfartsmuseets Årbog* (1973), 94–121.

9. VVFO, Archief C00 nr. 4, f° 515–45; C. Pfister-Langanay, *Ports, navires et négociants à Dunkerque (1662–1792)* (Dunkirk, 1985), 333 and 447.

10. A. Cabantous, 'Les gens de mer de Dunkerque entre 1695 et 1725 d'après les dénombrements' *Revue des Amis du Vieux Dunkerque*, 4 (1975), 27–39.

11. J. Parmentier and K. Degryse, 'Maritime Aspects of the Ostend Trade to Mocha, India and China (1715–1732)' in *Company and Shipping* (Leiden, Forthcoming).

12. ARB, Secretarie van Staat en Dorlog (SSO) nr. 2184.

13. Rijksarchief Brugge (RAB), Notariaat Van Caillie nr. 1941, 1781–3.

14. ARB, SSO nr. 2184.

15. Pfister-Langanay, 'Ports', 472.

16. *Ibid*, 460 and 578.

17. *Ibid*, 143.

18. J.M. Price, *France and the Cheseapeake. A History of the French Tobacco Monopoly, 1674–1791* (Ann Arbor, 1970), 497–502.

19. ARB, SSO nr. 2184.

20. RAB, Notariaat Van Caillie nr. 1941, Nov.–Dec. 1781.

21. P. Daudry, *Familles de la marine dunkerquoise* (Dunkirk, 1979), 556.

22. Pfister-Langanay, 'Ports', 133.

23. *Ibid*, 334.

24. VVFO, Archief COO nr. 4, f° 519. Joseph Stival became *poorter* of Ostend in April 1781.

25. ARB, SSO nr. 2184.

26. ARB, Raad van Financiën nr. 5150.

27. Pfister-Langanay, 'Ports', 453.

28. H. Lüthy, *La Banque Protestante en France, de la Révocation de l'Edit de Nantes à la Révolution* (Paris, 1961), vol. II, 609.

29. P. Dardel, *Navires et marchandises dans les ports de Rouen et du Havre au XVIIIe siècle* (Paris, 1963), 384 and 662–3.

30. Besides the firm Famin & Rigoult the imperial merchant houses Romberg & Co., W.J. Van Iseghem, J.J. Chapel and the foreign companies Pierre Gavanon & Co., Schultz, Tamme & Serruys and Dangirard & Co., who were all three established in Ostend, appeared as so-called 'owners' of Le Havre ships bound for Africa and the Antilles.

31. ARB, SSO nr. 2184 and P. Butel, *Les négociants bordelais, l'Europe et les Isles au XVIIIe siècle* (Paris, 1975).

32. C. Carrière, *Les négociants marseillais au XVIIIe siècle* (Marseille, 1973), vol. II, 499; O. Feldbaek, *Dansk Neutralitetspolitik under krigen 1778–1783: Studier i regeringens prioritering af politiske og økonomiske interesser* (Copenhagen, 1971), 106–14.

33. ARB, SSO nr. 2180.

34. ARB, SSO nr. 2160 bis.

35. ARB, SSO nr. 2179.

36. ARB, SSO nr. 2184.

37. RAB, Notariaat Van Caillie nr. 1941, vol. 113, Sept. 1782.

38. ARB, SSO nr. 2151.

39. Universiteitsbibliotheek Gent, *Gazette van Gent*, 27 Aug. 1781.

40. ARB, SSO nr. 2151.
41. Pfister-Langanay, 'Ports', 327.
42. ARB, SSO nr. 2151.
43. VVFO, Archief COO nr. 4.
44. Pfister-Langanay, 'Ports', 359 and 447.
45. ARB, SSO nr. 2184.
46. P. Butel, *Les Negociants*, 162 and 174.
47. ARB, SSO nr. 2184.
48. Besides the south coast of Ireland, the island of Madeira was a favourite port of call for outward-bound West Indiamen.
49. RAB, Notariaat Van Caillie nr. 1941, vol. 107–115 (1781–2) and ARB, SSO nr. 2184.
50. E.S. van Eyck van Heslinga, 'De vlag dekt de lading. 'De Nederlandse koopvaardij in de Vierde Engelse oorlog' *Tijdschrift voor Zeegeschiedenis,* 1 (1982) 2, 105.
51. E. Jacobs and S. Walda, 'De vlag dekt de lading. Scheepsverkopingen in Rotterdam en Amsterdam naar neutrale mogendheden tijdens de Vierde Engelse oorlog (1780–1784) (unpublished doctoral seminar-report, Leiden 1981/1982), 46.
52. VVFO, Archief COO nr. 4.
53. ARB, SSO nr. 2152.
54. ARB, SSO nr. 2184.
55. RAB, Notariaat Van Caillie nr. 1941, vol. 108, Feb. 1782.
56. ARB, SSO nr. 2184.
57. Jacobs and Walda, 'De vlag', 33.
58. RAB, Notariaat Van Caillie nr. 1941, vol. 110, Mar.–Apr. 1782.
59. ARB, SSO nr. 2184.
60. ARB, KNW nr. 651.
61. Lüthy, *La Banque*, 411.
62. ARB, SSO nr. 2184.
63. RAB, Notariaat Van Caillie nr. 1941, vol. 113, Sept.–Nov. 1782.
64. ARB, SSO nr. 2179.
65. ARB, SSO nr. 2184.
66. RAB, Notariaat Van Caillie nr. 1941, vol. 107, 31 Dec. 1781.
67. ARB, SSO nr. 2184.
68. F. Thesée, *Négociants bordelais et colons de Saint-Domingue: La maison Henry Romberg, Bapst & Cie, 1783–1793* (Paris, 1972), 5–10.
69. Y. Vanden Berghe, *Jacobijnen en Traditionalisten: De reacties van Bruggelingen in de Revolutietijd 1780–1794* (Brussels, 1792), 28–9.
70. P. Verhaegen, 'Le commerce des esclaves en Belgique à la fin du XVIIIe siècle' *Annales de la Société d'Archéologie de Bruxelles,* 15 (1901), 259–60.
71. RAB, Notariaat Van Caillie nr. 1941, vol. 107–113 (1781–2) and ARB, SSO nr. 2184.
72. ARB, SSO nr. 2184.
73. ARB, Raad van Financiën nr. 4401.
74. Stadsarchief Brugge, Wettelijke Passeringen 1779–1783.
75. ARB, SSO nr. 2173bis.

76. RAB, Notariaat Van Caillie nr. 1941, vol. 107–108, Oct. 1781–Jan. 1782.
77. Klem, 'Om Fr. de Conincks', 108–9.
78. ARB, SSO nr. 2150.
79. K. Degryse, 'De Antwerpse fortuinen. Kapitaalaccumulatie, -investering en - rendement te Antwerpen in de 18de eeuw' (unpublished doctoral thesis, Gent, 1985), 145.
80. ARB, SSO nr. 2184.
81. Museum Plantin-Moretus Antwerpen, archief nr. 1821.
82. ARB, SSO nr. 2184.
83. Degryse, 'De Antwerpse fortuinen', 147–8.
84. The Admirality registers mention only three merchants living in Ghent who became shipowners during the period 1781–3.
85. Rijksarchief Gent, Familiefonds de Potter d'Indoye nr. 244.
86. ARB, SSO nr. 2184.
87. Stadsarchief Gent, Familiefonds L. Janssens nr. 3301/4.
88. Lüthy, La Banque, 91.
89. Jacobs and Walda, 'De vlag', 23–7.
90. G. Dalle, 'De Nieuwpoortse vloot in 1778–1783' Handelingen van het Genootschap voor Geschiedenis, 128 (1991) 3/4, 190.
91. RAB, archief Brugse Vrije nr. 17.174.
92. ARB, SSO nr. 2150.
93. J. Decavele (ed.), Poorters en buitenpoorters van Gent 1477–1492, 1542–1796 (Gent, 1986), 262–90.
94. J.P. van de Voort, 'De Nederlandse Maatschappij voor Nijverheid en Handel (1777–1977) en de bevordering van de zeevisserij' in Ondernemende Geschiedenis. 22 opstellen bij het afscheid van Mr. H. Van Riel (s'Gravenhage, 1977), 201.
95. ARB, SSO nr. 2160bis.
96. ARB, SSO nr. 2184.
97. RAB, Notariaat Van Caillie nr. 1941, vol. 61, 19 Nov. 1781.
98. ARB, SSO nr. 2160bis.
99. ARB, SSO nr. 2151bis.
100. ARB, SSO nr. 2180.
101. ARB, KNW nr. 512.

CHAPTER 13

Privateers, Piracy and Prosperity: Danish Shipping in War and Peace, 1750–1807

Ole Feldbaek

The Danish Background

The second half of the eighteenth century witnessed the so-called 'Period of Flourishing Trade' for shipping sailing under the Danish flag. The years of the War of the Austrian Succession (1740–8) were good ones for shipping and trade, and those of the Colonial War (1756–3) were even better. The real boom came, however, with the American War of Independence, the Revolutionary Wars and the Napoleonic Wars. In 1807 this fabulous period came to an abrupt end when Britain forced Denmark into the war on the side of Napoleon.

Danish ships could claim harbours in the kingdoms of Denmark and Norway, and the duchies of Schleswig and Holstein, as their home port. Some could claim colonial ports: in the West Indies the harbours of Charlotte Amalie on the island of St Thomas and Christianssted and Frederikssted on the island of St Croix, and in India there were the settlements of Tranquebar on the Coromandel Coast and Serampore in Bengal.

The prosperity experienced by shipping and trade under the Danish flag was based upon two interdependent factors. One was the general growth and diversification of the European economy: the intensified trade between the states and regions of Europe as well as the growing trade between Europe and the overseas regions in the wake of the rising

Fig. 13.1 Anonymous watercolour of the sixty gun ship of the line *Indfødsretten* returning from the Cape of Good Hope in 1781 with a convoy consisting of the Danish Asiatic Company's China ships *Kongen af Danmark* and *Disco* and the Swedish East India Company's China ship *Finalda*. In the League of Armed Neutrality of 1780 the contracting parties had agreed to convoy each other's ships. (Museum of National History, Frederiksborg Castle, Hillerød)

consumer demand for overseas products. This general economic growth was immediately observable to the Danes at the time. In 1730 ships calling at Elsinore to pay Sound dues to the king of Denmark on their way in and out of the Baltic had numbered 4,000. In 1800, their number had risen to 10,000, and the ships had become larger.

The other factor was neutrality. Territorially Denmark as a state belonged to *les satisfaits*.[1] Neutrality in the wars of the great maritime powers was, therefore, her natural policy. And the exploitation of that neutrality would be her obvious endeavour. This exploitation of neutrality was very successful, whether measured by the number of ships sailing under Danish colours or by the value and quantity of the goods transported. Moreover, it was not just exploitation with a short-term perspective. Admittedly it was the temporary vacuum in transport caused by war that provided the precondition for the steep rise in the number of Danish ships after the outbreak of the wars. Nonetheless, the Danish government was very well aware that, through the exploitation of war and neutrality, long-term economic growth could be generated. It has to be acknowledged that the number of Danish ships did decrease with the return of peace. But it did not fall to the pre-war level, but was stabilized at a higher level than before the war. During the war years Danish ships had plied new routes and had entered new markets and thus established valuable contacts, and the Danish shipowners and merchants regularly proved able to hold on to a good deal of the market share they had gained.[2]

The Danish exploitation of neutrality, therefore, was not just a matter of money. It was a matter of very high economic importance. It is, of course, difficult to quantify such an importance, but it might give an idea of the magnitude of economic interests behind Danish shipping to report that in 1801 the mercantile marine of the kingdom of Denmark amounted to at least 0.17 tons per capita, while the corresponding figure for Britain was only 0.11 tons.[3]

The basic problem for the exploitation of neutrality was that neutral shipping invariably aided the weaker belligerent against its stronger opponent. Or, put more directly: neutral Danish shipping generally benefited France and her allies, at the same time undermining the war effort of the British navy and British privateers. Conflicts over the exploitation of Danish neutrality were, therefore, basically an Anglo-Danish matter.

These conflicts were formally fought out on the basis of the Anglo-Danish Treaty of Alliance and Trade dating from 1670, which was remarkably unclear about the principles of neutrality. For example, contraband of war, which the two monarchs solemnly promised not to transport to each other's enemies, was defined as a range of specified military equipment *et alia bello gerundo apta et necessaria*. It was thus up to the British judges to decide whether, for instance, timber, iron, sailcloth and foodstuffs were both suitable and necessary for the waging of war. Furthermore, at times Whitehall exercised very little authority over faraway Courts of Vice-Admiralty such as the notorious prize court on the West Indian island of Tortola, where the judge invariably sided with the local privateering interest. Similarly, it was common knowledge that the judge at the High Court of Admiralty in London allowed his decisions to be guided by directions from the cabinet. Moreover, half the members of the court of appeal, the Lords Commissioners of Prize Appeals, were privy councillors.[4]

Formally, Denmark claimed far-reaching principles of neutrality which gave Danish shipping the right to trade where it pleased, with what it pleased and with whom it pleased. Denmark thus insisted on the right to transport goods belonging to the enemies of Britain, to trade with the colonies of Britain's opponents, and to enter all belligerents' ports, unless they were effectively blockaded. Denmark admitted the right of British naval officers and privateers to board and search Danish merchant ships at sea, and to take them into port for further inspection of the papers and cargo if there were any just grounds for suspicion. However, Denmark opposed the right of British naval officers and privateers to board and search Danish merchant ships under convoy of ships and vessels of the Danish navy. In such cases Britain should accept the verbal assurances of the Danish naval officer who was in charge of the convoy.

None the less, the Anglo-Danish neutrality conflict was not fought out on the basis of principles of international law and obsolete treaty paragraphs. The outcome would be decided not by the relative strength of Britain and Denmark—where it was foreseeable—but by the ever-changing political and military factors of the war. If Britain found herself in a strong position she set very narrow limits to the Danish exploitation of neutrality. In times of strain, on the other hand, she would order her naval officers to put the telescope to their blind eye when confronting Danish convoys, rein in the British privateers and instruct the judges of the prize courts to be lenient in cases concerning Danish ships and cargoes.

Denmark, likewise, based her policy *vis-à-vis* Britain on her evaluation of the overall political and military situation. In general, she pursued what might be termed a defensive neutrality policy. She claimed her far-reaching principles of neutrality, but only to the point at which Britain showed signs of putting power behind her interpretation of the contested principle or signalled her intention to force Denmark into formally giving up the principle in question. In such cases, Denmark would stop claiming her rights and safeguard the contested principle for a future occasion when Britain might find herself in a tight corner. This defensive neutrality policy was followed by Denmark for most of the eighteenth century. The Danish government was under no illusion that it would ever be able to make Britain formally renounce the neutrality principles on which her position as a great maritime power was based. In her defensive neutrality policy Denmark aimed at a tacit British acceptance of the manifold activities carried out under the Danish flag.

Denmark had, of course, an alternative option: to pursue an offensive policy of neutrality. In situations in which she considered Britain would be responsive to pressure, Denmark might enter into alliances with other neutrals, which she did in the Leagues of Armed Neutrality in 1780 and in 1800, with the intention of forcing Britain to accept the Danish neutrality principles. Similarly, she might consider the political and military situation propitious for fitting out convoys and insist on the inviolability of neutral convoys, thereby challenging Britain's rule of the seas. She actually did so in 1798 in order to protect her richly laden ships from the East against British warships and privateers. Whether the policy Denmark pursued was defensive or offensive, her exploitation of neutrality depended on might rather than right.

Areas of Operation

Towards the end of the eighteenth century roughly half the tonnage operating under the Danish flag came from Norway, while Denmark and the duchies each had a quarter of the total tonnage. The complex economic structure of the conglomerate state influenced the ways in which Danish shipping operated. Norway had a substantial export trade in timber, fish and iron. Therefore we see a good deal of the Norwegian tonnage engaged in landing timber in England and fish in the Roman Catholic countries of southern Europe. But it should be borne in mind that this Norwegian export trade was the exception to the rule. Denmark and the duchies had no significant export trade of their own and a home market for imported products was very limited. The predominant part of the shipping under the Danish flag was, therefore, not engaged in trade, but in freight.

Another feature is the strong concentration of overseas shipping in very few ports. Some ships from Norway and from the duchies were engaged in the West India trade, but very few from the Danish provincial towns. The main part of the West India trade was carried on by ships from Copenhagen and from Altona in Holstein. In the East India trade this concentration was even more pronounced. Until 1772 the East India trade was a Copenhagen monopoly, and the trade with China and in Chinese goods remained so. A few Altona ships did participate in the East India trade towards the end of the period, but to all intents and purposes this trade was and would stay the preserve of the capital of the state.

Although shipping under the Danish flag was not divided up into watertight compartments, five areas of operation can be clearly singled out: the home waters; the European waters; the Mediterranean; the West India trade; and the East India trade.

A good deal of the shipping operated in home waters, the main features being a regular exchange of agricultural products from Denmark and the duchies for Norwegian timber, iron and fish, and a re-export trade in imported goods from Copenhagen to the various ports of the state. Some of the larger vessels engaged in this traffic would now and then venture into the Baltic.[5]

The main part of the shipping engaged in foreign trade would operate in European waters: that is, the Baltic and the northern and western coastline of the European continent, including the British Isles.[6] This was an old and well-established area of operation with a well-functioning network of business contacts and with Danish consuls and vice-consuls in all the important ports.

The Mediterranean, on the other hand, was a new area of operation.[7] Because of the harassment of the North African corsairs it had been virtually closed to Danish shipping until the middle of the eighteenth century. Then in 1746 the king of Denmark had chosen to follow the example of the other European maritime states and had concluded a treaty with the *dey* of Algiers, followed in 1751–2 by treaties with the *bey* of Tunisia and the *pasha* of Tripoli. In 1756 a treaty was concluded with the formal overlord of the Barbary rulers, the *sultan* in Constantinople, and the way was thus clear for Danish participation in the flourishing freight trade between ports in the

Mediterranean, and between southern Europe and the ports of north-western Europe and the Baltic.

The West Indies was not a new area of operation.[8] The Danes had acquired the island of St Thomas in 1672, St John in 1718 and finally St Croix in 1733. Until 1754 the West India trade had been a monopoly of the West India-Guinea Company. It had then been thrown open to all the king's subjects, but the mercantilist economic policy had, in practice, linked that trade very closely to Copenhagen where most of the government's growth-promoting activities were concentrated. Some ships on their outward passage would take on board negro slaves at the Danish settlement on the Gold Coast and then proceed to the Caribbean,[9] but the majority sailed directly between their home ports and the Danish islands in the West Indies. In peacetime there was a regular trade in sugar produced on the Danish islands. In wartime very considerable quantities of sugar from the colonies of the belligerents reached the European market by way of Copenhagen, covered by more or less fictitious Danish owners. During the wars, therefore, a large number of smaller vessels under Danish colours operated in Caribbean waters, supplying the isolated colonies with European goods and carrying their export sugar to the Danish islands where it was transshipped for Europe.

Asian waters had been an area of operation for shipping under Danish colours since 1619, when the first Danish vessel cast anchor off Ceylon.[10] In 1620 the Danes acquired Tranquebar, and in 1755 a permanent settlement in Bengal: Serampore. Trade with China and in Chinese goods remained the monopoly of the Danish Asiatic Company during the entire period under review. The remainder of Asian trade, however, was thrown open in 1772 by the Crown, and in 1777 it took over the administration of the Danish settlements in India in order to facilitate private trade. From the early 1770s, therefore, we encounter a flourishing India trade under the Danish flag, but to a large degree for Anglo-Indian account.[11] From the outbreak of the Revolutionary Wars large numbers of ships under Danish colours also participated in the trade between Europe and the isolated Dutch and French colonies in the Indian Ocean: Java and Mauritius. This traffic was a typical wartime phenomenon, as was the large number of so-called country ships with papers from Tranquebar and Serampore which entered the intra-Asian trade under the Danish flag.[12] These waters were the eighteenth-century areas of operation where Danish ships might meet foreign warships, privateers and pirates.

Warships, Privateers and Pirates

Did Danish ships in the second half of the eighteenth century really encounter pirates? The answer is probably no. Although many a ship's captain would swear that the Barbary corsairs were pirates, the king of Denmark, like other Christian monarchs, had concluded treaties with the North African rulers. He had formally accepted that the corsairs were entitled to seize Danish ships which had not been furnished by the Danish authorities with the official safe conducts in the form of Algerian sea passes. Even if ships' masters in Caribbean waters insisted that the Tortola privateers were nothing but freebooters and pirates, the latter were nevertheless furnished with lawful letters of marque by the British authorities. Pirates according to the law of nations were highwaymen at sea who had placed themselves beyond national and international law and the protection of the law. Such pirates did operate in the Straits of Malacca and in the Sunda Strait. The Asiatic Company's China ships passing these Straits would have their guns loaded and ready and boarding nets fitted along the gunwale to prevent Malay pirates from getting on board. But none of the Danish China ships were ever harassed by pirates, and neither were the smaller vessels from Tranquebar and Serampore operating in the waters 'to the Eastward'.

As far as Danish shipping in the second half of the eighteenth century is concerned, pirates should, therefore, be excluded from the list of the dangers of the sea. The warships of the belligerent powers should, however, be included. From the point of view of Danish ship-owners and merchants and of the Danish government, foreign warships and foreign privateers posed exactly the same threat: both were entitled to board and search Danish ships at sea, and both were entitled to bring the Danish ships into port in order to unload and investigate the cargo on grounds of any well-founded suspicion. In the period under review, Danish merchant ships might meet with foreign warships and privateers in all the five areas of operation outlined above.

Strange as it may sound they might even encounter them in home waters. In the early years of the Revolutionary Wars, French privateers would shelter from the cruising British warships among the countless skerries along the Norwegian coastline and occasionally break out and raid on the North Sea. Some enterprising British naval officers reacted by pursuing the French privateers into Norwegian territorial waters, and some even succeeded in eradicating the privateers. This regularly

Fig. 13.2 Aquatint 1805 by Niels Truslew showing an English privateer visiting and searching a Danish vessel. The demonstratively peaceful manner is typical of the way in which most of the English naval ships and privateers carried out their control of neutral shipping. (Museum of Shipping and Trade, Kronborg Castle, Elsinore)

led to unpleasant encounters between the Danish foreign minister and the British envoy in Copenhagen. A solution to the problem was eventually found when Britain put pressure on Denmark and made her forbid the sale of French prizes in Norwegian ports, thereby removing the economic incentive for the French privateers to operate in these waters. British warships and privateers regularly cruised off the Norwegian coast, hoping to catch some of the Dutch East India Company's ships which had sought shelter in the ports of Bergen and Trondheim and were waiting for a chance to cover the last dangerous passage to Texel. And occasionally British warships cruised in the Skagerak, the waters between Norway and Denmark, hunting for richly laden Danish ships returning from Batavia with cargoes on a Dutch account.

The activities of foreign warships and privateers in home waters were a nuisance to shipping under the Danish flag, whereas their activities in European waters constituted the greatest risk to neutral shipping. British and French privateers were literally swarming in these waters, and both the eastern and, particularly, the western entrance to the English Channel were their favourite hunting grounds. On their outward voyage some Danish ships therefore chose the route north of Scotland, and not a few of the ships returning from the East were instructed to keep a western course close to Newfoundland and then steer north of Scotland, in order to slip into a Norwegian port and get the latest information about the political situation in Europe. From Norway these ships might be escorted on the last stage of their passage to Copenhagen by a Danish naval brig. After the opening of the Eider Canal in 1784, ships from Copenhagen and the Baltic en route for Amsterdam could use this route and then proceed in the shallow waters along the North German coast—where British warships and privateers lay in wait for them when they had to pass the deep water in the river mouths of the Elbe, the Weser and the Ems on their way to the safety of the Zuider Sea. While the European waters in general constituted the greatest risks to neutral Danish shipping, the Baltic occupied a special position. British and French warships and privateers had no tradition of operating there, and the Leagues of Armed Neutrality of 1780 and 1800 actually contained provisions for keeping the Baltic a sea of peace.

In the Mediterranean Danish shipping might meet warships and privateers of all the belligerent powers. In the almost endemic warfare between Spain and Algiers, many Danish vessels were boarded and searched for naval and military equipment destined for the North African states. The main threat, however, came from the Barbary corsairs. Normally Danish ships furnished with Algerian sea passes could feel safe. But this was not always so. Now and again the North African rulers would demand higher payments, for instance when a new *dey* ascended the throne. Or they would react on suspicion—not always unfounded—that the Danish authorities had clandestinely sold Danish sea passes to ships from Hamburg. The reaction of the North African states was to allow their corsairs to seize Danish ships and to sell the crews as slaves.

The West India trade also had to reckon with harassment from warships and privateers, partly when running the gauntlet in European waters on their outward and homeward voyages, partly out in the open waters of the Atlantic. And in the Caribbean swarms of small privateers would be lying in wait for the Danish ships in the numerous creeks and bays of the islands.

The East India trade, likewise, had to run the gauntlet in European waters, and in the Atlantic they might encounter cruising warships as far south as the Azores. On the southernmost stage of their route they might meet with British warships and privateers operating from the Cape of Good Hope at periods when the Cape Colony was in British possession and a Court of Vice-Admiralty was established there. In the eastern seas Danish shipping might meet with British or French naval squadrons which were cruising there. The main threat to ships under neutral Danish colours was the French privateers operating from Mauritius, or Isle de France as it was then called. Their favourite hunting ground would be the track followed by the richly laden India, China and Batavia ships returning with the north-east monsoon en route for Europe. Occasionally the French privateers would also cruise in the Bay of Bengal, clearing the sea of vessels passing in and out of the Hughli.

In fact, none of the five areas of operation of Danish shipping in the second half of the eighteenth century was free from the dangers of warships and privateers. The question is: what did the Danes do to evade or minimize the risks connected with these encounters at sea? What losses did they sustain? And what was—in the broader sense— the price of prosperity?

The Price of Prosperity

One way to evade the dangers was of course to choose passages where
the foreign warships and the privateers did not operate and to abstain
from transporting unlawful goods. But that was easier said than done.
Firstly, the warships and the privateers were of course cruising in
waters through which the neutral ships had to pass. Secondly, if they
refused to take on board war contraband or goods actually belonging to
the belligerents, others would accept the freight and they would be left
behind with an empty hold. What they could do—and actually did—
was to procure the most convincing invoices and ship's papers. But in
some situations they could do nothing, when, for instance French
privateers were authorized to seize every ship which had the smallest
item of British origin on board—be that a carpet in the master's cabin
or a bucket of coal in the galley.

Then they could insure the ship and the cargo against the risks of
the sea and the war, which indeed the shipowners and merchants did
with insurance companies and underwriters in Copenhagen, Hamburg,
Amsterdam and London. But occasionally the insurance rates would
rise to virtually prohibitive levels, as they did in the summer of
1798.[13] At a time when the premium for voyages between Copenhagen
and ports in the Baltic and Norway was between 1 and 2 per cent, the
premium for voyages to and from the West Indies was 8 to 10 per cent,
to ports in the Mediterranean 20 per cent, and to and from the East
Indies between 20 and 30 per cent. Even then the underwriters refused
to insure against French privateers.

On the political level the Danish government did what it could to
make the belligerents order their naval officers and privateers to respect
neutral Danish shipping. But in periods of intense warfare at sea, such
démarches were of little avail. In Paris the revolutionary government at
times exercised very little authority—if any—over privateering bases
such as Nantes, Bordeaux and Marseilles.

The last resort of a neutral state like Denmark was to provide the
merchant marine with naval protection. The use of force had
occasionally been tried against the Barbary states: in 1770, for instance,
a squadron had blockaded and bombarded the port of Algiers, and in
1797 Danish naval ships gave battle to the *pasha*'s corsairs off the
port of Tripoli. Using force against a great maritime power such as
Britain was, however, quite another matter. At the outbreak of the
Revolutionary Wars, therefore, when Danish shipowners asked for a

convoy system, they had received a very cool answer from the foreign minister: 'Do you want war? I can take you into the war tomorrow. But taking you out again—that is beyond my power.'[14] Count Bernstorff knew only too well that neutral convoys were political brinkmanship. For one thing, the number of Danish warships was limited—some 20 ships of the line and a similar number of frigates and brigs; and most of them had to remain in the port of Copenhagen, in readiness to repel a surprise attack by the Swedes.[15] But more importantly a challenge to Britain in the form of Danish convoys, whose commanders were ordered to refuse any British demand to board and search the merchant ships under their protection, might trigger off a grave political crisis, even war.

The Danish government did not suffer any delusions of naval grandeur. They had sent out Danish convoys during the Colonial War, and also during the American War of Independence, when convoys had been sent all the way to the West Indies and to India,[16] but they had only been sent out after a careful calculation of the political risks. In the Colonial War, Denmark had miscalculated the risks and had been forced by Britain to give up her convoys. In the American War, however, Britain had tacitly chosen to accept the Danish convoys— already being at war with France, Spain, the Netherlands and the American Colonies, and not wishing to make more enemies.

In 1793, Count Bernstorff foresaw an intensification of the war at sea, and he vetoed the demands of the shipping interest for convoys until his death in 1797. But his young son and successor, Christian Bernstorff, did not have the authority to refuse the combined pressure of the shipping interest and the navy, and in 1798 the Prince Regent sanctioned Danish convoys in European waters, in the Mediterranean and to and from the East Indies. He did so in the expectation that in her precarious political and military position Britain would once again abstain from taking up the challenge—an expectation which was actually fulfilled, at least for the time being.[17]

However, neither safer routes, political *démarches* nor convoys could safeguard neutral Danish shipping against damage inflicted by warships and privateers. Damage might be anything from an insignificant loss of time to a wholesale condemnation of the ship and her cargo. Boarding and searching of the ship's papers at sea cannot be—and was not—looked upon as damage. Damage began to pile up when the ship was brought into port for further inspection of her cargo. Then the owner lost valuable time; the cargo might be damaged; and if it was ordered to be sold, the owner invariably found the sale price too low. The lawyers' fees were staggering, and if the verdict went against the naval officer or the privateer who had brought in the neutral vessel, it often proved impossible to make them pay the compensation awarded by the judge.

It is unlikely that all this minor damage can be registered—and unlikely that the work would be worth the historian's while. Occasionally we do come across lists of Danish ships brought in for inspection and adjudication. Although they are by no means explicit with regard to the actual expenses incurred by the Danish owners, they do give an impression of the magnitude of the damage. In the period from 1793 until 1802, French warships and privateers are said to have seized 467 Danish ships.[18] From 21 March 1799 until 14 January 1801 the British seized 156 Danish ships.[19] From the autumn of 1796 until the end of 1797 the French seized 75 Danish ships, and 91 during the first five months of 1798.[20] These data would suggest that in the Revolutionary Wars the French annually seized between 1 and 1½ per cent of the Danish ships and that the British seizures were between 3 and 3½ per cent. The British figure, though, is undoubtedly too high, as it is based upon data from a period when the British war effort at sea was much more energetic than usual.

Seen in the longer perspective, therefore, the economic damage done by warships and privateers to neutral Danish shipping seems to have been limited, even bordering on the insignificant. What characterized the wars was not losses but prosperity. Admittedly there were cases where staggering sums of money were involved—and lost. These cases, however, were chiefly connected with ships and cargoes from the East, where the judge—like the historian today—suspected the Danish papers and the Danish flag to be mere camouflage covering the property of the belligerents. When, in such cases, the judge did condemn the ship and the cargo as good and lawful prize, the real losers were not the Danes providing the neutral façade, but the French, the Dutch and the British owners.

The contemporary lists of seizures do not give information about the areas of operation of the ships seized. For one area of operation, however, we are in a position to present concrete figures for the damage done by warships and privateers to Danish shipping. That is the Asian trade. During the Colonial War none of the Asiatic Company's India and China ships were lost; and during the American War of Independence no ships trading to India, China or Mauritius—be they

Company ships or private vessels—were taken either.[21] The Revolutionary Wars from 1793 to 1802, on the other hand, witnessed remarkable losses. But as will be seen, the losses were almost exclusively connected to one particular branch of the East India trade: that with Batavia. None of the Asiatic Company's ships trading to India, China, Batavia or Mauritius were taken. Of a total of 26 ships under Danish colours *en route* from Mauritius to Copenhagen, only one was lost: the *Lolland*, which was taken by the British and condemned as prize.[22] The losses sustained by the private ships leaving India for Copenhagen were equally small. Of a total of 50 ships leaving India, only three were taken by French privateers. Two—the *Bornholm* and the *Juliana Maria*—were brought in to Nantes and condemned as Anglo-Indian property, which they actually were. The third, the *Duntzfelt*, was retaken by a British frigate and lost at sea.[23]

In the Batavia trade we bound with an entirely different pattern. Some 40 ships under Danish colours left Java for Copenhagen. At least 17 were taken, two by the French and 15 by British warships and privateers. One remarkable trait here is that seven of these ships took part in the so-called Batavia speculation: a venture in which the great Copenhagen merchant Frédéric de Coninck tried using his name and the neutral Danish flag to cloak a fleet of 19 large ships with cargoes for Dutch account.[24] Moreover, nine of the Batavia ships taken were on so-called direct voyages; that is, ships fitted out in the East and dispatched to Europe with Danish names and Danish papers. It is typical of the highly speculative nature of the early Batavia trade that all the ships taken set sail from Java in the years 1797 and 1798, immediately after the news that the Netherlands had entered the war. After this initial period of heavy losses the Batavia trade under Danish colours changed its character. The Dutch and their Danish agents had learned their lesson: that the British would not tolerate such excessive exploitation of neutrality and that they were able to curb it. From then on the Batavia trade was carried on by Danish ships coming out from Europe.

The short-lived peace of Amiens (1802–3) hit the Danish East India trade hard. After the outbreak of the Napoleonic Wars in May 1803 the Danish government and Danish shipowners and merchants accepted as a proven fact that the British warships and privateers effectively commanded the sea lanes, and when the Danish East India trade was resumed all parties concerned kept a low profile. And this cautious line paid off. No Danish ships from the East were taken and condemned as prizes.

But this was not to last for long. After the British attack upon Copenhagen in the late summer of 1807, Denmark was no longer neutral, and the British hunt for the Danish East Indiamen was on. Some reached safety in a friendly or a neutral port. But most of the ships were taken, either while lying in the Hughli or at sea, and summarily condemned as enemy property.

The Danish East India trade had been a flourishing one. In the period from 1772 to 1807 a total of 350 cargoes sold at the Copenhagen auctions had netted approximately 135 million rixdollars.[25] The damage done to this trade by warships and privateers had been modest and the economic losses had mostly been borne by Dutch and Anglo-Indian investors trying to carry on an illicit trade under a neutral flag. The figures from the Danish East India trade and the general picture of the damage done by warships and privateers to a neutral trade such as the Danish in the second half of the eighteenth century should, I think, be taken as a warning against overestimating the effects of this kind of early economic warfare.

If one looks for really serious damage, one should rather seek it at the political level. In 1798, Denmark had reacted to the intensified warfare at sea by sending out convoys to protect her trade. Initially Britain had ignored this challenge to her exercise of seapower. In 1800, however, the British government decided to contest Denmark's interpretation of the principle of the inviolability of neutral convoys. When Denmark refused to give in and joined the League of Armed Neutrality with Russia, Sweden and Prussia, Britain retaliated by declaring war. In the battle of Copenhagen on 2 April 1801, Nelson crushed the Danish naval defences and forced Denmark to give in to Britain's demands.[26] The price Denmark was forced to pay for her challenging exploitation of neutrality was her formal renunciation of the contested neutrality principles she had so consistently claimed during the wars of the eighteenth century.

Notes

1. Ole Feldbaek, 'Eighteenth Century Danish Neutrality: Its Diplomacy, Economics and Law' *Scandinavian Journal of History*, 8 (1983), no. 1; Ole Tuxen, 'Principles and Priorities. The Danish View of Neutrality during the Colonial War of 1755–63' *Scandinavian Journal of History*, 13 (1988), no. 3.
2. Ole Feldbaek *Dansk neutralitetspolitik under krigen 1778–1783: Studier i regeringens prioritering af politiske og oekonomiske interesser* (Copenhagen, 1973).
3. Ole Feldbaek, 'The Anglo-Danish convoy conflict of 1800: A Study of

Small Power Policy and Neutrality' *Scandinavian Journal of History,* 2 (1977), 162.

4. E.S. Roscoe, *A History of the English Prize Court* (London, 1924), 40–41; Isabel de Madariaga, *Britain, Russia and the Armed Neutrality of 1780: Sir James Harris' Mission to St. Petersburg during the American Revolution* (New Haven, 1962), 70, 144 and 154. See also Henry J. Bourgignon, *Sir William Scott, Lord Stowell, Judge of the High Court of Admiralty, 1798–1828* (Cambridge, 1987).

5. Anders Monrad Moeller, *Fra galeoth til galease, Studier i de kongerigske provinsers soefart i det 18. århundrede* (Esbjerg, 1981).

6. A general account of Danish shipping in European waters in the eighteenth century does not exist.

7. The only work on Danish activities in the Mediterranean in the eighteenth century is the now obsolete, C.F. Wandel, *Danmark og barbareskerne 1746–1845* (Copenhagen, 1919). A good presentation of the Algerian sea pass system is given by Erik Goebel, 'De algierske soepasprotokoller: En kilde til langfarten 1747–1840' *Arkiv,* 9 (1982–3).

8. Erik Goebel, *Dansk sejlads på Vestindien og Guinea 1671–1807* (Handels-og Soefartsmuseets Aerbog, 1982).

9. A preliminary account of the Danish slave trade is given by Svend Erik Green-Pedersen, 'The History of the Danish Negro Slave Trade 1733–1807: An Interim Study Relating in Particular to its Volume, Structure, Profitability and Abolition' *Revue française d'Histoire d'Outre-Mer,* 62 (1975), 226–7. See also his 'Colonial Trade Under the Danish Flag: A Case Study of the Danish Slave Trade to Cuba 1790–1807' *Scandinavian Journal of History,* 5 (1980), no. 2.

10. Kristof Glamann, 'The Danish Asiatic Company 1732–72' *Scandinavian Economic History Review,* 8 (1960); Erik Goebel, 'The Danish Asiatic Company's Voyages to China, 1732–1833' *Scandianivian Economic History Review,* 27 (1979); and Ole Feldbaek, 'Danish East India Trade 1772–1807, Statistics and Structure' *Scandinavian Economic History Review,* 26 (1978).

11. Ole Feldbaek, *India Trade under the Danish Flag 1772–1808: European Enterprise and Anglo-Indian Remittance and Trade* (Odense, 1969).

12. Ole Feldbaek, 'Country Trade under Danish Colours: A Study of Economics and Policy around 1800', in Karl Reinhold Haellquist (ed.), *Asian Trade Routes: Continental and Maritime* (London, 1991).

13. Johannes Werner, *Christian Wilhelm Duntzfelt: En dansk storkboeomand fra den glimrende handelsperiode* (Copenhagen, 1927), 63–4.

14. The anecdote is in Louis Bobé (ed.), *August Hennings' dagbog under hans ophold i Koebenhavn 1802* (Copenhagen, 1934), 198.

15. Ole Louis Frantzen, *Truslen fra oest: Dansk-norsk flådepolitik 1769–1807* (Copenhagen, 1980.

16. Ole Feldbaek, *Ostindisk konvoj i den florissante handelsperiode.* Handels-og Soefartsmuseets Aerbog, 1981.

17. Ole Feldbaek, *Denmark and the Armed Neutrality 1800–1801: Small Power Policy in a World War* (Copenhagen, 1980).

18. W. Alison Phillips and A.S. Reede, *Neutrality: Its History, Economics and Law. II. The Napoleonic Period* (New York, 1936), 216.

19. Axel Linvald, 'Bidrag til oplysning om Danmark-Norges handel og skibsfart 1800–1807' *Historisk Tidsskrift*, 8 (1917), no. 6, 396.

20. Axel Linvald, *Kronprins Frederik og hans regering 1797–1807: I. Styrelsen og dens maend. Çkonomisk og social politik* (Copenhagen, 1923), 111.

21. The information about the seizures of East India ships under Danish colours is based upon material too disparate to be quoted in detail. For a presentation of the sources, see my 'Danish East India Trade 1772–1807'.

22. Rigsarkivet. Kommercekollegiet. Ostindiske Kontor, *Ostindiske journalsager* 1799, 171 and 1802, 177.

23. The papers of the cases against the *Bornholm* and the *Juliana Maria* are kept in the Archives départementales de la Loire Atlantique in Nantes. Those of the *Duntzfelt*, like most of the other cases concerning Danish ships taken by British warships and privateers, are in the High Court of Admiralty papers in the Public Record Office. London.

24. Ole Feldbaek, 'Dutch Batavia Trade via Copenhagen 1795–1807: A Study of Colonial Trade and Neutrality' *Scandinavian Economic History Review*, 21 (1973). See also Els van Eyck van Heslinga, *Van compagnie naar koopvaardij: De scheepvaartverbinding van de Bataafsche Republiek met de kolonien in Azie 1795–1806* (Amsterdam, 1988).

25. Ole Feldbaek, 'Den danske Asienhandel 1616–1807: Vaerdi og volumen', *Historisk Tidsskrift*, (1990), no. 2. English version in *Scandinavian Economic History Review* (1991), no. 1. By way of comparison, the state revenues of the kingdom of Denmark around 1772 were some three million rixdollars. Around 1800 they had risen to between four and five millions, equivalent to one million pound sterling.

26. Ole Feldbaek, 'The Anglo-Russian Rapprochement of 1801: A Prelude to the Peace of Amiens' *Scandinavian Journal of History*, 3 (1978), no. 3. See also the same author's monograph on the battle of Copenhagen: *Slaget på Reden* (Copenhagen, 1985).

CHAPTER 14

The Voyage of the *Bornholm*: Danish Convoy Service in the Caribbean, 1780–1781

Erik Goebel

The Political Background

In many ways the eighteenth century was characterized by the increasing dominance of the great powers; their rivalry gradually took on a global scope. The most important actors were France and Britain, whereas the double-monarchy of Denmark–Norway played the role of a decidedly small power.[1]

After the Great Northern War against Sweden (1709–20), Denmark–Norway had had to abandon its hope of re-conquering the provinces east of the Sound that had been lost to Sweden in 1658. Instead, the Danish government concentrated on securing the rest of the realm, which consisted of present-day Denmark and Norway together with the duchies of Schleswig and Holstein. In addition to these areas, the Danish king ruled over the Faroe Islands, Iceland and Greenland, as well as small but economically important tropical possessions in India, on the Gold Coast in Africa, and in the West Indies. The Caribbean possessions included the three small Virgin Islands of St Thomas, St John and St Croix. In this chapter the terms Denmark and Danish refer to the whole of this territory.

Another vital government interest was to keep the nation out of the conflicts of the great powers as far as possible, and to promote national prosperity by turning neutrality to profit. The Danish authorities possessed rather limited means to achieve these ends. Neither the army nor the navy was strong enough to protect Denmark, mainly because of the weak economy of the realm. It was therefore necessary to position the double-monarchy as favourably as possible in the arena of international politics, with its shifting alliances among the great powers. After the peace of 1720, Denmark allied itself with Britain. From 1740 on, however, Denmark sided instead with France, which was still Europe's strongest power. After 1765 and for the rest of the century, Denmark joined forces with Russia, an arrangement which allowed it to retain possession of Norway and the duchies.

An extremely important element of Danish policy was the promotion of trade and shipping under the Danish flag. As the major warring nations were France and Britain, neutral tonnage and capital was able to take over a considerable portion of the great powers' commercial activities in the second half of the eighteenth century. In practice, Britain was master of the seas, and could put high-handed limits on the freedom of action of a small power. The Danish government, on the other hand, knew very well how to take advantage of Britain's difficult situation. Copenhagen carried out a pragmatic policy of neutrality, pressing the English as far as possible but withdrawing immediately when necessary.

Denmark formally insisted on the following four main rights of neutrals: first, to call at all ports belonging to belligerents; second, to carry all kinds of goods, except actual war materiel; third, to carry goods belonging to belligerents; and fourth, to refuse visitation and search of neutral merchantmen under escort. During the Seven Years War between Britain and France (1756–63), it had often been necessary to abandon these principles, as Britain was powerful enough to impose by force its own interpretation of the principles of neutrality. This included a broad definition of war contraband; rejection of the principle that a neutral flag protected the cargo as well as the ship; the right to search all neutral convoys; and finally the 'Rule of 1756', i.e. denial of the right of neutrals to call at foreign colonies to which they had not been permitted to navigate before the war. As the war went on, the Danish government reluctantly had to accept these principles, which were quite opposite to its own points of view. The acceptance was tacit, however; officially, the old Danish principles were insisted upon.

During the American War of Independence (1776–83), the same positions were taken, with the important difference that Britain was now much harder pressed by France and its allies, Spain and Holland. Britain therefore refrained from enforcing the Rule of 1756, although Danish vessels engaged in intensive shipping to French and Spanish islands in the Caribbean. Britain also reluctantly accepted Danish convoys in Asian waters and the Caribbean. These concessions were made in order not to force Denmark into the enemy camp.

This pragmatic and defensive exploitation of neutrality was on the whole extremely lucrative for Denmark–Norway. It was therefore most inconvenient when Catharine II of Russia, in the summer of 1780, forced the double-monarchy to join the Armed League of Neutrality directed against Britain. Only five days before, however, the Danish foreign minister, Andreas Peter Bernstorff, skilfully seized a chance to persuade Britain to enter into a separate Anglo-Danish contraband convention. Denmark thereby gave up its central demand that a neutral flag should cover any cargo; in return, Britain explicitly excepted all important Danish-Norwegian export commodities, i.e. foodstuffs, timber and iron, from the definition of contraband.

This was the culmination of Bernstorff's foreign policy as far as Danish independence is concerned. The government in Copenhagen quite correctly expected to profit more by acting on its own than by acting in strict concert with the Armed League of Neutrality. In 1781, the Danish prime minister expressed his attitude this way: 'It is the more prudent to push our own interests and slip through as best we can.' The highly favourable conditions for an independent Danish exploitation of neutrality prompted the Danes to press Britain for economic concessions, which made possible extensive and extremely profitable trade and shipping under the Danish flag. This apparently rather risky small-power policy was mastered by the Danish regime, and the desired economic result was in fact achieved.

In this atmosphere of hectic exploitation of neutrality, merchants and shipowners urged the government to assign the Royal Danish Navy to convoy duty. As early as 1779, naval frigates provided escort to vessels going back and forth between the Danish West Indies and the warring powers' colonies in the Caribbean, the French islands in particular.

In this chapter we will follow the Danish man-of-war *Bornholm* on her voyage across the Atlantic and in West Indian waters in 1780 and 1781. The captain was Peter Schioenning, 48 years of age. He and his crew experienced on the way simple shipboard routine as well as some extraordinary incidents. The main emphasis will be laid on naval rather than on the political or economic aspects of the voyage. Our main source is the captain's letters and general report to the Admiralty in Copenhagen.[2]

Convoys and Privateers

During the American War of Independence, shipping was not threatened so much by the great powers' men-of-war as by the numerous privateers. These were private vessels with official letters of marque issued by the warring governments, authorizing them to participate in hostilities at sea, especially by capturing the enemy's merchant vessels or other ships carrying his cargoes. Special prize courts ruled on the legality of seizures, deciding if the cargoes contained contraband.

Besides these legal privateers there were considerable problems with the fractious North African privateers. These infested the Mediterranean but also sailed west of Gibraltar. Like other European maritime nations, Denmark entered into treaties with these Moslem Barbary States between 1746 and 1753. Denmark paid substantial annual tributes, in return for which the king's subjects were allowed to sail unmolested.

These problems are alluded to even in the prologue of the Royal Instructions, dated 24 January 1780, to Peter Schioenning.[3] He was ordered with his naval frigate, *Bornholm*, to escort a small armed merchant vessel, *St Jan*, from Copenhagen to Algiers. Her captain, lieutenant commander Adolph Tobias Herbst, was to deliver Denmark's annual presents to the *dey* of Algiers. In addition, the *Bornholm* was to give escort to a Danish Asiatic Company's East Indiaman as far as Cape St Vincent, as well as to all private West Indiamen under the Danish flag that might request such protection on the first stretch of their long voyage.

Schioenning was not to allow anyone to search the convoy, not even to examine the ships' papers, either on the voyage out and home, or in the Caribbean. Instead he was to invoke the right of neutrality and affirm his convoy's adherence to the treaties, declaring that no contraband was carried by the ships, of which fact he had to assure himself before a vessel was allowed to be taken under escort in the first place. If necessary, he should resort to force in order to prevent foreigners from searching the convoy. As the king explicitly expressed it, the purpose of the escort was 'to protect the shores of Our West Indian Islands, to develop and secure Our subjects' West Indian trade in order to extend the welfare and flourishing of the country'. The orders required Schioenning otherwise to conform to the Danish Navy's Articles of War.[4] 'In conclusion, you may exert what seamanship and discretion you find appropriate.' By adding this sentence, the Admiralty in effect placed all responsibility on the captain.

In Copenhagen Harbour

Peter Schioenning was born in 1732 and became a midshipman when he was 14. Since then he had made excellent career progress in the navy. Having received good recommendations from his superiors, he had been a captain on men-of-war in home waters since 1770.[5]

Schioenning reported the *Bornholm* ready for sea on 17 January 1780. The *St Jan*, however, was not yet ready, and the two ships became icebound in Copenhagen harbour, together with several other vessels. A most dramatic episode occurred on the night of 27 February.[6] A violent fire broke out on board a brand new East Indiaman, which was frozen in the ice only one and a half cable lengths from the two frigates, and their supplies of powder had to be sunk underwater. Early in the morning the fire reached the powder room of the burning ship, and it blew up. Schioenning acted very courageously on this occasion. After many conventional attempts to extinguish the fire had failed, he tried to chop a hole at the waterline to allow sea water to flow into the hull of the merchantman. Unfortunately this attempt was also in vain. Nevertheless his action was regarded as so praiseworthy that it was explicitly mentioned among the grounds of the sentence imposed on Schioenning by a court martial the following year.

The *Bornholm* was an ordinary Danish naval frigate, built by the well-known naval architect Henrik Gerner in 1774. Her overall length was 130 ft, the beam 35 ft, and the draught 15 ft. The armament consisted of 24 12-pounders and 10 4-pounders. The hull was painted black, the gun ports were yellow, and the masts and yards were pale yellow and black respectively. To this must be added the beautiful carving and gilt ornamentation fore and aft.[7] The crew for this long voyage was 226 men. The ship had been given the name of a Danish island in the Baltic. All this was typical of Danish naval frigates at that time.

Fig. 14.1 Commander Peter Schioenning, born 1732, died 1813. Painting by Johan Hoerner 1763. (Museum of National History, Frederiksborg Castle, Hillerød)

The Voyage Out via Algiers

At last, on 12 March 1780 at dawn, the two vessels departed the roads of Copenhagen, but on the very first night, westerly winds drove them irretrievably apart. When the current also became unfavourable, the

Bornholm had to anchor at Elsinore until 6 April, without any further news of the *St Jan*. A week after leaving Elsinore, Schioenning passed south of the Faroe Islands. From there he went west of Ireland and arrived at Lisbon on 20 April. This was the agreed-upon *rendez-vous* under circumstances like this, and the *St Jan* was found there safe in port. Having victualled, watered and taken some wine on board, the two Danish frigates again sailed together. The day after, at Cape St Vincent, they were hailed by a British naval frigate of 60 guns. The Danes at once beat to quarters, but as soon as the English had ascertained that they were not Dutch or French, they sailed on their way.

Schioenning and Herbst anchored off Algiers from 12 to 30 May 1780, while the latter executed his errand to the Algerian prince. While they were there, the need for the treaty was made evident, as the Algerians brought in a Venetian and a Neapolitan vessel. Both were condemned as good prize and the crews were kept as hostages, to be ransomed at great cost. Returning through the Strait of Gibraltar was difficult for the two Danish vessels because of strong westerly winds, but no problems were encountered with the Spanish guard ships. In the Atlantic Schioenning and Herbst set their course to the south of Madeira, which was sighted on 20 June. A little more than three weeks later, the Caribbean island of Antigua was sighted. The ships let go their anchors at Christiansted on the Danish island of St Croix on 13 July 1780.

First Convoy in the Caribbean

Peter Schioenning at once reported, in accordance with his instructions, to Major-General Peter Clausen, governor-general of the Danish West Indies. Clausen had authority to decide where and when Danish escorting vessels were to be sent out, and what ships would be allowed the protection of Danish convoys in the Caribbean. On the next day, the governor-general wrote ordering Schioenning to go to the French island of Guadeloupe, escorting three vessels on the way, and returning to St Croix with two ships belonging to the Royal Chartered Danish West Indian Trading Company. Schioenning pointed out that it was a difficult and dangerous time of the year for sailing ships in these waters but was obliged to leave St Thomas on 25 July—the day that inaugurates the hurricane season in the Caribbean.

The vessels arrived safely at Guadeloupe, which is situated about

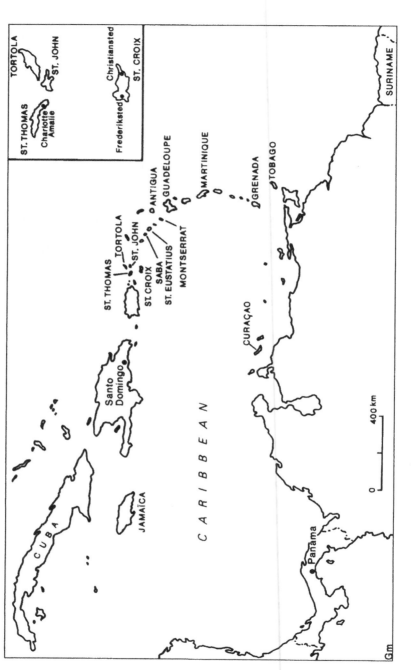

Map 14.1   The Caribbean (inset: the Danish Virgin Islands)

300 nautical miles south-east of the Danish islands, on 6 August. The *Bornholm* then had to wait, cruising offshore for a week and a half, until the Trading Company's two ships were ready for departure. The convoy that weighed anchor on the morning of 15 August consisted of the two company vessels as well as two of the three vessels Schioenning had escorted from St Thomas. In addition, moreover, two other small ships under Danish colours followed in the wake of the convoy. The Danish commander notified the newcomers that only under express orders from his governor-general was he allowed to escort them, and that under no circumstances could he take them to any other port than St Thomas. None the less, the two vessels could keep close to the convoy, as he was authorized to protect all Danish ships against privateers, although not against naval men-of-war.

At dawn the next day, Schioenning learned that an unknown merchant vessel had joined his convoy in the dark of the night. At exactly the same time, he received the alarming news that three warships were approaching the eight vessels. Firing a shot, they showed English colours and laid themselves close to the *Bornholm*. Both parties cleared for action. The three small merchant vessels that did not properly belong to the convoy fled at once. Schioenning explained to the English that the three were not under his protection. At the request of the British, the *Bornholm* fired a gun, upon which two of the fugitives returned flying Danish colours. The third one did not turn around and showed no flag at all. The British men-of-war gave chase but did not catch the small vessel before they all disappeared from the sight of the convoy.

It was then learned, to Schioenning's astonishment, that the fleeing vessel was registered at St Croix, and that the stranger that had entered the convoy during the night was Dutch, although it had had the audacity to hoist the Danish flag! It also turned out that a schooner which had been under escort from Guadeloupe, flying Danish colours the whole time, was French-owned! Both sailed on with the convoy to St Thomas, although Schioenning tried several times to get rid of them.

Back home again, Schioenning notified the governor-general Peter Clausen of this unfortunate affair, drawing Clausen's attention to the serious consequences if the British authorities could justly point out that Denmark had not strictly observed the conditions of neutrality. In Schioenning's opinion the two captains ought to be punished, and the British should be informed of the facts of the case. The governor-general, an experienced official, brushed aside the arguments of the newly arrived commander: it was not necessary at all to interrogate or bring a charge against the foreigners, 'as such conduct always has been resorted to to save oneself'. This concluded the affair, and nothing more happened.

Peter Schioenning later learned with satisfaction that the fleeing schooner eventually had been overtaken and captured by the British the following day. It was ruled a good prize at Antigua. His feelings were probably mixed, on the other hand, when he was informed that the British commander who had let the Danish convoy pass had been relieved of his command by Admiral George Rodney.

More Convoys in the Caribbean

Schioenning was now ordered to patrol the waters around the three Danish islands until January 1781. The frigate soon came upon one of the notorious British privateers from Tortola, but unfortunately it was impossible to overhaul her, as she beat better to windward than the *Bornholm*. On 26 September, 1780, Schioenning departed from St Thomas as escort for five ships bound for Guadeloupe, which was reached without event. At Guadeloupe, however, a hurricane passed over on 11 October. Even by Caribbean standards it was an extremely violent one. Schioenning saved his ship by resolutely cutting away his anchors and letting the *Bornholm* be driven out to sea, a fine show of seamanship, indeed.

The other five vessels ran into trouble, however. Two of them capsized immediately in the heavy seas and went down; one snow broke her cable, was driven to sea, and was taken by British privateers from St Christopher; one schooner drifted to sea in a very bad condition and vanished without a trace; and one brig cut away her anchors and headed for the open sea. Eight days later, Schioenning came across this last vessel by coincidence and found it 'in miserable condition, without anchors, boats or fresh water, and with a crew on the verge of killing the captain'. Mutiny was prevented by the appearance of the naval frigate.

The *Bornholm* left Guadeloupe again on 28 October, in the company of a merchant frigate and the mutinous brig. All three arrived at St Thomas four days later without encountering any problems on the way. On this occasion also, two French merchant ships stayed very close to the convoy all the way into the Danish harbour. For some time thereafter the *Bornholm* patrolled the waters near the Danish West Indies.

The Catastrophe

On 16 November 1780, Schioenning was ordered once again by governor-general Clausen to escort one of the West Indian Trading Company's ships to Guadeloupe, together with any other merchantmen that might wish to be protected. Unfortunately, 11 members of the *Bornholm's* crew had died and 13 others were so ill that they had to be left in St Thomas. The only other Danish man-of-war in the Caribbean, another frigate, had lost all three masts during the hurricane, and was being repaired at St Croix. This being so, Peter Schioenning was called on again. The *Bornholm* sailed on 29 November with a convoy consisting of 12 ships. Nine of these arrived at Guadeloupe on 15 December, three having been oblidged to turn back due to rough weather.

Schioenning departed again on Christmas Eve. Under his escort were eight of the ships he had brought to Guadeloupe (the Trading Company's vessels remained there), and two small Danish vessels with cargoes for St Thomas. By this time more than 60 members of the *Bornholm's* crew had died or were so ill that they were unable to work, and an equal number of men on board were convalescent from the attacks of various tropical diseases.

In the afternoon of 28 December, between Guadeloupe and Montserrat, an armed frigate was sighted, crowding on sail after the convoy. As the stranger approached she hoisted the White Ensign and a masthead pennant. She carried 26 guns. Her captain declared that he was instructed to search all ships sailing from Guadeloupe, which Schioenning refused, in accordance with his orders. When the British vessel tried nevertheless to search the convoy, Schioenning fired four shots at her. The stranger then disappeared.

The next day at dawn, however, the English vessel was right back, now accompanied by two more frigates. One of these flew the White Ensign and a masthead pennant and carried 22 guns; the other one displayed no distinguishing naval marks, but carried 20 guns. All three resembled typical British warships, and officers in uniforms could be seen aboard all of them. The Danes probably did not consider the possibility that the three ships might not be British men-of-war.

At any rate, the Danish commander at once cleared his ship for action. At the same time, he signalled to his convoy to keep close to him and if possible to increase speed. The British demanded permission to search the convoy, but as on the day before, Schioenning refused, declaring to his British counterpart that all was in accordance with the right of neutrality. In the meantime, another of the British ships approached the merchant vessels, until she was forced by the *Bornholm* to withdraw.

After this the three foreigners stayed away for an hour and a half. At eleven o'clock, when the convoy was a little to the south-west of Saba, the English reappeared ahead and to starboard. This time they requested very politely only to inspect the ships' papers, as they supposed there were French and North American vessels among them. This request also was refused by Schioenning.

Thereafter a tense situation developed very quickly. Briefly, this is what happened. The convoy was sailing before the wind with the *Bornholm* sternmost, and behind came the British. At a quarter past eleven, the British commander hailed one of the merchantmen, which had fallen a little behind the rest of the convoy and the Danish man-of-war. The *Bornholm* hauled up into the wind, turning to starboard, and fired a shot at the impudent British frigate. The Englishman was undismayed and hailed another merchantman, and Schioenning luffed right round in order to bring his broadside to bear on his enemy. All three English vessels dropped to leeward, thereby placing themselves a cable length astern of the Danish frigate, which they began to rake with all their might, firing broadsides from their main gun decks and round shot and grape from swivel guns in the tops.

Strangely enough, no one on board the Danish ship was hit by this cannonade. However, the mizzen mast, an anchor stock, and all the sails were seriously damaged. The crew of the *Bornholm* tried to return the fire but could bring only the aftermost guns on the starboard side to bear. The depletion of the crew by illness furthermore meant that men from the quarterdeck guns constantly had to assist in handling the sails,[8] and two 12-pounders on the gun deck remained unmanned. In addition to all this, the frigate had lost steerage way, and would not answer the helm in the light winds and swell. Soon the ship was completely immobile, exposed to the enemy's heavy fire from astern. No more than three cannon shots were fired from the Danish ship.[9]

In this precarious situation, Peter Schioenning had to acknowledge 'the disadvantageous position in which I found myself without any hope, . . . with the prospect of having the ship and crew quickly

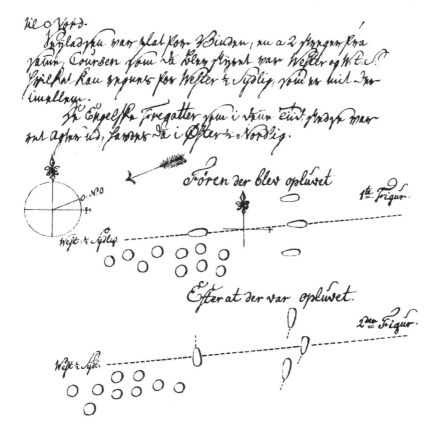

Fig. 14.2 Peter Schioenning's personal sketch of the situation off Saba, before and after the *Bornholm's* hauling to the wind. (Royal Library, Copenhagen)

destroyed. In these circumstances I had to give in to the superior enemy, as it would not be possible to prevent the searching of the convoy. . . . As I thought it highly improper to attend, flying the Danish flag, the detaining and searching of the convoy, I decided to strike my colours.' This happened at a quarter to twelve, and all firing ceased soon after.[10] The Danish commander's intention had only been to make known that he did not see his way to defend the convoy any more, it had certainly not been to surrender to the enemy.[10]

Schioenning relates: 'I sent one of my officers in a boat to the British commander in order to learn his intentions for the convoy. I realized with astonishment that they were instructed to seize it, but we [i.e. the

Bornholm] could sail where we would.' His surprise was well-founded, or was probably rather a feeling that something was completely wrong. At any rate, it must have been with heavy hearts that the ship's council decided to head directly for St Thomas instead of following the captured ships. The Danish frigate had provisions for only two weeks, and they certainly could not count on any help in whatever British port the convoy was now bound for.

Upon his arrival at St Thomas on 30 December 1780, Schioenning was informed that the convoy had been taken to St Christopher and that the three British frigates were not men-of-war, they were privateers! The air was thick besides with rumours, which Schioenning had quite a job trying to suppress. The argument he repeated again and again ran as follows: 'I deeply regret that this accident should happen on top of several other dangers and troubles that have taken place on this voyage to Guadeloupe. I can assure you that everything was done that in my best judgement should and could be done in the circumstances, over which we had no control.'

Governor-general Clausen at once demanded the immediate release of the ten seized ships, for the present without any effect.[11]

The British Reading of the Facts

The first privateer to approach the Danish convoy had been the *Stag*, whereof John Carey was commander, the other two were the *Regulator*, commanded by James Wolcott, and the *Mercury*, commanded by Robert Craggs. Usually, when British ships-of-war had met with a Danish frigate with ships under her convoy in the Caribbean, whether going or coming from any French island, they would not in the least manner molest or search them, but only hail the frigate. On being assured by her commander that the vessels under his convoy were Danish property they would let them proceed quietly on their voyage. This time, however, the Britons insisted upon seeing the papers of the Danish fleet. Commander Schioenning refused, 'saying that the vessels and cargoes were all Danish property, and that his orders were, not to let any of the vessels or their papers be examined'. The Britons promised him that 'if the papers showed the ships and cargoes to be Danish property upon a legal trade they were welcome to proceed, and that he would be detained less than half an hour'.

Finally, Robert Craggs explained to the Prize Court:

the frigate fired several shot at the deponent's [i.e. Robert Craggs'] ship the *Mercury*, some whereof passed over the said ship's quarter deck. The fire was thereupon returned by the *Stag* and the *Mercury*, (the *Regulator* being at a distance to prevent the fleet from dispersing), and again returned by the frigate. During the firing on both sides as aforesaid the said frigate being then going before the wind, the ensign on board the frigate was seen to fall, but the pennant at the main-topgallant masthead, another pennant at the mizzen peak, another pennant at the fore topsail yardarm, and a jack at the foretop masthead were still flying. Instead of backing her sails or laying to, the said frigate set her foresail and hauled her wind and endeavoured to run from the said privateers. Whereupon it not appearing whether the ensign had been struck or shot away, (and the said privateers having reason by the conduct as aforesaid of the said frigate to suspect that she might be an enemy), some shot were fired at her to bring her to, when the said frigate then—and not till then—backed her sails, hauled down her other colours, and lay to. And on her so doing, all firing instantly ceased.[12]

It may be added that later on, in the neutral port of the Azores on 1 July 1792, Captain Craggs confessed to a group of Danish naval officers that the three privateers deliberately had pretended to be British men-of-war.[13]

After having been captured off Saba, the ten merchant vessels were carried into the roads of Basseterre in St Christopher, which was in British hands at that time. The Vice-Admiralty Court of that island condemned all vessels as lawful prize on 24 February 1781. Most prominent among the Danish vessels was the schooner *Jenny*, mastered by John Elwood, and owned by Troels Smith Munthe af Morgenstierne and John Elwood, who were both citizens of St Croix; the cargo was the lawful property of Niels Ryberg, who was one of the largest merchants of Copenhagen. The case was appealed to the High Court of Admiralty in London. There it was established that no French or North American ships whatsoever had been in the convoy. All the vessels were Danish, and none of them carried any kind of contraband.

Voyage Home via Saint Domingue

The other Danish naval frigate in the West Indies was operational again on 21 January 1781. Two weeks later the *Bornholm* departed for Europe. In accordance with orders from the governor-general, the voyage went via the French port at Cap Francais in Saint Domingue. A Danish ship had to be escorted from St Thomas to that port, and two of the West Indian Trading Company's ships needed naval protection on their voyage from Cap Francais to Copenhagen. Just before his

departure, Schioenning was given ten men as partial replacement for
the many deceased members of the crew. The voyage to Saint
Domingue went smoothly. The *Hertug Ferdinand* and the *Grev
Schimmelmann* had completed their preparations, and departed on 16
February under the *Bornholm*'s escort. Only a couple of days later, one
of the merchant ships sprang a leak, forcing the small convoy to return
to Cap Francais for repairs.

The *Bornholm* added ten more men to her crew at Saint Domingue,
and on 26 February 1781 the three ships sailed once more for
Denmark. East of Bermuda, unfortunately, Schioenning lost contact
with the *Hertug Ferdinand*, but by that time the Danish ships had left
the privateer-infested waters of the Caribbean. The *Bornholm* and the
Grev Schimmelmann passed the Azores on 10 April. Two weeks later they
had left the English Channel behind them—and therewith the last of
several privateers which had assailed them on the voyage home.

A good impression of the great compass of the war at sea is provided
by the following account of vessels that contacted the Danes on their
way home from America. On 20 February 1781, at Cap Francais, they
met three North American naval frigates; on 9 March, another naval
frigate of the same nationality; east of Bermuda, on 18 March, they
encountered an armed frigate that first hoisted the North American
flag, replaced it with the White Ensign, but when all came to an end
appeared to be an ordinary British privateer. In the open Atlantic, the
Danish convoy did not come across any privateers. At the entrance to
the Channel, on 15 April, the *Bornholm* and the *Grev Schimmelmann*
again met with privateers. This time two frigates and a brig, all armed,
and flying masthead pennants, first showing North American colours
but shortly afterwards the White Ensign instead. These three vessels
were actually British privateers, and for three days they sought
opportunities to search the merchantman. At the Lizard, five days later,
a large British man-of-war hailed the Danes; later on the same day they
met a naval frigate of the same nation. Finally, on 22 April, the
Bornholm and the *Grev Schimmelmann* were hailed by two British naval
frigates accompanied by three heavily armed cutters.

In his general report Schioenning pointed out that 'we have sighted
several more privateers that have not approached or hailed us'. The last
time this happened was on 7 May in the Kattegat close to the Danish
west coast, where a large British privateer frigate was sighted. Before
that, the *Bornholm* and its charge had been forced to put into a port of
refuge on the Norwegian coast. After having been at sea for nine

weeks, many members of the crew were ill, and butter, spirits and firewood were in very short supply. On top of this, the wind was contrary, blowing from the south and east, so the ship's council decided to put into the port of Eggersund in Norway. After a couple of days there, the two ships were able to proceed to the entrance to the Sound, where they were forced by wind and current to lie at anchor for another couple of days.

Peter Schioenning concluded his report with some remarks about the condition of the crew and ship at the end of the voyage, which had taken nearly a year and a half. The hurricane in the Caribbean and the equinoctial gales in the North Atlantic had taken their toll on masts, rigging and sails. The hull had sagged and was rather leaky. A total of 70 members of the crew had died, and many were ill, some apparently incurably, even though the *Bornholm* had been spared the worst infectious tropical diseases.

At Home Again

Finally on 17 May 1781 the *Bornholm* arrived back home in Copenhagen. News had arrived long before, however, of the unfortunate circumstances of the seizure of the valuable convoy, and an investigation by a specially appointed tribunal was immediately commenced.[14] As soon as the frigate arrived in Copenhagen her crew was detained incommunicado on board, except for the most seriously ill, who were transferred to the Naval Hospital.[15] Beyond these, Peter Schioenning was immediately taken ashore to the naval base—but under arrest and closely guarded.

The affair in the Caribbean on 29 December 1780 was regarded with great seriousness and displeasure by the Danish government because of the substantial political and economic interests at stake. Just at that time, the government was struggling fiercely to make Britain accept Denmark–Norway's right to call at the French colonies in the Caribbean. In addition, the whole situation was aggravated by the fact that Denmark's national prestige was involved. The affair was a common subject of conversation in Copenhagen in those days: everybody had an opinion on the matter. The young Crown Prince repeatedly said that Schioenning deserved to lose his head. The hostile public attitude toward the commander, however, was soon tempered by other points of view.[16] Half a year later, having thoroughly investigated the case, the tribunal and the regent agreed upon the following: Peter

Schioenning had struck his colours, i.e. his flag and masthead pennant, without first offering adequate resistance. This ignominious conduct had disgraced the Danish flag and posed a threat to the nation's flourishing trade and shipping.

Schioenning was therefore sentenced, in November 1781, to be 'dismissed as unworthy of serving His Royal Majesty'. The officer second-in-command was reduced to an ordinary seaman, and all other officers on board were severly reprimanded.[17] It may be added that even the *Bornholm,* after another unsuccessful voyage to the Caribbean, was considered unfit for normal employment. Instead she was anchored as a guard ship at Elsinore, where all foreign ships had to pay Sound Toll dues, for the rest of her lifetime.[18]

A direct consequence of the *Bornholm* affair was the following amendment to Article 752 of the Danish Navy's Articles of War.[19] The article, in force since 1752, explained that any commander in case of action had to do everything in his power to defend his ship; surrender might only be chosen when there was no longer any hope at all. In January 1782 a royal amendment to the Articles of War explained that if a commander did not do his utmost, for example 'if he stroke his colours without being in extreme peril' or in any other way dishonoured the flag, then he should be sentenced to death, no matter if the reason was 'personal fear, lack of skill, want of careful deliberation, or any other flaw with the commander'.[20]

The Danish government certainly considered the *Bornholm* affair to be very important and serious, the national objective being first and foremost to encourage the flourishing trade and shipping under the neutral Danish flag, and at the same time to preserve the intricate balance of the monarchy's foreign policy.

Manuscript sources

Danish National Archives, Copenhagen:

Soeetaten: Embeds-, kommissions- og andre lignende arkiver: Peter Schioennings embedsarkiv (i.e. Peter Schioenning's official records);

Soeetaten: Admiralitetets kongelige resolutioner (i.e. royal resolutions concerning the Admiralty);

Soeetaten: Admiralitetets indkomne sager (i.e. records received by the Admiralty);

Soeetaten: Admiralitetets kopiboeger (i.e. the Admiralty's letter copy books);

Soeetaten: Admiralitetets generalkrigsretssager (i.e. the Admiralty's tribunal records);

Kort- og   tegningssamlingen: Soeetaten: diverse tegninger vedroerende Bornholm (i.e. constructional drawings of the *Bornholm*).

Danish Royal Library, Copenhagen:
Haandskriftafdelingen: Schioennings samling (i.e. Schioenning's private papers).

Public Record Office, London:
High Court of Admiralty: Prize Papers 32/366 no.14 (Schooner *Jenny*) and 42/130 (Schooner *Jenny*).

Notes

1. The political background is thoroughly described in Ole Feldbaek, *Dansk neutralitetspolitik under kirgen 1778–1783: Studier i regeringens prioritering af politiske og oekonomiske interesser* (Copenhagen, 1971) (with an English summary); 'Eighteenth-Century Danish Neutrality: Its Diplomacy, Economics and Law' *Scandinavian Journal of History,* VIII (1983); *Danmarks historie IX: Den lange Fred 1700–1800* (Copenhagen, 1990); and *Konovoj* (Copenhagen, 1992).
2. Schioenning's letters of 27 May 1780, 15 July 1780, 18 August 1780, 3 November 1780, and 28 January 1781 are in Admiralitetets indkomne sager; his general report is in Schioenning's embedsarkiv. Where nothing else is stated reference is to these letters and general report. See Erik Goebel, 'Dansk sejlads paa Vestindien og Guinea 1671–1807' *Handelsog Soefartsmuseets Aarbog,* XLI (1982) (with an English summary); and 'Volume and Structure of Danish Shipping to the Caribbean and Guinea, 1671–1807' *International Journal of Maritime History,* II (1990), for a general survey of Danish shipping to the Caribbean.
3. Instructions in Kogelige resolutioner no. 18, 19, and 20 of 24 Jan. 1780; sailing orders in Kopiboeger same date.
4. Kong Friederich den Femtes Soee-Krigs-Artikels-Brev dateret 8de Jan. 1752 (Copenhagen, 1811).
5. T.A. Topsoee-Jensen and Emil Marquard, *Officerer i den dansk-norske Soeetat 1660–1814 og den danske Soeetat 1814–1932 I–II* (Copenhagen, 935), vol. 2, 455–7.
6. Benny Christensen, *Den gode Hensigt 1780* (Copenhagen, 1784), 4–13.
6. Kort-og tegningssamlingen, espec. drawings A 1208f, A 1208g, A 1220g, B 82I, B 82II, B 82III, and G 4579. Seven frigates were constructed, between 1774 and 1783, according to this set of drawings.
8. Kay Larsen 'Orlogsfregatten Bornholm's onde Aar' *Vikingen,* XV (1938), 17.
9. See the story as told in George F. Tyson, *Powder, Profits and Privateers: A Documentary History of the Virgin Islands During the Era of the American Revolution* (St Thomas, 1977), 50–1 (letter of 23 Jan. 1781 from James Ramsay to Major General Vaughan) according to whom to Danish frigate fired four guns.
10. O. Eidem and O. Luetken, *Vor Soemagtes Historie* (Copenhagen, 1906), 603–4.
11. Tyson, *Powder, Profits and Privateers,* 51 (letter of 13 May 1781 from Samuel Johnston to Lord George Germain).
12. Prize papers HCA 32/366 no. 14 and HCA 42/130.
13. Admiralitetets indkomne sager: Jens Gerner's report of 2 Aug. 1781.
14. Admiralitetets kongelige resolutioner 18 May 1781; Admiralitetets kopiboeger same date.

15. *Ibid.*, 24 May 1781.
16. Schioennings samling.
17. Admiralitetets kongelige resolutioner 5 Nov. 1781 (i.e. Royal confirmation of the Tribunal's sentence dated 9 Oct. 1781).
18. Larsen, 'Orlogsfregatten', 18.
19. Kong Friederich den Femtes Soee-Krigs-Artikels-Brev, Article 752.
20. *Ibid.*, Appendix 4.

INDEX

(pmw = privateer; pir = pirate; mm = merchant vessel; nv = naval vessel)

Printed and bound by CPI Group (UK) Ltd, Croydon, CR0 4YY

23/04/2025

14660992-0004